Indian Women and French Men

D1559290

A VOLUME IN THE SERIES
Native Americans of the Northeast
Culture, History, and the Contemporary

EDITED BY
Colin G. Calloway and
Barry O'Connell

Indian Women and French Men

Rethinking Cultural Encounter in the Western Great Lakes

Susan Sleeper-Smith

University of Massachusetts Press *Amherst*

Copyright © 2001 by University of Massachusetts Press
All rights reserved
Printed in the United States of America

LC 2001026716
ISBN 1-55849-308-5 (library cloth); 310-7 (paper)

Designed by Dennis Anderson
Set in New Baskerville by Graphic Composition, Inc.
Printed and bound by Sheridan Books, Inc.

Library of Congress Cataloging-in-Publication Data

Sleeper-Smith, Susan.
Indian women and French men : rethinking cultural encounter in the Western Great Lakes / Susan Sleeper-Smith.
p. cm. — (Native Americans of the Northeast)
Includes bibliographical references and index.
ISBN 1-55849-308-5 (cloth : alk. paper) — ISBN 1-55849-310-7 (pbk. : alk. paper)
1. Indian women—Northwest, Old—History. 2. Indians of North America—Commerce—Northwest, Old. 3. Indians of North America—First contact with Europeans—Northwest, Old. 4. Fur trade—Northwest, Old—History. I. Title. II. Series.
E78.N76 S54 2001
977'.01'082—dc21
2001026716

British Library Cataloguing in Publication data are available.

To Bob, my partner in love and life

Contents

	Illustrations	ix
	Tables	xi
	Acknowledgments	xiii
	Introduction	1
1	Fish to Furs: The Fur Trade in Illinois Country	11
2	Marie Rouensa and the Jesuits: Conversion, Gender, and Power	23
3	Marie Madeleine Réaume L'archêveque Chevalier and the St. Joseph River Potawatomi	38
4	British Governance in the Western Great Lakes	54
5	Agriculture, Warfare, and Neutrality	73
6	Being Indian and Becoming Catholic	96
7	Hiding in Plain View: Persistence on the Indiana Frontier	116
8	Emigrants and Indians: Michigan's Mythical Frontier	141
	Notes	165
	Index	223

Illustrations

Figures

1 The Great Lakes heartland 13

2 Principal Indian portages 20

3 The expansion of Potawatomi lands from the seventeenth to the nineteenth century 39

4 Family names in the Catholic kin networks of the western Great Lakes fur trade 51

5 Ancient garden beds, rectangular, St. Joseph River valley, Michigan 79

6 Ancient garden beds, patchwork, St. Joseph River valley, Michigan 80

7 Ancient garden beds, circular, Prairie Ronde, St. Joseph River valley, Michigan 81

8 Ancient garden beds, arrowhead, St. Joseph River valley, Michigan 81

9 Indian Villages in Southwest Michigan Territory, c. 1830–1840 107

Color Plates

(*following page 110*)

1 *Miss En Nash Go Gwah* by George Winter

2 *Nan-Matches-Sin-A-Wa, 1839, Chief Godfroy's Home* by George Winter

3 *The Deaf Man's Village* by George Winter

4 *D-Mouche-kee-kee-awh* by George Winter

5 *Mas-Sa* by George Winter

6 *Te-quoc-yaw* or *Bouriette—Indian Interpreter* by George Winter

7 *Pot-Ta-Wat-Ta-Mie Chief, I-O-Wa* by George Winter

8 *Wewissa* by George Winter

9 *Kee-waw-nay Village* by George Winter

10 *Rescue Group* by Horatio Greenough

11 *Frances Slocum* (with her daughters) by George Winter

12 *Frances Slocum* by George Winter

Tables

1 Abstract of payments made by John Tipton for clearing land, building houses, etc. for Potawatomi Indians, 1829 121

2 Payments made by John Tipton in fulfillment of treaty with Thorntown Indians, October 31, 1828 122

3 European trade goods in the western Great Lakes, 1715–1760 126

Acknowledgments

THIS BOOK was written with the encouragement and assistance of a large scholarly community as well as many friends and my family. That support crosses a multiplicity of disciplines, spans a universe of graduate and undergraduate students, and includes numerous conversations at conferences, libraries, and museums. Unfortunately, I can personally thank only those people whose repeated efforts made this book a reality.

I am particularly indebted to three people whom I met at the outset of my academic career: R. David Edmunds, Nancy Shoemaker, and Jeani O'Brien-Kehoe. They commented on my first papers at national conferences, and they have been there ever since, offering not just scholarly expertise but friendship and continuing moral support. Dave Edmunds read several versions of this manuscript, encouraged the direction of my work, and always provided insightful written commentaries. Nancy Shoemaker and Jeani O'Brien helped me to conceptualize this project innovatively and transform a traditional narrative about war and diplomacy in the western Great Lakes into one that focused on community, kinship, and trade. Both Nancy and Jeani read numerous shorter monographs, helped me work through major revisions, and then read the entire final version. Nor will a simple thank-you ever be sufficient to acknowledge the contribution of Kerry Trask. His willingness to identify himself as an anonymous reviewer was crucial in helping me understand the parameters and form of publishable research. I also owe a tremendous debt of gratitude to Barry O'Connell, who read my final manuscript and ushered me in the direction of a truly superb university press.

I am indebted to Alfred Young and Helen Hornbeck Tanner at the Newberry Library; to Jacki Rand, LeAnne Howe, Elden Lawrence, and Bob Craig, who were part of the ethnohistory seminar organized by Gary Anderson at the University of Oklahoma; the staff of the Warren Center (1996–1997) and the participants of Bernard Bailyn's Atlantic World

Seminar, held at Harvard University. Richard White read an early version of this manuscript and offered both support and suggestions for the future direction of my work. Lucy Murphy, Jennifer Brazille, Daniel Richter, Alice Nash, Jacki Peterson, Rebecca Kugel, and Clara Sue Kidwell have provided insightful comments as co-panel members and commentators at numerous national conferences. Above all, countless members of the Society for Ethnohistory have provided an ongoing forum for the exchange of ideas that has proved central to my work.

Numerous archives graciously opened their collections to me, even when they were not equipped to accommodate researchers. Several merit particular note, including the Tippecanoe County Historical Association, the Historical Society of Porter County, the Provincial Archives of the Brothers of the Holy Cross at Notre Dame, St. Mary's College Archives, and the Northern Indiana Historical Society. I also thank the archivists and librarians at the Indiana Historical Society, the Chicago Historical Society, and the Newbury Library; their tireless efforts to assist with my research made it a pleasure to work in these archives.

The Michigan State University History Department is my academic home, and this book became a reality because of the supportive environment provided by my fellow scholars and friends. David Bailey was there from the beginning, but best of all, he shared tea and sympathy, readings and suggestions on a weekly basis during the final six months of the revision process. Gordon Stewart had the Scottish good sense to help me rethink how to proceed after my first revision had added several hundred unnecessary pages. My fellow New Yorker Emily Tabuteau focused her attention on randomly scattered commas and obscure sentences in need of firmer direction. My other comrade from the Big Apple, Peter Levine, read the earliest version of my work and provided continuing encouragement during the revision process. My chair, Lewis Siegelbaum, read the entire manuscript as it neared completion and helped me obtain financial support for the color plates that appear in this book. My department provided me a public forum for my scholarship, allowed me to structure seminar courses around my research, and provided me with release time to complete the book.

My university has a diverse body of scholars who share my interests, particularly Keith Widder, whose highly respected work on the fur trade paved the way for me to think about Indian women as cultural mediators. His careful reading has saved me from many embarrassing errors. My good friend Dawn Martin and two of my graduate students, Patrick Lucas and John Thiel, are the real footsoldiers of this work. Dean Patrick

McConeghy as well as the Office of the Vice President for Research and Graduate Studies provided financial assistance that enabled the printing of the color plates.

I have saved two of my fondest debts of gratitude for last. I had the good fortune to attend the University of Michigan, where I encountered a superb group of scholars. The faculty encouraged my intellectual development, and they pushed me to extend the boundaries of American history to include Native people in the Great Lakes. James Turner is a valued mentor; his kindness, encouragement, and intellectual honesty are a continuing inspiration. Maris Vinovskis, Carol Karlsen, Michael McDonald, David Hollinger, John Shy, and Ken Lockridge transformed my graduate training into a worthy and rewarding intellectual endeavor.

Finally, no book could ever have been completed without my family, who have put up with interrupted vacations, curtailed holidays, and missed birthdays. My husband, Bob, and his children, Becky, Julie, and Jim, have made my world very special. Their spouses, Charlie, Kent, and Suzanne, have richly given of themselves. Nor could any book ever take the place of knowing "Jamaica Me Crazy": Andrew, Alex, and Channing.

MATERIAL FROM my articles "The World of Marie Madeleine Réaume L'archêveque Chevalier" in *New Faces of the Fur Trade,* ed. Jo-Anne Fiske, Susan Sleeper-Smith, and William Wicken, and "'Ignorant bigots and busy rebels': The American Revolution in the Western Great Lakes" in *The Sixty Years' War for the Great Lakes, 1754–1814,* ed. David Skaggs and Larry L. Nelson is used here by permission of Michigan State University Press.

A version of chapter 2 first appeared as "Women, Kin, and Catholicism: New Perspectives on the Fur Trade," in *Ethnohistory* 47 (spring 2000): 423–52, and is used by permission of the American Society for Ethnohistory.

S. S. S.

Indian Women and French Men

Introduction

OUR UNDERSTANDING of Indians is primarily obscured by our stereotypes. Scholars often attribute these fictive Indians to James Fenimore Cooper's *Last of the Mohicans,* Henry Wadsworth Longfellow's *Song of Hiawatha,* or the romanticized descriptions of Pocahontas and Sitting Bull. But these images are benign when compared with the more brutal and aggressive Indians television has created. During the 1960s and 1970s, when Indians appeared on the television screen dreadful things happened. Indian violence became increasingly graphic as men, women, and children were brutally murdered and scalped or burned at the stake. Blood-curdling Indian war cries on *Wagon Train* and *The Rifleman* horrified young audiences.[1]

At the same time that television viewers identified violent behavior with Indians, historians in the 1960s began to reassess the role that Indians played in history. Social historians replaced the "simple decline and death theme so prevalent in the writing of [early] Indian history" with an examination of how Indians blended old and new ways to survive in a world transformed by the Columbian encounter.[2] Although Indians played a vital role in the process of encounter, demise remained a common outcome, now frequently depicted as a nineteenth-century, rather than a seventeenth- or eighteenth-century, phenomenon. Although census figures indicate a sizable, present-day Indian population in the United States, we often see little connection between the Indians of the past and those of the present.[3]

The television image of the violent Indian is difficult to counteract when historians provide few examples of viable, peaceful Indian communities. Simultaneously, Indian communities that accommodated to and incorporated characteristics of their Euro-American neighbors are often regarded with suspicion by both historians and the lay public. The stereotypically correct Indian remains a "primitive" figure clad in animal skins and moccasins who disappeared long ago. This depiction encourages us to discount the cultural revitalization of Indian people. Thus, nations such as the Pequots, whose reemergence has been facilitated by the influx of casino money, often are dismissed as though they were not "genuine" Indians. Although general comments about people who do not look like Indians are disturbing, this notion of the "primitive but genuine" Indian is reinforced by historical explanations that rely on notions of "demise."

In this book I maintain that Indians have existed as viable, distinct people from the earliest times to the present and contend that, while encounter changed indigenous communities, it also encouraged the evolution of strategic behaviors that ensured cultural continuity.[4] I focus on the prolonged interaction between Native Americans and Euro-Americans in the western Great Lakes fur trade and on the adaptive behaviors Indians employed to deal with both amicable and hostile strangers. During the colonial period, there were few similar North American regions where interactions between diverse people and disparate economic systems occurred on a daily basis. The fur trade was not an avenue to demise, but a laboratory of social experimentation that lasted for almost two hundred years.[5]

I have not attempted a comprehensive study of the fur trade or a description of all the Indian people in the Great Lakes region.[6] That history has been well detailed by both historians and anthropologists.[7] Rather, this is a more particular story about persistence strategies that evolved in the southern Great Lakes River basin, in those villages east of the Mississippi and north of the Ohio River valley, in what today constitutes southwestern Michigan and parts of Indiana and Illinois.

This book is indebted to and builds on the work of numerous social historians who have brought a new perspective to the process of encounter. Of all the books written within the framework of the new Indian history, it is Richard White's *The Middle Ground* that has drawn attention to the importance of the western Great Lakes as a coherent geographical entity and, more important, as a region where encounter entailed a process of negotiation, where neither Europeans nor Indians could win through force. As White so clearly demonstrates, "The middle ground grew according to the need of people to find a means, other than force, to gain the cooperation or consent of foreigners."[8]

This book, however, differs with *The Middle Ground* on the outcome. Although White offers important perspectives on a negotiation process not dominated by Euro-Americans, he also argues that the nineteenth-century dissolution of the middle ground led to indigenous demise. The middle ground was destabilized by the British withdrawal from the Great Lakes following the War of 1812, and, according to White, Native people found negotiation with the new United States a one-way process, with their fate being dictated to them. White concludes that the failure of the middle ground resulted in both the voluntary and forced removal of Indian people from the Great Lakes.

The depth and richness of White's research suggests alternative scenarios, and, for this reason, I pose a different thesis: The way in which Indian people responded to the challenges posed by American arrival was shaped by the way they had responded to aggression by the Iroquois in the seventeenth century, to the influx of French fur traders in the early eighteenth century, and to the arrival of the English during the last half of the eighteenth century. Nineteenth-century U.S. people were, for Indians, another stage in a continuous process of encounter with foreigners. The struggle to maintain or improve their position in relation to others, less or more powerful than themselves, invoked a well-established repertoire of responses. In the western Great Lakes, Indian people persisted, despite forced removal, because diaspora, both forced and voluntary, was a significant part of their past. Indians were practiced in the arts not just of accommodation but also of resistance. In the face of overwhelming odds, Indian people were still far from powerless.

The theoretical framework of *The Middle Ground* relies on the work of Marshall Sahlins and Anthony Giddens. For White, the middle ground "resulted from the daily encounters of individual Indians and Frenchmen with problems and controversies that needed immediate solution." The middle ground was a "jointly invented world" that arose because divergent cultural forms required new and more suitable means of interaction. Innovative cultural practices were negotiated on the middle ground and then incorporated into French and Indian societies. White views the middle ground as a cultural invention, an example of Giddens' structuralism, and, therefore, it possessed a logic that was neither fully European nor Algonquian.[9] My work is indebted to this perspective but relies more heavily on Pierre Bourdieu's concepts of the *habitus of behavior* and *symbolic capital,* because they describe both the continuity and the patterned nature of indigenous social practice. Bourdieu maintains that kin-based societies are shaped by the power of habit and that future behaviors are heavily influenced by repetitive behavioral patterns. The habitus of behavior is inculcated in each person as he or she grows to adulthood within a community; daily behaviors are not consciously constructed. When confronted with new situations, people engage in correcting the results of practiced behaviors by developing new strategies. In kin-based societies, behaviors change as people struggle either to attain or to retain symbolic capital—what people sense as honor, prestige, respect, or authority. Central to this idea of symbolic capital is the prestige and renown that attaches to a family name or a kin network and can be converted into economic capital. These were behaviors based on such concepts as obligation, personal loyalty, or, perhaps, a code of honor. In the fur trade, the obligations entailed in kinship controlled both entrance into the trade and access to peltry.[10]

Marital and kinship strategies transformed trade into a social process and mediated the disruptions inherent in disparate and competing economic systems. Indian communities successfully incorporated European traders as well as other strangers, and even enemies, through intermarriage. Marriage, either sacramentally sanctioned or in "the manner of the country," transformed French fur traders into friends, family, and allies.[11] Kinship transformed the impersonal exchange process characteristic of capitalism into a socially accountable process.

This book is different from many histories of the fur trade because it examines the kin-based nature of the exchange process, the face-to-face exchange of peltry for trade goods. Most fur trade histories focus on other stages of this very complicated and lengthy process. The core archival sources for historians of the fur trade have usually consisted of the letters exchanged between North American officials and the centers of power at Versailles and Whitehall, along with the business records and the correspondence of traders, merchants, and priests. These documents are accessible at national archives and provide much information. Unfortunately their "top-down" view often obscures the exchange process that took place at a local level. The adaptive strategies that Native communities employed to structure exchange and their accommodation to a changing world are not readily apparent in these traditional archival documents.

Indigenous exchange strategies emerge more clearly from sources that describe daily life. This research incorporates records located in local and state-level archives because they are more closely attuned to the kin-based nature of the Great Lakes trade. My work relies on baptismal and marital registers and the account books and correspondence of local traders who married into indigenous society. Religious records describe the Catholic kin network that evolved in conjunction with the trade and linked numerous fur trade communities. Inventories of trade goods provide evidence for the affluence of many Indian villages involved in the trade. Indigenous prosperity emerges even more clearly from the watercolors and sketchbooks of the English immigrant artist, George Winter. His nineteenth-century portraits, housed in a county historical society, provide the visual evidence of Potawatomi and Miami men clothed in trade goods: silk turbans, waistcoats, and ruffled shirts. Female dress was equally elegant, but even more lavishly adorned, often with trade-silver pendants. Local archives coupled with material culture provide evidence for indigenous communities that accommodated to change and persisted.

The primary focus of my narrative is the often misunderstood but highly important role that Native women played in establishing the fur trade as an avenue of sociocultural change. Native women who married fur traders successfully incorporated their French husbands into their communities. These women were important links in the exchange process.[12] They did not "marry out" of the villages in which they were raised and they ensured that exchange remained defined by kinship behaviors.[13] In addition, they were the progenitors of Catholic kin networks that eventually controlled a large share of the Great Lakes trade. These networks evolved because many of these Native women were Christian converts; and they, as well as their fur-trader husbands, repeatedly served as godparents to those involved in the trade: often hunters but, more frequently, the female processors and the male transporters of furs and goods.[14] Traders and Indians became part of a kinship system that established familial bonds often as secure as those of written contracts. Catholic kin networks linked Indians and French; they paralleled, but did not displace, the kin networks of indigenous society.

The Native women who married fur traders not only mediated the exchange of furs for trade goods but often used their intermediary role and their access to trade goods to augment their own authority and that of their households.[15] Native women, whose marriages were sacramentally sanctioned, often emerged as the cultural progenitors of new communities of fur trade kin. These women lived in matrifocal households, and they raised agricultural produce and manufactured products for the trade.[16] Many of the households and Indian communities that were agricultural suppliers of the trade had demographically stable populations.[17] Because of the scarcity of priests, the Native converts often fostered the emergence of a frontier Catholicism that proved sympathetic to indigenous beliefs.[18]

Women, kinship, and Catholicism shaped the dynamics of the exchange process and minimized the intrusion of market forces. This, coupled with the longevity of the fur trade, contributed to Indian persistence. In this book I contend that much of the Great Lakes fur trade remained viable from the precontact period to the late nineteenth century. The bulk of the beaver trade moved permanently into the Canadian Northwest during the 1820s and 1830s, but in the marshes and river valleys south of Lake Michigan, often assiduously avoided by eastern settlers, fur exports continued to increase. Black raccoon replaced beaver, and this proved strategic to Indian persistence, for the river valleys that were the traditional homelands of the Potawatomi and Miami people were the breeding grounds of these animals.[19]

I also explore the ways in which cultural processes become more important than the formal structures of political power in understanding the transformative nature of contact with Euro-Americans. Because the adaptive behaviors of Native people were determined by the complex social structures of kin-based societies, Europeans experienced difficulty in exerting claims of sovereignty. They encountered resistance from a Native social and cultural system that was highly coherent and, because of its social complexity, proved difficult for outsiders to understand. The adaptive behaviors that evolved among Native people over a prolonged period of time frustrated first the French and then the British.

The fur trade also provides a glimpse into how Europeans were changed and transformed by their encounter with Native people. Europeans never dominated the seventeenth- and eighteenth-century Great Lakes, and their attempts to impose formal governance were continually frustrated by the kin-based consensual nature of authority in the indigenous society. Cultural change was a two-way process: Each society had an impact on the other. The changes in French behavior were often more dramatic than the changes in Indian behavior. As the Jesuits frequently lamented, French fur traders were more inclined to become Indian than to remain Frenchmen.[20]

Finally, this book also reintegrates the natural landscape with the fur trade and shows how environmental factors not only shaped cultural encounters, but led to indigenous persistence.[21] The quest for furs led France to explore and claim the St. Lawrence River valley, the gateway to the western Great Lakes, rather than the more fertile lands along the Atlantic seaboard. While the geographically accessible western Great Lakes provided the largest quantity of colonial peltry, this swampland habitat proved problematic during the nineteenth century. The rivers that transported the French to the western Great Lakes became formidable obstacles to the overland westward movement. Even the most determined Americans were thwarted by seasonal rains and floods that transformed swamplands and rivers into insurmountable barriers. Some emigrants chose alternative paths, and, consequently, Native people were often left unmolested by westward expansion. Swamplands frequently remained unclaimed and, therefore, persisted as part of an indigenous landscape. Both northwest Indiana and southwest Michigan afforded long-term havens for those Indians who resisted removal.

THERE ARE many reasons historians of the antebellum midwestern frontier do not incorporate those Indian communities that persisted. For instance, Indians who effectively thwarted removal often relied on anonymity as a protective device. Others constructed white facades through the use of Christian names: they took title to lands in Euro-American names and relied on mixed-ancestry kin to speak for them—usually men with Indian mothers and French fathers. Identity was refashioned to ensure persistence. In an increasingly racist society, being white became more important than the public evidence of "civilized" behaviors. "Red men and women" were subject to removal; white men and women were not.

The midwestern frontier remains a blur of fact and nostalgia for many historians, where the pioneer farm family displaced a few adventuresome French fur traders and nomadic Indians.[22] The construction of whiteness as a conscious Indian strategy encouraged this myth making; consequently, the writers of pioneer histories often misconstrued the evidence of accommodation for assimilation. When the Census Bureau announced the closing of the frontier in the final decades of the nineteenth century, the search for evidence of white pioneer families further obscured Indians who had persisted. Writers became obsessed with proving that the frontier, with its access to land and participatory, democratic processes, was the building block of United States uniqueness. Even mixed-descendants of Native people, shamed by their Indian blood, homogenized the midwestern frontier and described it as settled by "white" pioneer families.[23]

The idea of a sparsely populated Indian frontier landscape has been successfully challenged by western historians.[24] Their depiction of the Far West as a geographical region inhabited by diverse peoples is also useful for understanding how the antebellum frontier of the Great Lakes was shaped by geography and forged against an established Indian presence. To appreciate the diversity of this frontier requires that the chronological span be broadened to incorporate the colonial past. The western

Great Lakes, or *pays d'en haut,* as the French referred to the region, was far from monolithic. Just as recent studies of communities have revealed that no one village typified all of New England, so in this research I hope to establish that no one Indian people was emblematic of the larger, more diverse society. Nor did changes brought about by the fur trade impact Native people uniformly or always lead to their demise.

This book focuses on the malleable nature of human interaction, where we can comprehend only a fraction of the changes and interactions that occurred. Thus, a diversity of terms is employed to describe the numerous people of the western Great Lakes. Terms used to identify the original inhabitants are always capitalized: Indian, Native American, and Native. Various terms were used to describe the French who arrived and settled among the Native people. Some French who settled among the Indians became primarily farmers and were referred to as *habitants* by colonial French authorities. When the British took possession of the western Great Lakes, they failed to distinguish between the *habitants* and the fur traders and disparagingly referred to them as the Interior French. Many historians use the term *Métis* to describe the mixed-ancestry descendants of traders who married Native women. This term, however, presents considerable confusion. The use of *Métis* is rare in seventeenth- and eighteenth-century manuscript sources. At many smaller posts, such as Fort St. Joseph in Michigan and Ouiatenon in Indiana, identity was defined by kin rather than by ethnicity or nationality. In the colonial world of the *pays d'en haut,* a distinctive Métis population evolved at the larger fur trade communities, such as Michilimackinac and Green Bay. In Canada, the term *Métis* is also capitalized, but this is because generations of mixed-ancestry offspring have themselves sought reservation lands as a sovereign people. Thus, terms such as *Métis* are reminders of the malleable boundaries that characterized colonial society in the western Great Lakes. Identity was multidimensional, and often terms used to identify one group did not have resonance for every region and time period.[25]

This book provides one perspective on a colonial world where kinship determined identity. When the nineteenth-century Americans arrived, they were surprised by the significant numbers of Indians who lived on and farmed the lands that speculators had advertised as vacant. If we reestablish the Great Lakes as a socially diverse land where malleable borders changed the human landscape of Indian communities, it will help us to understand why some Indian villages thwarted removal by successfully shielding themselves behind a facade of whiteness. They became so successfully involved in their own construction of whiteness that they became invisible: They hid in plain view.[26]

The fur trade provides a means to examine the variety of interactions that took place as Native Americans encountered diverse Euro-American people. Indians lived side by side with Europeans, and both groups exhibited a variety of good and bad behaviors. Interaction was never a monolithic experience. The Native and French communities that evolved in the interior of North America during the colonial period, although far removed from the coastline where English settlement took place, were pivotal in the Franco-English struggle to achieve North American supremacy. Native people affected the course of that struggle and allowed France, despite limited resources, to persist in staking its claim to the North American interior until 1763. In the nineteenth century, the mixed-ancestry descendants of that interaction facilitated indigenous persistence when the United States established sovereignty over Native lands in the western Great Lakes.

1

Fish to Furs

The Fur Trade in Illinois Country

In 1993, when the Mississippi River reclaimed its natural domain and swept aside towns and settlements, it also engulfed 15 million acres of farmland.[1] The flood inundated lands from Minnesota to Louisiana and reestablished the lakes, causeways, and keys of early-contact America. Floods are the foils of today's technology, but they also re-create, in however transitory a fashion, the landscape of an earlier time—when spring thaws and fall rains fused previously separate bodies of water and facilitated intracontinental travel.

Waterways were the highways of the preindustrial world. They led Europeans west and shaped encounters in North America. Division of the continent among the French, English, and Dutch was influenced by the configuration of its riverways. Early in the sixteenth century, Europeans, especially the French, braved the hazards of transatlantic travel to fish the Grand Banks.[2] The search for a passage to China led France along the St. Lawrence River, west through the Great Lakes, to the Mississippi.[3] The St. Lawrence was the only river that extended from the coastline to the interior, and French imperial claims followed that river's pathway.[4]

While sixteenth-century European monarchs commissioned exploratory voyages to search for a Northwest Passage, European merchants focused their attention on a more mundane transatlantic expedition, the annual fish harvest. By 1580, as many as twenty thousand sailors may have spent their spring and summer months on the North Atlantic coast.[5] At the century's end, as consumer demand for felt hats increased, economic attention shifted to peltry.[6] The fur of the beaver, extinct in Europe, formed the soft, downy surface of the felt hat.[7] The demands of fashion commodified North America's animal resources.[8]

The Great Lakes area was a rich source of furs, highly accessible because of the Indian trade routes that moved furs eastward along the

St. Lawrence River to the Atlantic coast.[9] This interior trade was controlled by the Huron, who functioned as middlemen.[10] In 1649, this exchange process was destroyed when the Iroquois started the Fur Trade Wars. Europeans, anxious to enhance profits, became ensnared in a web of competitive Indian intrigue.[11] English and Dutch traders encouraged Iroquois aggression and supplied them with firearms, while France encouraged Huron retaliation against the Iroquois.[12] Fur trade rivalry sparked a war in which most of the Huron were killed. A fortunate few were adopted by the Iroquois or fled west.

Events in the western Great Lakes were influenced by what happened in the east. The heavily armed Iroquois, no longer contained by the Huron, pushed into the Great Lakes region and attacked and annihilated villages. An Iroquois-driven diaspora changed the demography of the region. Villages were abandoned as unarmed people sought refuge along Lake Michigan's western shore.[13] Large numbers of Indians temporarily banded together near present-day Green Bay: Potawatomi, Miami, Fox, Sauk, Huron, Erie, and Neutral. But even this distant community was not immune from turmoil. These people lived in a hostile, unfamiliar land, threatened on the west by the Sioux and on the east by the Iroquois.

During the last half of the seventeenth century, the lands that bordered the Great Lakes were Iroquois hunting grounds. Overland, the Iroquois, no longer blocked by the Huron, had unrestricted access to the west. They journeyed through present-day Canada to the lands that bordered Lakes Huron and Michigan. The Iroquois also relied on the Allegheny River, which flowed through their homelands, to take them to the Ohio River valley. They traveled west along the Ohio to the Mississippi and relied on the Wabash drainage as a northern passage to Lake Michigan.

The network of rivers that circumscribed the southern boundary of the Great Lakes gave the lands of this region a distinctive heart shape (see fig. 1). It was these lands, where furs were plentiful and easy to transport, that the Iroquois terrorized throughout the seventeenth century. Periodic incursions kept this heartland region an Iroquois hunting ground.

Until the eighteenth century, intermittent warfare continually plagued the people of the Great Lakes. Interruptions in the fighting led to the temporary migration of refugees from Green Bay. Unfortunately, when Iroquois attacks resumed, resettled villages were dispersed, and survivors again fled west to the overcrowded refugee center at Green

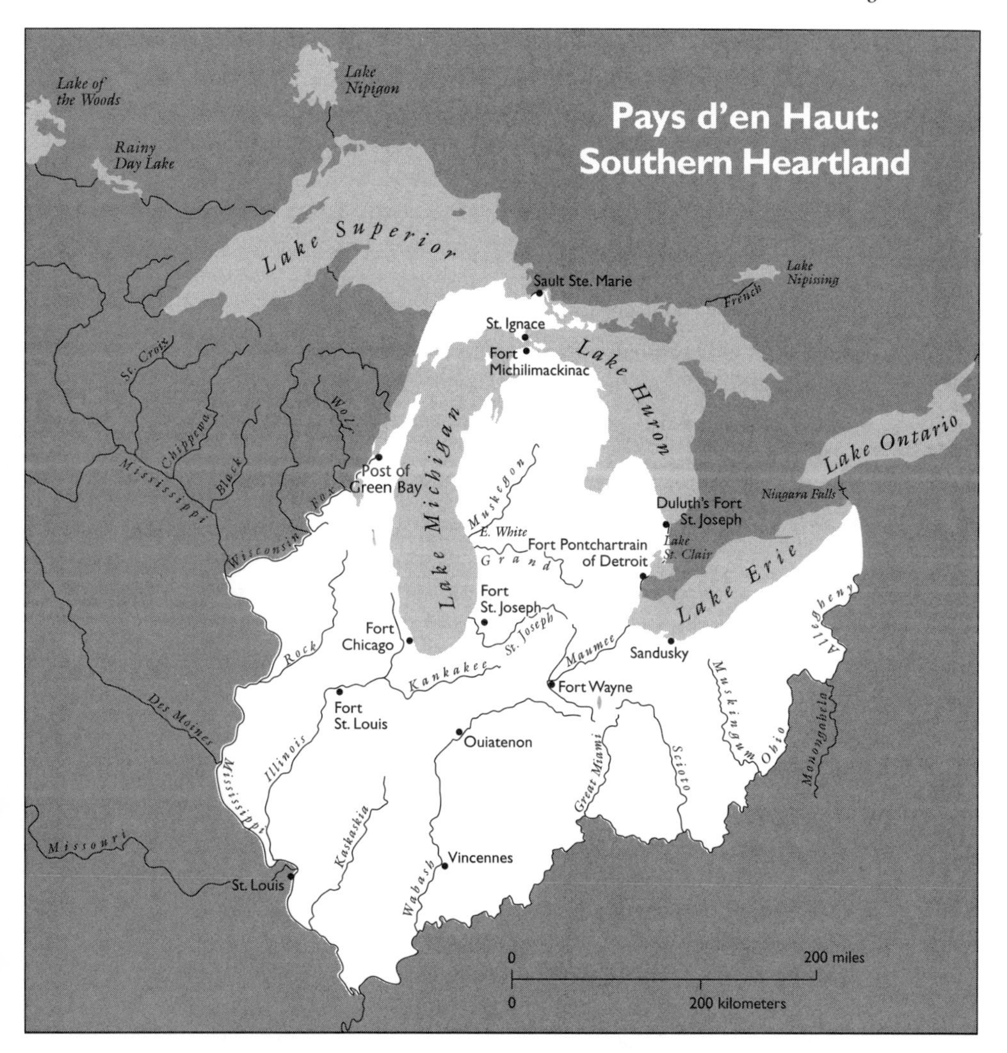

FIGURE 1. *The Great Lakes heartland.* The rivers that bordered the southern Great Lakes gave the lands of this region a distinctive heart shape. French forts of the seventeenth and eighteenth centuries are shown.

Bay. Influxes of refugees continually recast the human landscape of this ethnically diverse community.

The Fur Trade Wars transformed the beaver trade into a high-risk venture. Most Indians avoided the hazardous journey east to Montreal. Instead, French traders went west, motivated by Pierre-Esprit Radisson's 1650 trading expedition into present-day Minnesota. Radisson had returned to Montreal with sixty birch bark canoes overflowing with furs. For many Frenchmen, the wealth garnered from furs outweighed the dangers of war. This exodus of traders into the west would permanently relocate the exchange process from Montreal to the western Great Lakes, the *pays d'en haut,* or Upper Country.[14]

The Iroquois' most formidable foe was the Iliniwek Confederacy, or people of the Illinois Country, who remained in their homelands.[15] The French mistakenly assumed that a political affiliation existed among the Ilini and attributed to them a status akin to a confederacy.[16] The Ilini, like their northern refugee neighbors, banded together for defensive purposes. As the Fur Trade Wars intensified, the size and diversity of the refugee villages continued to increase. For example, in 1673, Father Jacques Marquette described Kaskaskia as a community with seventy-four cabins. When Marquette returned to preach Easter Mass at Kaskaskia in 1675, his audience reportedly consisted of five hundred chiefs and elders, seated in a circle around him. The rest of his audience included fifteen hundred young men, as well as women and children.[17] Kaskaskia was then located on the Illinois River, just south of Lake Michigan.[18] Four years later, the Jesuits described it as a "great" village that housed perhaps as many as eight thousand people.[19] Father Claude Jean Allouez tells us,

> I found this village largely increased since a year ago. Formerly, it was composed of but one nation, that of the Kachkachkia; at the present time, there are eight tribes in it, the first having summoned the others, who inhabited the neighborhood of the river Mississippi. . . . One cannot well satisfy himself as to the number of people who compose that village. They are housed in 351 cabins.[20]

Illinois Country encompassed almost the entire present-day State of Illinois as well as southern Wisconsin and Iowa.[21] The Ilini were spread over so vast an area that the French referred to present-day Lake Michigan as the Lake of the Illinois.[22] The Iliniwek occupied the terminus of a vast river network that included the Wabash watershed and southern Lake Michigan. They also controlled access to the Lower Mississippi, and to the north, they had peripheral access to Green Bay. Consequently, the Ilini protected the Green Bay region from a southern assault by the Iroquois and also blocked European access westward to the plains tribes and the bison trade.[23]

Agriculture, well established before the Europeans arrived, accounted for the high precontact population levels among the Ilini. The multitude of rivers, streams, and marshlands created lush vegetation and fertile soil. Annual spring floods deposited topsoils on the lowlands, while adjacent marshlands provided a rich animal habitat. Abundant harvests, access to well-stocked hunting grounds, and highly navigable rivers encouraged the Ilini to fight to retain their lands rather than flee.

The region was one nexus of the continent's riverways, and people moved back and forth across the continent to and from the Mississippi River valley. Thus, its inhabitants were also involved in trade well before European arrival.[24] Between A.D. 900 and 1200, Cahokia flourished as a center of continental trade. Between ten and thirty thousand people lived in Cahokia, which was governed by a powerful social hierarchy and linked to numerous peripheral population centers. Peripheral trading communities emerged astride tributaries of the Mississippi. Archaeologists have found "exotic goods" at all these trading centers, particularly among the grave goods. Funerary objects include copper and mica hammered into elongated hands and stylized faces and exotic stones that were refashioned into ornamental animal shapes for pipe stands, storage jars, and food vessels.

Cahokia and its network of smaller trading centers declined sometime after 1300, and Indians gradually dispersed into smaller settlements. These population shifts continued well into the sixteenth century. The migrations noted by European explorers were frequently deliberate rather than random.[25]

Precontact population centers linked by intercontinental trade routes characterized societies that were not static. The multiple rivers that crisscrossed Illinois Country provided a highly accessible transportation network. Indeed, when Illinois was carved out of the Northwest Territory, the state's length was defined by 1,160 miles of navigable rivers.[26] Unfortunately, in this fertile, lush land, there were no natural barriers—no mountains or dense forests—in any direction to shield the confederacy from the westward pressure of the Iroquois. During the seventeenth century, the accessibility of the region thus subjected the Ilini to repeated Iroquois invasion.

In 1680, the Iroquois initiated a war of extermination against the Iliniwek Confederacy, which had steadfastly refused to bring its furs to the Iroquois. Instead, the Ilini continued to trade with the French. Hostilities further intensified when René-Robert Cavelier de La Salle arrived in Illinois Country.[27] The Iroquois had driven La Salle from the east, and they were angered by his warm welcome to the refugee communities of the western Great Lakes.[28] La Salle sailed west aboard the *Griffon,* the first large ship built to traverse the waters of the Great Lakes.[29] By the time La Salle reached Green Bay, the *Griffon* was so laden with furs that it was dispatched to Montreal.[30] La Salle constructed forts for the collection and storage of furs. He established one collection point at Green Bay and another at the Miami River on Lake Michigan's eastern shore; the river was later renamed the St. Joseph by the Jesuits.

In Montreal the Iroquois complained bitterly of La Salle's activities to Governor of New France Joseph-Antoine Le Febvre de La Barre.[31] The Iroquois rejected all French attempts at pacification and, instead, escalated their war against the Iliniwek. La Salle prepared for the Iroquois' onslaught by constructing forts in the *pays d'en haut,* and among the Iliniwek the first was near Lake Peoria. The second was Fort St. Louis, a larger and more elaborate structure built on a 125-foot rock that rose out of the Illinois River.[32]

La Salle's attempts to secure the area against the Iroquois changed the demography of the western Great Lakes. La Salle encouraged the resettlement of eastern Indians and relied on trade goods to transform strangers into allies.[33] In present-day southwest Michigan, La Salle's gifts successfully aligned the Abenaki, Mohegan, Shawnee, and Miami.[34] In Illinois Country, Ouilamette, an eastern refugee, spoke for La Salle. His skill as a negotiator and proficient linguist was enhanced by his access to trade goods.[35] Ouilamette successfully gained the support of the Indians who lived in Illinois Country, a task complicated by the large, ethnically diverse population. Directly north of Fort St. Louis there were twelve hundred Ilini warriors. To the south of the fort was a village of two hundred Shawnee, and nearby were villages of Wea (Ouiatenon), Ouabona, Kilatica, Pepikokia, Miami, and Piankesha. Directly north of the Ilini resided the Kickapoo and another group identified as the Mascoutin or Fire Nation.[36]

Gift-giving transformed strangers into allies, and access to trade goods was ensured by the settlement of French fur traders among the Ilini. This diverse Great Lakes population was further complicated by the intermarriage of Frenchmen and Native women. According to the Jesuits, these young men "acquired" Indian women in accordance with indigenous custom, and instead of farming, relied on their wives to sustain agricultural production. The horrified Jesuits complained directly to the New France governor.

> M. de la Salle has made grants at Fort St. Louis to several Frenchmen who have been living there for several years without caring to return.

> This has occasioned a host of disorders and abominations. These people to whom M. de la Salle has made grants are all youths who have done nothing toward cultivating the land. They keep marrying after the manner of the savages of the country.[37]

La Salle's plans for the *pays d'en haut* expanded when his explorations confirmed that the southern Mississippi emptied into the Gulf of Mexico. La Salle planned to bypass Montreal and to extend New France's boundaries into the western Great Lakes. He and his backers hoped to increase their fur trade profits by shipping Great Lakes furs south and then east across the ocean to France.

La Salle's plans were opposed by a highly disparate but vociferous group of people: Iroquois, Jesuits, Montreal merchants, and New France's Governor La Barre. The Jesuits were infuriated by the influx of fur traders who, they believed, corrupted the Indians and undermined their missions. Meanwhile, the Montreal merchants feared that La Salle's activities might shift the fur trade from the St. Lawrence to the Mississippi River valley. The Mississippi was navigationally preferable to the St. Lawrence, for it did not freeze during the winter months.[38]

Governor La Barre, who was allied with the Montreal merchants, disliked and distrusted La Salle and removed him from command at Fort St. Louis, but La Salle returned to France to obtain the financial and political support denied him in the colony. He freely conceded that his plans were detrimental to the Montreal merchants but he reasoned that, if "this affair should prove hurtful to New France, it will [still] contribute to its security, and render our commerce in furs more considerable."[39]

La Salle's fur trade activities, supported by members of the French Court, further disrupted this already strife-torn region. The financial backing that he received from men such as the Prince de Conti and the Marquis de Seignelay, Jean-Baptiste Colbert's son, fueled La Salle's conflict with the Montreal merchants and La Barre. While La Salle was in France, the Montreal merchants sent their own traders west to counter La Salle's growing influence in the *pays d'en haut.* Governor La Barre simultaneously and surreptitiously granted a portion of La Salle's lands to the Jesuits to establish a mission.[40]

Colbert opposed westward expansion of New France, but his support of La Salle furthered that process.[41] To help defray the cost of his exploratory venture down the Mississippi, La Salle was granted the right to establish trading posts and to trade for furs in the Mississippi Valley.[42] His exploration of the Mississippi supported France's claim to all the lands from Hudson Bay to the Gulf of Mexico. France became engaged in a colonial conquest that committed the nation to the defense of half the continent with little regard for the economic balance sheet.[43] By 1681, Colbert, no longer able to confine the Canadians to the St. Lawrence River valley, attempted to restrain the westward population by licensing only twenty-five canoes a year to travel west to trade; the licensing system, however, did little to stem the increasing number of men illegally engaged in the trade.[44]

Iroquois hostility and La Salle's fur trade activity, however brief, changed the western Great Lakes. First, the region became ethnically more diverse as people were forced west and were integrated into existing refugee communities. Refugees rarely established separate villages. Second, in this demographically diverse and turbulent world, trade goods acquired an increasingly important function. They facilitated the negotiation of indigenous alliances and transformed strangers and even enemies into allies. Third, the pattern of Frenchmen transporting goods to the Indians of the western Great Lakes became firmly established. Fourth, as the numbers of traders in the western Great Lakes increased, the conflict with the Iroquois intensified. These Frenchmen became increasingly dependent on Indian people not only for furs but also for protection. However intense the warfare, the French continued to go west—no other occupation offered rewards so lucrative as those of the fur trade.

Moreover, a class of illegal traders emerged, known as *coureurs de bois*, or runners of the woods. Although French *habitants* were forbidden to leave the settled areas without permission from the government of New France, this restriction was routinely ignored. By 1680, there were reported to be as many as eight hundred illegal traders in the west, but this was a far from accurate assessment, because, as one of the New France officials said, "Everyone associated with them covers up for them."[45] When New France first issued trading licenses in 1681, many *coureurs de bois* simply ignored the new restrictions.

Seventeenth-century life in the western Great Lakes was a perilous venture for Frenchmen, especially for illegal traders. Warfare did not diminish until the 1690s, when the French finally recruited sufficient Native allies to move the fighting from the *pays d'en haut* to Iroquois lands. Only in 1701 did the Iroquois sue for peace.

The landscape of warfare, coupled with the distance from Montreal to the western Great Lakes, encouraged the establishment of Indian villages at or near river junctions and portages. The French established forts where large numbers of Indians lived in adjacent villages, but most of these were neither very large nor heavily fortified. They would be referred to more aptly as trade outposts (see fig. 1). The French military presence proved too limited to guarantee protection, and these forts depended on the support of indigenous people. When Indian support failed, these posts were abandoned by the French.[46]

The Fur Trade Wars destroyed long-established indigenous trade routes, and no one group again dominated the trade as the Huron had initially done with the French. The Odawa tribe, located on Lake Michigan's eastern shore, failed in its attempt to assume the middleman role previously held by the Huron along the St. Lawrence River. The natural landscape of the Great Lakes provided multiple pathways to the same destination. In Michigan, for instance, the Maumee, Raisin, Saginaw, Au Sable, Manistee, and St. Joseph Rivers provided access from Lakes Huron and Erie to the interior without hazarding confrontation with the Odawa (see fig. 2). Logistically, it was impossible for one people to dominate the western Great Lakes fur trade.

Fur traders also discovered that the exchange process was embedded in an indigenous social context and was defined by friendship and kinship. Exchange occurred primarily at wintering grounds or in villages. Consequently, fur traders attempted to position themselves within the kin networks of indigenous society. Marriage, either in the "manner of the country" or performed by missionary priests, assured traders inclusion as Native allies, secured personal safety, and facilitated access to furs.[47] Traders fortunate enough to marry socially prominent Indian women, particularly those with extensive kin networks, had an advantage over their rivals. As Jennifer Brown's work demonstrates, not only did Native women enhance the success of the exchange process but a woman's absence might lead to the failure of a trading expedition.[48] Intermarriage continued into the nineteenth century when one of the best-known examples was John Johnston's marriage to O-shaw-gus-co-day-way-quah, whose father was the powerful Ojibway leader, Waubojeeg. Johnston's marriage transformed him into a successful Lake Superior trader, and his wife became one of the most powerful women in the region.[49] One of their daughters, despite being educated in Ireland, retained her Indian name and identity and became the wife of Henry Schoolcraft, who was the Indian agent at Sault Ste. Marie from 1822 to 1832 and became a well-known folklorist of Indian legends.

Trade in the western Great Lakes was complicated by the Fur Trade Wars as well as by the cultural context that defined exchange for the

Indians. A trader's success depended on his ability to understand and negotiate the symbolic consequences of exchange. Consequently, Native wives became indispensable intermediaries for their fur trader husbands. These women facilitated communication among people who spoke different languages by serving as interpreters and by arbitrating the negotiation process.

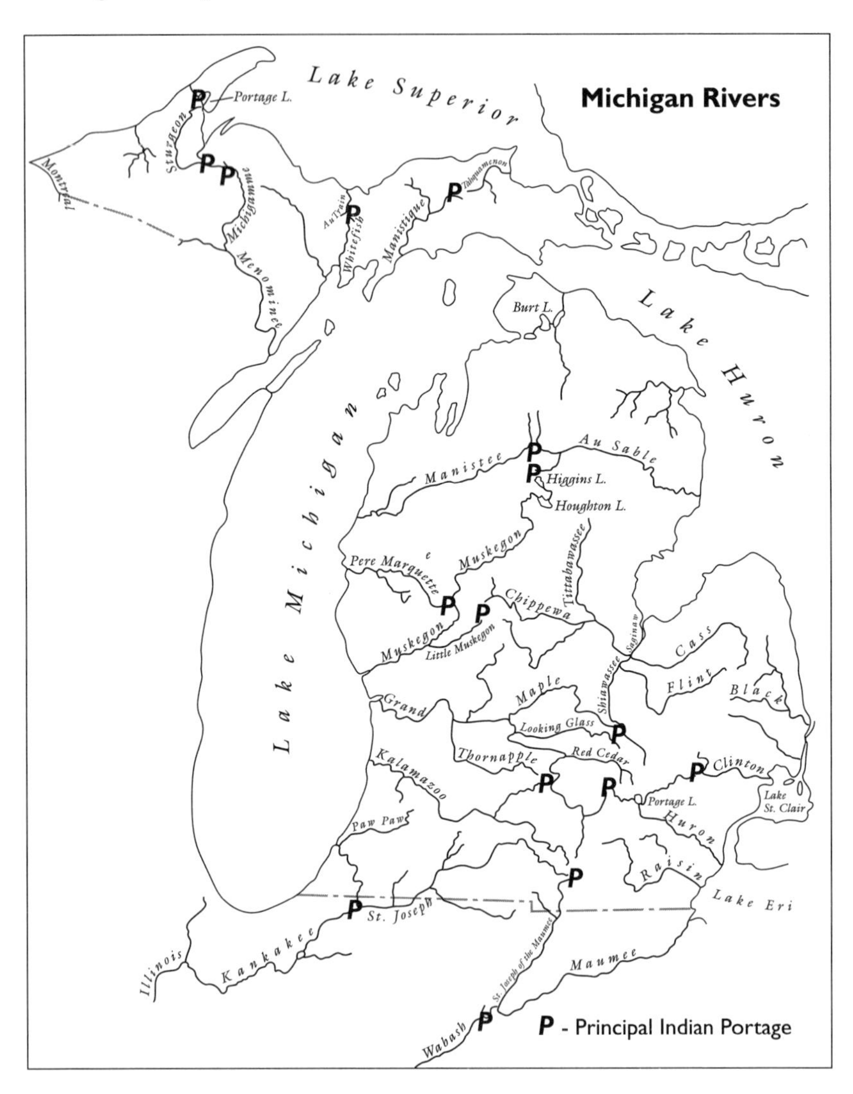

FIGURE 2. *Principal Indian portages.* During the seasonal fall rains and winter thaws these portage areas became part of the rapidly flowing riverways and made it difficult for one community or people to dominate the trade.

Early Jesuit records, particularly marital and baptismal registers, provide an opportunity to study the lives of some of these women. Even though the Indian women mentioned in these records became Catholic converts, they did not simply reinvent themselves as French. As we shall see, these women retained their Indian identity, as evidenced by their language, names, and tribal affiliations.[50]

Catholicism had important social and cultural consequences and often served as the means through which Native women enhanced their own prominence and authority.[51] It was women whom the Jesuits recruited and trusted to become catechizers, instructors, and interpreters. Some Native women became devout Catholics, but Christianity did not uniformly transform gender-egalitarian societies into communities where male authority prevailed.[52] For the tumultuous years of the Fur Trade Wars, from 1650 to 1700, *The Jesuit Relations* provide detailed descriptions of a diverse spectrum of Native people as well as the varieties and vagaries of their interactions with each other and with the French. The *Relations* were yearly accounts, often lengthy narratives, submitted by the missionaries to their superiors in New France. Many of these accounts were printed in France and were then read by other Jesuits and wealthy patrons. Embedded within this Jesuit literature is the record of an oral culture, one that left few written records. But, by reconstructing an oral culture from this textual mode, we can extract the history of everyday communication and hear, in however fragmentary a fashion, the language of face-to-face association and firsthand experience. Most important, we can begin to see how individuals and groups established their core identities, how much and what type of variation they permitted around that core, and what they deemed unacceptable. Interrogating the Jesuit written record allows us to understand something of how individuals not only shaped and reshaped their identities but also connected with large-scale historical processes.[53]

In the western Great Lakes the fur trade was part of an ever-evolving arena of cultural negotiation. Indians and Frenchmen "who shared neither their values nor their assumptions about the appropriate way of accomplishing tasks" met on the middle ground.[54] By broadening this middle-ground arena of cultural negotiation to include both Native women and Christianity, we see how women's participation in the fur trade ensured an exchange process governed by kinship.

The next chapter, by following the Jesuits into the *pays d'en haut,* shows how they gravitated, like the traders, toward refugee centers. Illinois Country proved receptive to the Jesuits' message, and in a profusion of letters and journals, the Jesuits reveal how Catholicism and the fur trade evolved as a mutually constitutive middle ground. Through the eyes of Father Jacques Gravier we see how Marie Rouensa, the young daughter of a prominent Kaskaskia headman, used her conversion to Catholicism to assert control over her life. An examination of her life reveals why the Ilini were receptive to the French and how women emerged as cultural mediators of the middle ground.

2

Marie Rouensa and the Jesuits

Conversion, Gender, and Power

The prolonged fighting of the Fur Trade Wars encouraged the employment of adaptive strategies, but the Ilini were not one people before the onset of war and then an entirely different people at the end of the fighting. Nor was warfare the single transformative agent that led to Catholicism at a "moment in time when competing interests clash[ed] in a visible and tangible way."[1] Indian conversions to Christianity resulted from a larger, ongoing social contest about the nature of authority and the role of women and men in Ilini society. Christianity was integral to the adaptive behaviors of the Ilini as they responded to encounter and involvement in the fur trade. Catholicism appealed to Ilini women because it often offered an alternative to abusive, polygamous marriages. Even before the arrival of the French or the conflict with the Iroquois, the number of Ilini men had declined dramatically, reduced by warfare with the Winnebago and Sioux.[2]

The constant threat of warfare and its devastating consequences, coupled with repeated relocations to avoid attack, stressed social relationships within Ilini communities. Female oppression and abuse, perhaps a consequence of skewed sexual ratios, were not unusual among the Ilini. One early French account contends that there were four women to every man. Both Fathers Jacques Marquette and Claude Allouez confirmed the high incidence of serial polygamy. La Salle reported that men could have as many as ten or twelve wives.[3] Women were brutally punished for marital infidelity, and one Frenchman, a young observer named Pierre Deliette, described how an unfaithful wife was punished through gang rape.[4] This punishment was condoned by the husband, who admonished his wife, "As I know you are fond of men, I offer you a feast of them—take your fill."[5] Even a widow's mourning behavior could be publicly policed by the dead man's family. Any woman who failed to honor the customary one-year mourning period might be scalped by "the relatives of the deceased," who "would take her scalp as if she were one of their enemies, would put it in a hoop and hang it at the top of their cabin."[6]

The arrival of the Jesuits and French fur traders offered women an opportunity to challenge abusive treatment openly. Catholicism enhanced their authority and power within their villages. This chapter focuses on Marie Rouensa, the daughter of a prominent Kaskaskia headman. Conversion transformed her into a public figure and allowed her to challenge the authority of both her father and her French fur trader husband.[7] Father Jacques Gravier's message proved particularly appealing to young women. Catholicism celebrated female celibacy and allowed women to refuse offers of marriage. For those who elected marriage, the monogamous Christian sacrament proved particularly appealing and replaced indigenous practice. Both polygamous marriages as well as "country" marriages to French fur traders were rejected by these Christian converts.[8] Women, aided by Catholicism, gradually transformed polygamy into monogamy.[9]

Although the process of conversion and intermarriage differed by community, young women like Marie Rouensa often became Catholic converts before marriage. Her Catholicism led her to challenge her father's decision that she marry a French fur trader, an apostate Catholic known for his mockery of the Jesuits.[10] When Marie opposed her father's marital demands, a public struggle ensued that shows how Catholicism both encouraged and facilitated Marie's success in challenging male authority. Marie asserted authority and autonomy over her own life and, eventually, over her household, including its male members.

In Marie Rouensa's village, social dynamics overshadowed Christian dogma when Marie negotiated a compromise that led to her marriage and converted her parents and her village to Catholicism.[11] Many men as well as women—old and young—eventually became Catholic. Even some of the village elders became Catholic converts. These men, who represented traditional sources of authority in Indian society, also reasserted their own authority through Christianity and eventually challenged the ascendant authority of Christian proselytizers, such as Marie Rouensa.

It is from Father Jacques Gravier's perspective that we learn the specific details of Marie Rouensa's life.[12] By 1688 Gravier lived among the Iliniwek and became one of the more successful Jesuit missionaries. He fostered a cadre of female proselytizers who, as professed Christians, behaved more assertively. They publicly challenged the non-Christian elders of their village. According to Gravier, these female converts acquired notoriety because they openly rejected the customs of their society:

> Although this nation is much given to debauchery, especially the men, the reverend Jesuit fathers . . . manage (if one may so say) to impose some check on this by instructing a number of girls in Christianity, who often profit by their teaching, and mock at the superstitions of their nation. This often greatly incenses the old men.[13]

Father Gravier's letters also enthusiastically described Marie Rouensa's prominent public role as a Christian proselytizer. He portrayed her as an able assistant who translated his Christian teachings into the Ilini language. It was Marie's translations from French to her Native language that situated Christianity within an Ilini context. Marie's repertoire of Biblical tales provided an array of new stories that resonated with their indigenous oral traditions. Christian stories had familiar themes, and those with endings that rewarded pain and suffering were in concert with the trials the Kaskaskia endured: Abraham's sacrifice, Job's trials, and Samson's strengths and failures. Even the lamentations of Jeremiah would have found resonance among the Kaskaskia, whose world was plagued by Iroquois hostilities.

Father Gravier reinforced the public drama that surrounded Marie's public storytelling by lending her his Bible. Father Gravier's large copperplate Bible provided a visual cue card for each of Marie's stories. Those pictures drew people throughout the village to her father's cabin to hear her speak.

> This young woman, who is only 17 years old, has so well remembered what I have said about each picture of the Old and New Testament that she explains each one singly, without trouble and without confusion, as well as I could do—and even more intelligently, in their manner. In fact, I allowed her to take away each picture after I had explained it in public, to refresh her memory in private. But she frequently repeated to me, on the spot, all that I had said about each picture; and not only did she explain them at home to her husband, to her father, to her mother, and to all the girls who went there, as she continues to do, speaking of nothing but the pictures or the catechism, but she also explained the pictures on the whole of the Old Testament to the old and the young men whom her father assembled in his dwelling.[14]

To Father Gravier, Marie was an instructor for the adults and children of her village, an interpreter who was recognized as a gifted storyteller. Even the elders came to hear her. Among Native people, it was these men who usually served as the repositories of oral traditions, but they listened attentively to this young woman. Father Gravier's appreciation of Marie's proselytizing skills allowed him to go about his daily round of devotional duties while Marie drew new converts to his mission.[15]

Marie Rouensa's effectiveness as a proselytizer was enhanced by the large number of women in her Kaskaskia village. Polygamous marriages increased the number of adult women in each household. Therefore, households were a natural site for proselytization and conversion. As the Jesuits explained, "We call those instructors, who in other missions are called catechists, because it is not in the Church, but in the wigwams that they instruct the catechums and the proselytes."[16]

Christianity evolved into a shared female experience that expanded the roles available to women. Father Gravier told stories of female Catholic saints and provided Native women with new and very powerful models of assertive behavior.[17] Although it is impossible to understand just how the Kaskaskia women actually comprehended Catholicism, it is not difficult to understand how the transforming hand of the Jesuits made Christianity attractive to Ilini women who had been degraded and, often, physically abused. Catholicism's multiplicity of female saints proved particularly appealing. They offered new behavioral roles that encouraged Kaskaskia women to dedicate their lives to the Church. Catholicism offered a celibate alternative to the narrow range of acceptable female behaviors among the Ilini. Before Gravier's arrival there was only one option for unmarried Ilini women: to enter warrior society.[18] Although indigenous women were often free to reject potential suitors, such behaviors were undoubtedly discouraged after prolonged warfare had substantially reduced the male population. Christianity offered its followers an alternative pathway.

As a young woman, Marie Rouensa "[resolved] to consecrate her virginity to God."[19] Her professed devotion to chastity and her love of Christ intensified when her parents chose a fifty-year-old veteran of the fur trade with an unsavory reputation for her husband. Michel Accault was a social reprobate, "famous in this Ilinois country for all his debaucheries."[20] He came west with René-Robert Cavelier de La Salle in 1679 and had lived and traded among the Ilini for twenty years. Although the marriage had been arranged by her parents, Marie refused to obey and relied on her Christianity to justify her decision. She was supported by Father Gravier.

She had resolved never to marry, in order that she might belong wholly to Jesus Christ. She answered her father and her mother, when they brought her to me in company with the frenchmen whom they wished to have for a son-in-law, that she did not wish to marry; that she had already given all her heart to God.[21]

Marie was banished from her mother's cabin and was then stripped of her clothing and driven outside by her father. She sought refuge with Gravier, who was blamed for her disobedience. Her father ordered the Kaskaskia to stay away from the chapel and posted armed observers near the entrance. This threat of force left Gravier with a nearly empty sanctuary. Even the fort commandant offered the Jesuit no assistance and, instead, reviled him with "a great many calumnies . . . in the presence of the French and of a large number of savages."[22] Marie's father, meanwhile, "assured her that, if she obeyed him not, she would be treated most rigorously by him; that assuredly prayers would no longer be said to God; that he would go to war, and that she would see him no more."

Father Gravier urged Marie to "fear not, because prayer was her refuge" against her irate parents. But two days later, Marie's attitude toward marriage changed. She relied on her father's behavior to justify this attitudinal shift and told Father Gravier that she "feared that her father would become still more furious and proceed to extremities." She proposed an alternative strategy, a compromise that even Father Gravier admitted "was a good one." Marie would "consent against [her] inclination" to this marriage, if her parents elected to become Christians. Gravier immediately supported Marie's marital decision. Subsequently, he provided her with new models of saintly behavior: Catholicism had a bevy of saints for married as well as single women. Father Gravier described Marie's choices,

She has taken for her special patronesses the christian Ladies who have sanctified themselves in the state of matrimony,—namely, St. Paula, St. Frances, St. Margaret, St. Elizabeth, and St. Bridget, who[m] she invokes many times during the day.[23]

Many saints, like Mary, the mother of Jesus, possessed dual natures. Mary could be prayed to as either the Virgin or as the Mother of God. Gravier assured the married Marie Rouensa that "she is not angry because you call her mother."[24]

Christian conversion presented no stumbling block for Marie's parents: Conversion was integral to the language of accommodation, and ensured their daughter's marriage and their village access to trade goods and French assistance. As Jacqueline Peterson has shown, "Relatives by marriage were expected not only to deal fairly, but to provide protection, hospitality, and sustenance in time of famine."[25] It is not surprising that, once Marie consented to marry Accault, her father "informed all the chiefs of the villages, by considerable presents, that he was about to be allied to a Frenchman."[26]

Marriage was viewed as a sacrament by the Catholic Church and this, undoubtedly, appealed to Marie Rouensa. In the late seventeenth century, "country" marriages offered Native women minimal control over their French husbands. For Marie Rouensa, a Christian marriage reshaped an otherwise dismal outcome. With the conversion of Marie's parents to Catholicism, the Christian strictures about the sanctity of marriage became enforceable community norms. Marie Rouensa's father gave the Jesuits control over marriage when he publicly proclaimed that "the black gowns were the witnesses of true marriage; and that to them alone God had given orders to pray for all who wished to marry, and they would be truly married."[27] Although marriages "in the manner of the country" often acquired long-term stability, marriage partners like Accault, better known for their wayward than their faithful behavior, were problematic husbands. Marie's household, reinforced by Christian strictures about the sanctity of marriage, was now ensured a steady supply of trade goods.

While Gravier's letters idealized the Kaskaskia as Christian, it was also apparent that religion was a contested middle ground. Christianity facilitated female challenges to male authority, but simultaneously provided avenues through which recent male converts might reassert their own authority. Catholicism became a more nuanced, socially combative arena once it included a larger, more diverse population. The authority of both Father Gravier and Marie Rouensa was immediately challenged when the village elders became Christians. Father Gravier skillfully rebuffed their first attempts when he retained control over the hours of Christian worship. "The elders called out the summons to prayers throughout the village; and I think that the whole of it—women, girls, children, and even old men—gathered round the chapel." Gravier resisted the elders' challenge by refusing to open the doors of the church. Since he "alone governed prayer . . . and since I had not announced it, or appointed any one to do so in my stead, there would be no prayer that day."[28]

Marie's Catholicism also encouraged her to resist those behaviors that threatened her autonomy. A French trader like Accault found it difficult to assert French notions of patriarchal authority. Father Gravier was justifiably reluctant to accord Michel Accault authority over his wife, who was both an effective Catholic proselytizer and a rigorous and faithful Christian. In this instance, Catholicism proved a socially innovative mechanism that enhanced female authority and mitigated female submission to male authority.

The French audience who read Gravier's accounts of Marie Rouensa may have questioned contributions to a mission that empowered women and curtailed male authority. Gravier, however, provided a reasonable Catholic answer when he ascribed transformative power to Marie's Christian piety. Gravier's description of Marie attributed to her the types of extraordinary behavior associated with saints and martyrs of the church. Marie became responsible for her parents' conversion and, quite amazingly, even her reprobate husband was transformed into a model Christian, and he publicly proclaimed himself a reformed man. Then, in Father Gravier's most lavish testament to Marie's miraculous power, he noted that two hundred Kaskaskia were baptized between March 30 and November 29, 1693. Gravier even counted more than three-quarters of the Kaskaskia population present during catechism. Father Gravier may have inflated the attendance or he may have reinvented "curious" Kaskaskia spectators as Catholic converts. Undoubtedly, his enthusiastic depiction of Marie led him to overemphasize her Christian influence. By describing her behavior as inspirational, however, Father Gravier also minimized Marie's challenges to patriarchal authority. When he associated Marie's miraculous behaviors with the conversion of her entire village, he described a conversion miracle that few seventeenth-century Jesuits ever witnessed.[29]

A rather singular but probably unspoken alliance joined female converts and the French priests. The priests identified the Kaskaskia as Catholic, while their female converts relied on Catholicism to assert their own autonomy and independence from Ilini men.

Fur traders who married Native converts joined their wives' households and complied with indigenous behavioral standards. Indigenous kin networks determined access to furs, and it was crucial that the behavior of the trader's wife remain consonant with indigenous society. Even the behavior of Christian converts remained consonant with the social mores of their households and their villages. Because trade goods were used to form or reaffirm indigenous alliances, fur traders were welcome additions to households and villages. Their presence ensured access to trade goods.[30] Fur trade marriages may have been governed by the consensual decision making of the community, rather than individually motivated.

Catholicism and the fur trade encouraged the formation and perpetuation of matrifocal households.[31] Among the Ilini, where women outnumbered men, the Frenchman who lived in his wife's household helped reinforce female residence patterns. The household's access to trade goods enhanced the prestige and power of its members. Moreover, these households were able to produce a food surplus that fed not only the fur trader but also the French canoemen or voyageurs who also arrived from Montreal. Western Great Lakes fur traders were dependent on Indians for their food supply. Licenses, or *congés,* limited the number of canoes sent into the western Great Lakes. Canoe cargoes consisted primarily of trade goods, and traders obtained their food supplies in the Upper Country. As one trader remarked, "The canoes, as I have already observed are not large enough to carry provisions."[32] Men who had the good fortune to marry into indigenous households had a distinct advantage over transient traders.

Agriculture remained women's work and the fur trade dramatically increased agricultural productivity.[33] In Illinois Country, matrifocal households produced both rich grain and vegetable harvests. Most historians have assumed that crops such as wheat, because they required extensive milling, were not grown by Native people, but in Illinois Country, wheat was harvested by both Natives and Jesuits.[34] Father Marest's Iliniwek village had three mills, the Jesuits had their own, and the Iliniwek operated two more.[35]

The increased emphasis on an agricultural surplus became apparent when Marie's Kaskaskia village resettled on the Mississippi's rich alluvial lands, near present-day St. Louis. Shortly after Accault's death, following seven years of marriage, Marie married another fur trader, Michel Philippe, who was far less prominent than Accault. Philippe arrived in Illinois Country an obscure voyageur, or canoeman, who probably earned less than 1,000 livres a year.[36] They were married for twenty years, and, although the Kaskaskia baptismal records tell us that Marie gave birth to six more children, we know very little about her everyday life during this period.

Marie died in 1725; she was about forty to forty-five years old. She was buried under the floor of the Immaculate Conception parish church in Kaskaskia. It is from the circumstances of her death that we see how her adult life was continually shaped by her Indian heritage, as she simultaneously and selectively incorporated practices and behaviors of the

French. Marie's Catholicism reshaped the framework of her life, and as death approached, she relied on French law and her priest to ensure her household's continuity. Marie left a written will that she dictated to Father Jean-Antoine Le Boullenger in her Ilini language. The priest simultaneously translated into French and the notary formally recorded Marie's bequests. The priest read it back twice, in Ilini, to Marie. This will, because it was recorded in French and notarized, was legally enforceable. This document had practical implications, but its formulation provides insight into a household that remained rooted within indigenous society. Marie's dictating her will in her Ilini language was indicative of a household in which her children were conversant with her language.[37]

Marie relied on French law to impose the kinds of behaviors Ilini women expected of their children. Because her estate was large enough to probate and inventory Marie used legally enforceable conditions to divide her household's wealth and goods and in this way attempted to control the behavior of her wayward eldest son. She threatened to disinherit her son "as much for his disobedience as for the marriage he has contracted despite his mother and his relatives." There is no reference to the authority of her French fur trader husband. Instead, she refers to herself and her relatives as the authority figures in her son's life. Marie's son had left her household and had married and lived "among the savage nations," probably among the non-Christian Peoria.[38] She denied him his inheritance until he left his wife and returned to her household. Marie's son did eventually return, after his mother's death, and received his share of the inheritance.

Female converts like Marie Rouensa used the institutional framework of French religion and law simultaneously to accommodate to and to influence the behavior of male and female offspring. Marie divided her wealth and linked it to specifically required behaviors. Her sizable estate facilitated such control and also reflects the extent to which her Kaskaskia household became both acquisitive and accumulative. Marie's estate was valued at 45,000 livres, and her children, upon maturity or marriage or obedience, would receive equal shares. Marie's property included several tracts of agricultural land. Two houses, 36 by 20 feet, with stone fireplaces were located within the Kaskaskia village. Two barns, filled with hay, fed the livestock: oxen, thirteen cows, three horses, thirty-one pigs, and forty-eight chickens. There were oxcarts and horse carts and iron plows. She owned two African American married couples as well as an Indian woman slave.[39] The three women probably planted and harvested oats, wheat, and maize. The male slaves were more likely to work in the fur trade, but they were also woodcutters, for there were nine tons of wood, cut and debarked, in the estate. The barns also contained wheat and oats. The wheat, valued at 3,300 livres, had been sheaved but not yet ground at the nearby mill. Nineteen to twenty arpents of maize or Indian corn remained to be harvested.[40]

Marie's wealth rested on her household's agricultural productivity, and because she left sufficient property to inventory, we also see the material evidence of her second husband's continuing employment as a fur trader. Among the goods inventoried inside Marie's house were prodigious amounts of cloth, emblematic of a household that was directly engaged in the trade. Michel Philippe was a fur trader—he was not a French peasant farmer.

Many histories, however, mistakenly identify Kaskaskia as a French settlement, even though during the first twenty years of its existence, only one Frenchwoman lived here. Of the twenty-one recorded baptisms, only one was the child of a Frenchwoman.[41] The female French names that appear in marital and baptismal registers testify to the presence of Native women baptized by missionary priests.[42]

Neither Catholicism nor involvement in the trade transformed Native women into French housewives. Native women resisted the division of labor associated with European households. There were none of the traditional tools that characterized French home industry (spinning wheels, looms, or even knitting needles) among the probated wills and inventories of these river community residents.[43] Since Kaskaskia remained part of an indigenous universe in which agriculture remained a female responsibility, the viability of evolving matrifocal households was ensured through an ever-expanding labor pool that incorporated adult children and their offspring, as well as Native American and African American slaves and their children. Indigenous gender roles gave women the management and allocation of productive resources. Native women were even engaged in mining and among the Sauk, Mesquakie, and Winnebago influenced mining techniques and access to lead mines.[44]

Later, the nineteenth-century United States condemned Frenchmen as lazy, an adjective also indiscriminately applied to Native men, but this was because women's agricultural work went unnoticed. As Jacqueline Peterson has pointed out, most French fur traders, even those who retired, had little interest in farming and they "only pretended to cultivate the soil."[45] Instead, it was women's work that produced the food surplus that fed transient traders and was eventually exported to New Orleans for resale. The continued commitment of women to agriculture permitted French husbands to become traders rather than farmers. The Jesuits at Kaskaskia taught the Indians to use the *charrue,* a wheeled plow, and its use was reportedly widespread among the Kaskaskia. Fields may also have been mounded in Indian fashion.[46] An agricultural surplus, coupled with the fur trade, ensured the viability of these matrifocal households.

Catholicism further enhanced the social prominence of these women. Among the Ilini, Catholicism was integrated into the behaviors of women's daily lives. During Mass, for instance, prayers were often the responsibility of Indian women. Women also summoned their community to daily devotions. Mission chapel bells were often rung by Native women to signal the start of morning and evening services.[47] At the River L'Abbe mission, the French colonial church for the Cahokia Indians on Monks Mound, one Ilini woman was immortalized by being buried with the chapel's large bell.[48]

Historians often associate successful Indian conversions with the Jesuits' ability to locate sympathetic parallels between indigenous beliefs and Catholicism.[49] Among the Ilini, the Jesuits approached Catholicism through the lives of female saints, relying on a multiplicity of godlike figures. When the Jesuits entombed Native women in the churches of their Christian God, they not only publicly honored them, but these women also entered a female pantheon of the good and holy. The inclusion of indigenous role models, such as Marie Rouensa, unofficially expanded the body of Catholic saints.[50]

Father Gravier promoted a Christianity that publicly enhanced female power and authority, but he did so in a way that encouraged Indians to consider the multiple nature of the Christian God. This concept of multiplicity of godlike figures in Catholicism proved compatible with the numerous manitous, or spirits, that were integral to the beliefs of Algonquian-speaking people in the western Great Lakes. For Marie Rouensa's mother, for example, Christ became "'Manitoua assouv'—that is to say, 'the great spirit, or genie.'"[51] Among the Odawa, God became Gitche Manitou, the Great Spirit. Thus, Christ became one of the many manitous invoked at councils and feasts.[52]

Father Gravier's syncretic efforts were rewarded when Christian teachings resonated with women who sought to enhance their authority within their own communities. Jesuit writings are replete with examples of thinly veiled, but persistent indigenous behaviors that were often misinterpreted as the penitential behavior of religious fervor. For example, recurrent, prolonged fasting had long been integral to indigenous beliefs and proved "striking" when Jesuits described Catholic Indians. Scholars who have focused on well-known female converts, such as Kateri Tekakwitha, have noted the prominent role of penitential suffering in their lives. Marie Rouensa's life was also marked by this sympathetic relationship with Catholic penitential practice. For instance, Father Gravier urged her to stop her severe abuse of her body and urged her to treat herself more "tenderly." What Father Gravier viewed as the devout fervor of the converted Catholic also bore similarity to persistent Indian behaviors.

> Having heard me say that many Christians, penetrated with regret for their offenses and with sorrow for having crucified Jesus Christ by their sins, practice Holy severities upon themselves, she . . . made for herself a girdle of thorns. This she wore for two whole days, and she would have crippled herself with it, had she not informed me of this mortification.[53]

Father Gravier recorded these behaviors as the penitential evidence of Christian enthusiasm, but it was these behavioral extremes that Jesuits found difficult to control and that threatened the Jesuits' hold on Christianity. The specter of female mortification loomed as potentially more powerful than that of their long-suffering teachers. Among the Iroquois, for example, Nancy Shoemaker has shown how Kateri Tekakwitha's self-mortifications involved painful forms of physical suffering in the public arena. Native American converts were public, not private, sufferers. In public self-mortification they found empowerment.

> There were Savage women who threw themselves under the ice, in the midst of winter. One had her daughter dipped into it, who was only six years old,—for the purpose, she said, of teaching her penance in good season. The mother stood there on account of her past sins; she kept her innocent daughter there on account of her sins to come, which this child would perhaps commit when grown up. Savages, both men and women, covered themselves with blood by disciplinary stripes with iron, with rods, with thorns, with nettles. . . . They mingled ashes in their portion of Sagamité; they put glowing coals between their toes, where the fire burned a hole in the flesh; they went bare-legged to make a long procession in the snows.[54]

This sacrificial side of Christianity proved a powerful social force, and Father Gravier channeled the potentially disruptive behavior of female converts in alternative directions. Gravier encouraged Native women to assume the traditional behaviors assigned to Christian men.[55]

> I had but to tell her that, in addition to the prayers that I say every morning in the chapel, it would be good to say them in the house for the whole family, before retiring. I told her that it was also advisable to invite some persons from the other cabins to come at that time, so that the prayers might be said and the examination of conscience be made together . . . and from the month of October she never failed to do so after supper.[56]

At the time of Marie Rouensa's conversion and marriage, the Kaskaskia and Peoria were settled along the Upper Illinois River. By the time of Marie's death, the Kaskaskia had migrated south to escape the Iroquois and had settled near Cahokia.[57]

Marie Rouensa exemplified Catholicism as a source of female empowerment, but at the same time her life demonstrated that the language she spoke, the clothes she wore, and the household in which she lived were still rooted in an indigenous context. A life lived in the midst of a kin-based society encouraged Marie to refashion Catholicism within that familiar context, but Marie's life also suggests that compromises made on the middle ground were subsequently institutionalized in cultural practice. Christianity was negotiated and transformed on the middle ground.

Marie Rouensa was not an atypical historical figure. Certainly, much about her life remains unknown and only recently has she received historical attention. In *The Middle Ground* in 1991, Richard White referred to her as Aramepinchieue and relied on her marriage to Michel Accault to illustrate the kinds of compromises responsible for the evolution of the middle ground.[58] Carl Ekberg's article, published in 1991, refuted references to Marie Rouensa as Aramepinchieue.[59] But Ekberg, unlike White, focused on Marie's transformation into a Frenchwoman.

Marie Rouensa was not French, however. The Kaskaskia village population grew owing to the intermarriage of Frenchmen and Native women, not Frenchmen and Frenchwomen. In a world where Frenchmen preferred the fur trade to farming and Native women were skilled agriculturalists, any dramatic transformation in the productive roles of men and women was unlikely.

The marital behavior of Marie's children was prototypical of those involved in the fur trade. Mixed-ancestry daughters married Frenchmen and sons married Indian women. Marie threatened to disinherit her eldest son because he married a non-Christian Indian woman, but her threat proved difficult to enforce. It was too difficult to discipline young men who lived among Indians, especially young men of mixed ancestry.

Although Marie's son himself then disappeared from written record, Marie's memory was publicly perpetuated. In 1740, Marie's name reappeared when a priest recorded the marriage of a young Indian woman named Marie Rouensa to a French trader. Perhaps a naming ceremony bestowed Marie's name on a young Ilini woman, or perhaps a young Indian convert chose this as her baptismal name. Whether given to or taken by a young Indian woman, Marie's name was perpetuated beyond her death.[60]

There were other seventeenth-century indigenous parallels for Marie's Christian conversion and her social prominence.[61] The Erie–Oneida convert, Catherine Gandeateua, and her Mohawk successor, Kateri Tekakwitha, were also prominent converts.[62] Among the Iroquois, the Jesuits required "a massive reorientation of behavior and belief," but in the Great Lakes, they rarely achieved this type of committed Catholic orientation.[63] The Jesuits were dramatically disrupted by an eighteenth-century decline in their numbers, and by midcentury the order was disbanded. In Catholic communities among the Five Nations Iroquois, other Catholic orders replaced the Jesuits, but in the western Great Lakes, the Jesuits had few replacements. Instead, a type of "frontier" Catholicism evolved, and Native converts and their mixed-ancestry descendants assumed increased importance as lay practitioners. Despite the absence of priests, there exists substantial archaeological evidence that confirms the continuing burial of Native Catholic women.[64]

Marie was different from the Iroquois converts because her conversion foreshadowed the behaviors of Native women who became involved in the fur trade. Her alternative life choices were not made possible solely by the arrival of the Jesuits but also by the onset of the fur trade. Marie Rouensa's Catholicism evolved as she pursued "status and a firmer sense of her own identity."[65] She epitomized the type of Jesuit success that the historian Daniel Richter has characterized as being "won on the basis of diplomatic, political, and religious considerations that were essentially Indian and traditional rather than European and Christian."[66]

The life of another Catholic Ilini woman, Marie Madeleine Réaume L'archevêque Chevalier, who lived among the Potawatomi in the St. Joseph River valley, is examined in the next chapter. Where Marie Rouensa's life suggests how and why a sympathetic relationship evolved between Jesuits and Native women, Marie Madeleine's life shows how socially dynamic Catholic kin networks linked distant fur trade communities throughout the western Great Lakes.

The Ilini decision to remain on their homeland was disastrous. By

1700, their population was greatly reduced and dispersed. More than eight tribes disappeared: the Kouerakouilenoux, Raparouras, Maronas, Albivi or Amouoka, Chepoussa, Chinko or Coiracoenatanon, Espemikia, Tapoura, and several others.[67] Simultaneously, many Ilini Catholic women and their French fur traders moved north into Potawatomi communities.

3

Marie Madeleine Réaume L'archevêque Chevalier and the St. Joseph River Potawatomi

AT THE END of the seventeenth century, as the Fur Trade Wars ended, Indians and traders, the French military, *habitants,* and priests moved into the lakelands and river valleys of the *pays d'en haut.* Much of Illinois Country was claimed by the Green Bay Potawatomi, who had followed the Lake Michigan shoreline eastward.[1] The Potawatomi settled along the northern border of Ilini lands and established numerous villages adjacent to the Miami in the St. Joseph River valley (see fig. 3). By 1694, Antoine de la Mothe Cadillac, then the commandant at Michilimackinac and later founder of Detroit, estimated that over two hundred warriors could be recruited among the Potawatomi in southwest Michigan. This indicated a population of more than twelve hundred people.[2]

In the seventeenth and eighteenth centuries, when rivers were transportation conduits, the St. Joseph River portage to the Kankakee, where the French located Fort St. Joseph, was an important link between Lake Michigan and the Mississippi River valley.[3] During the spring, when the winter snow melted, and in the fall, when the seasonal rains arrived, the river valley flooded and the once-dry land took on a lakelike appearance. Indians journeyed south along the St. Joseph River, to the Kankakee, and then followed the Illinois River to the Mississippi. This river valley was a microcosm of the numerous Indian villages that had been settled in conjunction with the fur trade, and thus, there were clusters of communities at river entrances, crossings, and portages. Villages in the St. Joseph River valley attracted people as diverse as the Ilini, Miami, Potawatomi, Huron, Mahican, Fox, Sauk, and Wabunaki.[4] They were loosely joined fragments of a common society and culture that faced a continual influx of strangers.

Social flexibility was crucial in these diverse villages. The incorpora-

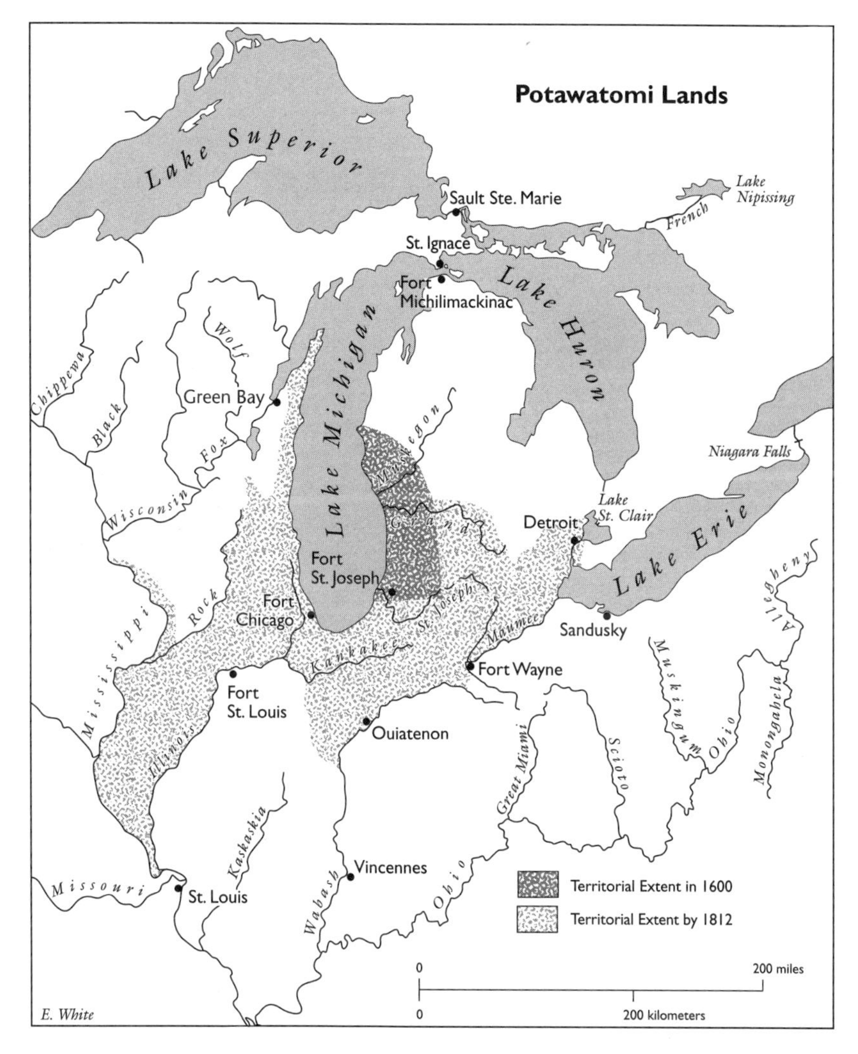

FIGURE 3. *The expansion of Potawatomi lands from the seventeenth to the nineteenth century.*

tion of strangers took place through intermarriage and, less frequently, through adoption. Kinship loyalties often transformed strangers into allies but, in other instances, magnified the volatility of society in the western Great Lakes. Marriage traditionally fostered alliances among clan members who lived at some distance from each other. When the Iroquois threat forced closer proximity, intermarriage increased the number of people with predetermined loyalties and further complicated local disputes. Marital alliances transformed personal disputes into potentially lethal social contests. One physical blow was often magnified by the large number of male allies who rushed into the fray and transformed a minor disagreement into a major confrontation. The incident below, which took place in seventeenth-century Green Bay, was similar to many that occurred throughout the western Great Lakes:

> Sharp words arose on both sides and they came to blows. The Frenchmen were vigorously attacked by the savages and a third man came to the aid of his comrades.
>
> The confusion increased; the Frenchman tore the pendants from the ears of a savage, and gave him a blow in the belly which felled him so rudely that with difficulty could he rise again. At the same time the Frenchman received a blow from a war-club on his head, which caused him to fall motionless.[5]

In this instance, three families, each with a distinct alliance to one of the combatants, joined in the fray. The head of the Bear family was an intimate of the Frenchman. He was immediately joined in the dispute by the Sauk chief, who had married the daughter of the head of the Bear family. The Potawatomi who felled the Frenchman was a member of the Red Carp clan with marital ties to the Black Carp. Only the fact that the Frenchman regained consciousness prevented further bloodshed.

This tumultuous landscape was further complicated by an intense rivalry between Jesuits and fur traders. Not all fur traders followed Michel Accault's example and were married in the eyes of the church. The Jesuits viewed "marriages in the manner of the country" as immoral and these adulterous fur traders as a threat to their missionary efforts.

The Jesuits also believed that fur traders hindered the Christian conversion of the Indians. In lengthy letters, the priests enumerated the nefarious behaviors of fur traders and blamed them for introducing "two Infamous sorts of Commerce which . . . brought the missions to the brink of destruction. The first [was] the Commerce in brandy; the second [was] the Commerce of the savage women with the French." The Jesuits were outraged by the traders' penchant for gambling and alcohol and they bitterly complained of drunken traders whose surly behavior was openly disrespectful. Alcohol disrupted their missionary efforts.

> What makes their misconduct on this score still worse is, that so persistent an attachment of the game is hardly ever unaccompanied by the general Intoxication of all the players; and drunkenness is always followed by quarrels that arise among them. When these occur publicly before the eyes of the savages they Give rise to three grave scandals: the

> first at seeing them intoxicated; the second, at witnessing them fighting furiously with one another,—sometimes to the extent of seizing their guns in order to kill each other; the third, at observing that the missionaries cannot Remedy these evils.[6]

The Jesuits regarded fur traders as serpents in the Garden of Eden. They cast Native women who dismissed their Christian message as the temptress Eve, especially those who discovered that their "bodies might serve in lieu of merchandise and would be still better received than Beaverskins."[7]

Fur traders deflected Jesuit accusations by offering an alternative interpretation for their behavior and depicting themselves as wilderness diplomats. Many embellished their reputations as skillful Indian negotiators. Traders described Native American society as plagued by warfare, portraying themselves as effective negotiators of indigenous rivalries who secured both peace and allegiance to New France. This argument rarely swayed the Jesuits, but it resonated with the attitudes of New France officials. Consequently, traders were used to distribute gifts to Native American allies, to summon various tribes to peace conferences, and to assess the loyalties of various villages.

The contentiousness between priests and traders has distorted much of the archival record. Letter writing became a literary battlefield, where Jesuits and traders justified their presence by providing harrowing and often exaggerated descriptions of warlike behavior among Native Americans. Intent on removing the fur traders, the priests blamed the traders when warfare erupted. Meanwhile, the traders depicted themselves as resourceful negotiators who brought peace to warring Indians.

French diplomacy rested on the loyalties of their indigenous allies, a loyalty that allowed New France to claim sovereignty over the vast North American interior. Unlike Britain, France lacked a sufficient population to appropriate and colonize Indian lands. Left with little choice, the French learned to negotiate the cultural landscape of an Indian world where friendships and alliances were sealed through the exchange of gifts. Consequently, both French traders and Indians became the beneficiaries of governmental largesse. The distribution of gifts from the French to the Indians was frequently the responsibility of fur traders, and it was this "diplomatic" form of gift-giving that enhanced a fur trader's ties to particular villages and augmented his fur trade profits. Indians reciprocated with presents of furs, but rarely did this peltry become government property.

Gift-giving became a government expenditure that fostered the successful negotiation of indigenous alliances. Unfortunately, many New France officials were trapped into stereotypically describing Indians as warlike to justify gift expenditures to Versailles officials, most of whom never understood this diplomatic process. Ironically, as Iroquois aggression and the Fur Trade Wars ended, the need for gift-giving increased. Versailles responded not with largesses but with a politically naive policy that threatened the stability of the entire region.

Jesuit complaints about fur traders were generally ignored by New France officials, and the disgruntled priests successfully lobbied Versailles to ban traders from the western Great Lakes. The Jesuits' demands, supported by the king's wife, Madame de Maintenon, coincided with an oversupply of furs in government warehouses. Consequently, on May 21, 1696, the king revoked all fur-trading licenses by royal ordinance and prohibited all French traders from carrying goods into the west. Native people were expected to transport their own furs to Montreal, and fur traders who ignored the edict faced confinement in French galleys.[8]

Just as the Fur Trade Wars were ending, Versailles jeopardized French control over the western Great Lakes. Stability in this demographically tumultuous world was maintained through the exchange of gifts, and villages required more, not fewer trade goods. Any diminution in trade goods undermined the ability of villages to incorporate strangers and to establish alliances. The Potawatomi were infuriated by the proposed trade restrictions. The Potawatomi spokesman, Onangizes, threatened General Frontenac with the dissolution of the French alliance. "'If the French leave us,' he said harshly, 'this is the last time we shall come and speak to you.'"[9]

Despite Indian protests, the trade ban went into effect. The 1696 edict transformed legal traders into illegal traders. Those who remained in the west sought the protection of Native communities, thus furthering their dependence on Indian people. During the nineteen years of the ban, traders and Indians became increasingly interdependent. The *coureur de bois* who found refuge in his wife's household accommodated to, and even assimilated into, a world structured by Native American custom and tradition. Because villages incorporated Frenchmen and rejected the possibility that Native women "married out," marriage, either sacramentally sanctioned or in "the manner of the country," transformed French traders into Indian husbands, fathers, and brothers.[10]

The western Great Lakes was a highly complex kin-related world where individuality was subsumed by a larger collective identity. This was a face-to-face world in which people were identified by their relatives and where the individual was suspect. An encounter between strangers required lengthy introductions, necessitated by the increasingly complex kin networks. The words used in most greetings indicated of whom one was a son or daughter or who was one's mother's brother. When the names of family members were unknown, introductions were extended until a familiar name was identified, even as distant as the brother of one's mother's father's sister's son. It was the reputation and prominence of kin networks that defined social acceptance and prominence.

Kinship was more flexible than nationality, ethnicity, or race in constructing identity. Kinship permutations were endless, and, in this already complex world, a new kinship structure grew out of the marriage of French fur traders to Native women that not only incorporated their mixed ancestry offspring, but also facilitated the expansion of the fur trade. The Catholic kin network that appeared during the years of the fur trade ban, 1697 to 1714, was firmly entrenched by the time many of the western posts were reopened between 1718 and 1720.

The exchange process was increasingly centralized in a fictive kin network in which the selection of godparents signified more about the trade than the nature of religious faith. Baptism affirmed the value of social relationships and "extended the bonds of social solidarity."[11] Godparents ensured entrée into the trade, and well-known fur traders and their wives were frequent godparents.

Catholic kin networks paralleled and were enmeshed in those of indigenous society. The fictive relationship created by godparenting bridged the social boundaries of the French and the Indian worlds, further complicating an already complex kin-based society. Entrée into the eighteenth-century trade was increasingly governed by Catholic kin networks, rather than by the regulating authority of the New France government. More formal structures of European governance had limited relevance in the western Great Lakes. The military men, legal fur traders, and even the Jesuits who arrived after the western trade was reopened and the forts were reestablished, discovered a world where kin networks had replaced the hierarchical patterns of French authority. In 1714, when New France again issued licenses to trade in the west, many traders simply ignored the new requirements. The exchange process continued to function as it had over the past two decades. The habitus of behavior, of inclusionary practices fostered by intermarriage and trade within kin networks, was not changed by the reinstatement of trade licenses. Without kin and allies, one could neither govern nor trade.

This Catholic kin network linked commandants to the larger, more populous indigenous world that surrounded them. They served repeatedly as godfathers to the children of Native women and Frenchmen. Unlike their seventeenth-century predecessors, these military commandants rarely engaged in confrontational struggles with the Jesuits. Eighteenth-century appointees were not only older but many had grown to adulthood in the Upper Country. For example, when Fort St. Joseph was reopened, forty-eight-year-old Jean-Baptiste de St. Ours was appointed commandant. His predecessors had been men in their twenties, often first-generation immigrants. St. Ours, like many commandants, was the descendant of New France settlers.[12] Few of these men had direct access to and influence at the French Court, which had previously undermined the authority of New France officials.

The Jesuits were also different from their seventeenth-century predecessors. During the eighteenth century, missionary fervor waned and the number of priests declined dramatically. The diminution of missionary priests opened the door for the expansion of lay Catholicism, with Native converts filling the void left by the shortage of priests.[13]

Genealogical research in marital and baptismal registers and in fur trade records of the Montreal merchants has yielded the names of many members of Catholic kin networks involved in the fur trade, but beyond their names, we often know very little about these individuals. In most instances, the jumble of names is difficult even to sort out. The diversity and multiplicity of names in baptismal registers contributed to an individual's anonymity, but it simultaneously contributed to that person's importance.[14]

This chapter focuses on Marie Madeleine Réaume whose life illustrates how kin networks were formed and how they became integral to the trade. She lived during two important periods of the fur trade. She was a child during the years of the fur trade ban, and her adult life was marked by the reopening of the trade, the reestablishment of the forts, and the expansion of Catholic kin networks. Marie Madeleine first appeared in the written records as a young woman and she can be traced in those records until she reached the age of seventy. Throughout her life she was an active fur trade participant and, consequently, was part of that broader, socially dynamic world where human interaction was shaped by both Indian and French cultures.

Marie Madeleine Réaume's life, glimpsed through parish and merchant records, reveals a bicultural world that shaped her behavior and was, at the same time, indicative of the broader social processes of accommodation apparent throughout much of the western Great Lakes. In Marie Madeleine's life we see how the fur trade created an arena of cultural experimentation for Native people, rather than precipitating their demise.

Marie Madeleine was the daughter of the Ilini woman, Simphorose Ouaouagoukoue, and Jean Baptiste Réaume, a Fort St. Joseph interpreter. She was a mixed-ancestry descendant whose childhood blurred the boundaries of her French and Indian heritage and whose adult identity was defined by the ever-expanding Catholic kin network of the fur trade. Marie Madeleine was raised in the *pays d'en haut* during the years of the fur trade ban when both her father and his brother served as interpreters for the king. Their official business was conducted in conjunction with their illegal trading activity. Marie Madeleine's uncle, Simon Réaume, was the more prominent of the brothers. He frequently served as the governor's official interpreter in meetings with the Odawa in Montreal. When the forts and the trade were officially reopened, both brothers left Montreal and moved permanently to the west. Simon lived in Illinois Country, where he was assigned in 1720 to "lead and maintain the Ouyatanon" Indians. He successfully recruited hundreds of warriors during the Fox Wars, and this led to his appointment as acting commandant at Ouiatanon in 1731.[15] Simon's brother and Marie Madeleine's father, Jean Baptiste Réaume, also lived and traded in Illinois Country. In 1720, he moved to Fort St. Joseph and, by 1732, had relocated in Green Bay, where he served as the post's interpreter and continued to trade.[16]

The Réaumes' ability to function effectively in the western Great Lakes relied on the women that the brothers married. Jean Baptiste Réaume's marriage to Simphorose Ouaouagoukoue assured both brothers access to the Illinois Country fur trade and protection while traveling and trading. Simon's marriage to Thérèse Catin assured the brothers an ample supply of trade goods.[17] Accorded her husband's power of attorney, Thérèse supplied not only her husband and brother-in-law but she also sold goods to other traders and soldiers. She never journeyed to the western Great Lakes but remained in Montreal, where she, in partnership with a man who lived in her house, acquired goods from France through the trans-Atlantic trade.[18]

A fur trader's success was often fostered by entrepreneurial Frenchwomen.[19] Thus, it is not surprising that French traders then relied on Indian women to mediate for them in the indigenous world in which they traded.[20] By 1720, when the French reestablished most of the western forts, the high rates of intermarriage became a matter of record. In her study of Michilimackinac, historian Jacqueline Peterson found that one-third of intermarriages involved Indian women and Frenchmen while another 20 percent involved Frenchmen and mixed-ancestry women.[21] Baptismal registers in smaller trading communities, like Fort St. Joseph, also confirm these high rates of intermarriage.

The female and male children of Indian women and French men were raised biculturally. From an early age, they functioned effectively as part of an indigenous world, while at the same time being raised in the French world of the fur trade. Baptismal registers confirm that children served as godmothers or godfathers and were incorporated into the emerging Catholic kin networks of the Great Lakes. Marie Madeleine's name first appeared in the St. Joseph baptismal record when, as a woman of eighteen, she became the godmother of Indian and mixed-ancestry children. She also served as a godmother to the children of French *habitants*.[22]

Marie Madeleine's role as a godmother illustrates how kinship mediated the ethnic diversity of small fur trade communities such as Fort St. Joseph. Following her marriage to the Illinois Country trader Augustin L'archevêque[23] and the birth of her first child, she chose godfathers for her children from Frenchmen involved in the trade. Commandants or other male members of their families served repeatedly as godfathers.[24] Even when the commandants' wives or daughters lived at the post, these Frenchwomen were not usually incorporated into these Catholic kin networks.

Commandants were willing and often eager godparents. They were motivated by their own involvement in the fur trade as well as by their military reliance on Indian warriors. With few Frenchmen to guarantee the "military" viability of the small posts, each commandant relied on Indian allies.

Native women, rather than Frenchmen, were more prominent in the growth of Catholic kin networks. Although Madeleine married Augustin L'archevêque, he never served as a godfather.[25] L'archevêque was identified as a trader in Illinois Country and the priest noted his residence as Quebec.[26]

Marie Madeleine was an increasingly frequent godparent and repeatedly appeared as a godmother to a host of collateral relatives and to

Native converts. *Habitants* and soldiers and even French couples who sought to enter the trade chose Madeleine as a godmother to their children. Often she was the godmother of a French couple's first child, but the subsequent children were given French godparents.[27] Marie Madeleine's daughters also served as godmothers, their names dutifully recorded in the baptismal registers by missionary priests.

By 1720, most Great Lakes missions faced a shortage of priests. In 1730, the full-time St. Joseph priest was replaced by the occasional visiting priest.[28] The social dimensions of Christianity quickly overshadowed dogma and many lay Catholics, like Marie Madeleine, played an increasingly important role in the mission church at Fort St. Joseph.

Marie Madeleine relied on the fictive kinship of godparents to link her household and her community to fur trading centers throughout the western Great Lakes. In the summer of 1749, Madeleine personally initiated an expansion of her Catholic kin network beyond the borders of the St. Joseph community. She was about thirty-nine and a widow when she took her three children on the long journey north to Michilimackinac. Here, her young son was baptized and two of her daughters were married. Members of two prominent fur trade families, the Langlades and the Bourassas, both signed as godparents at the baptism and as witnesses at the weddings.[29] Seventeen-year old Marie Catherine L'archevêque became the wife of a Trois Rivières trader.[30] Fifteen-year-old Marie Joseph Esther L'archevêque's bridegroom appears to have been related to a Montreal merchant with whom Madeleine's father had traded.[31] Joseph Esther's marriage at such a young age suggests her mother may have arranged this match.[32] Both daughters and their husbands returned to Madeleine's St. Joseph household.

Two years later, Madeleine further extended and complicated her Catholic kin network. At the age of forty-one, Madeleine gave birth to a son. The father was Louis Thérèse Chevalier, a well-known Michilimackinac trader.[33] Six months after young Louis' birth, Madeleine and Louis were married at the St. Joseph mission. She was forty-two; her husband was several years younger.[34]

Despite her age, Madeleine was an attractive marital prospect. Marriage offered her husband access to new sources of furs and extended the ties of his fur trade kin network into the southern Great Lakes. Louis had probably known Madeleine for twenty years and apparently had severed the less constrictive ties of his Odawa country marriage to marry and move to Fort St. Joseph.[35] Members of the Chevalier family had lived at Fort St. Joseph since its reestablishment. Louis' father had purchased a trade permit in 1718 but he subsequently returned to Michilimackinac. When the elder Louis reappeared in 1730, probably hired as a guide by two Montreal merchants, it was the same year that one of Louis' sisters, Charlotte, also moved to Fort St. Joseph with her blacksmith husband, Antoine Deshêtres.[36] In 1732, when both Charlotte and Marie Madeleine bore children they served as the godmothers to one another's children.[37]

Marriage to Louis Chevalier dramatically expanded Madeleine's kin network. Louis had fifteen siblings raised at Michilimackinac; each married into the fur trade. Several of Louis' brothers had married among the Winnebago.

The marriage of Louis to Madeleine rapidly integrated the unmarried members of the Chevalier family into the St. Joseph community. One of Madeleine's daughters married Louis' younger brother, Louis Paschal Chevalier.[38] Another daughter married her stepfather's Montreal trading partner, Charles Lhullic dit Chevalier. The groom was a forty-five-year-old recent widower; the bride, Angelique L'archevêque, was twenty-one.[39] Madeleine's youngest daughter, seventeen-year-old Anne, also married a fur trader and remained part of the St. Joseph community.[40]

Marriage integrated these two families and mobility extended the familial ties to the south, a relationship that became increasingly important to the entire St. Joseph River valley when the British took control of the western Great Lakes. Contemporaneous with Madeleine's marriage to Louis, her two eldest daughters, their husbands, and their children moved to Fort Pimiteoui, now Peoria, and then, eventually to Cahokia. Madeleine's fourth daughter, Marie Amable, and her husband also eventually joined their L'archevêque kin at Cahokia, while members of the Chevalier kin network also moved south.[41] Louis Chevalier's sister, Marie Josephe (Josette) moved to Cahokia with her husband, Pierre Renaud dit Locat, and their children.[42] Meanwhile, the children of Louis' sister, Charlotte, and Antoine Deshêtres, the former St. Joseph blacksmith, also relocated to Illinois Country.[43]

Kin linkages established by marriage were then reinforced by the godparent roles that siblings played to one anothers' children. Madeleine's daughters were frequent godparents to their nieces and nephews.[44] Twelve of her grandchildren were baptized at St. Joseph. Godparents often lived in the community, but they might also come from distant posts. Louis Chevalier's siblings became godparents to L'archevêque grandchildren, and Madeleine's daughters were godmothers of Chevalier grandchildren.

Although the fur trade entailed a continual influx and outflow of people, identifiable core families emerged. The Catholic kin network at Fort St. Joseph was integrated into the networks of other Great Lakes communities. Mixed-ancestry offspring identified themselves by kinship, but they might simultaneously identify themselves as either Indian or French. Initially, someone like Marie Madeleine could function both alternatively or simultaneously in two cultures.[45] Ironically, in the smaller communities like St. Joseph, mixed-ancestry offspring such as Marie Madeleine came increasingly to resemble their indigenous kin rather than their French relatives. Madeleine's world bore the imprint of the Ilini world in which she was raised and the Potawatomi community in which she would live for almost seventy years. Not surprisingly, her son Louison married among the Potawatomi.

By the mid-eighteenth century, when the Fort St. Joseph community was reclaimed as a predominantly indigenous settlement, Marie Madeleine also increasingly identified with her indigenous heritage. New France had offered free land and tools to French *habitants* and mixed-ancestry families that resettled at Detroit. Among the many St. Joseph *habitants* who moved east were Charlotte Chevalier and her husband, Antoine Deshêtres.[46]

The absence of French neighbors and priests transformed Madeleine into the community's most important Catholic lay practitioner, who played an important role in maintaining a Catholic presence there. Her faith was far different from that which we associate with twentieth-century Catholicism. Madeleine probably led daily devotions or prayers and on Sundays was certainly involved in more lengthy religious services. She may have administered the sacrament of baptism to a child threatened by death, but the sacraments still remained primarily the missionary priests' responsibility. Priests were infrequent visitors, however, appearing only once every several years.[47]

Catholicism did not demand of Native Americans that same personal transformation required of Protestant conversion. Consequently, Madeleine was able to employ religion as a socially integrative tool that incorporated increased numbers of Native people. Madeleine, for instance, was the godmother to Marie Jeanne, a thirteen-year-old Panis or Indian slave as well as to Therese, a forty-year-old Potawatomi woman.[48] One Miami couple, Pierre Mekbibkas8nga and his wife, had their "indian style marriage" sacramentally sanctioned by a visiting priest.[49] The incorporation into the church of their four adult daughters through baptism revealed even more strongly the influence of the L'archevêque–Chevalier family. One daughter selected Louis Chevalier as her godfather; two other daughters chose Madeleine as their godmother.[50] The midcentury departure of the French signaled a dramatic increase in such Catholic conversions among Indians.[51]

During the 1850s, there was a dramatic increase in the number of furs harvested in the St. Joseph River valley. More engagements or contracts for hiring canoemen were issued for St. Joseph during this decade than in any previous period.[52] Thus, fur exports, increased when the L'archevêque–Chevalier kin network and their Potawatomi allies controlled the trade.

Like the St. Joseph community, Madeleine's life underwent many changes, but those changes were always defined by the extensive kin networks that controlled and mediated the exchange process of the fur trade. She was the daughter of a fur trader, married successively to two fur traders, and her five daughters married fur traders. Two daughters lived in the community for thirty-five years. In the first half of the eighteenth century, Marie Madeleine's kin network revolved around Fort St. Joseph. By midcentury, when the French population had dramatically decreased, her world was increasingly defined by the Potawatomi who were her relatives and her trading partners. By 1760, all but one of her children had moved to larger fur trade communities, but they returned frequently to Fort St. Joseph to have their children baptized or to serve as godparents. Marriage served as a planned extension of kin networks, Catholicism further extended those linkages through fictive kinship, and mobility extended that kin network throughout the western Great Lakes.

IN 1711, MARIE Madeleine was born into a demographically chaotic and socially unstable landscape. Over time, seemingly disparate population clusters at places such as Fort St. Joseph were integrated across vast distances by consanguinal, affinal, and fictive ties. Recognized kin networks extended from Laurentian Canada to the fur trade communities of the Great Lakes and south to trading villages in the Mississippi River valley and along its tributaries (see fig. 4).[53]

The core of fur trade families that emerged from the intermarriage of Native women and fur traders evolved because Indian communities, like the Potawatomi of the St. Joseph River valley, sought sustained involvement in the fur trade. Those mixed-ancestry offspring who chose

Cahokia	Detroit	Green Bay	Michilimackinac	Ouiantanon	St. Joseph
	Baby				
	Bertrand		Bertrand		Bertrand
			Bourassa		Bourassa
		Chaboillez			
Chevalier	Chevalier	Chevalier	Chevalier		Chevalier
	Fafard				
			Grignon		
			Kewinaquot (Odawa)		
			LaForuche (Odawa)		
	LaFontaine				
		La Framboise	La Framboise		
			Langlade		
L'archevêque		L'archevêque			L'archevêque
			Menard		Menard+
			Mitchell (Bertrand)		
	Montour		Montour		
			Parent		
	Réaume	Réaume	Réaume	Réaume	Réaume
		Schindler*	Schindler		
			Villeneuve		

+dit LaFontaine
*Baird

FIGURE 4. *Family names in the Catholic kin networks of the western Great Lakes fur trade.* These names represent a small fraction of the families involved in the trade but demonstrate that each family had relatives at numerous fur trade communities.

to further extend their kin networks across time and space acquired increasingly important roles as cultural mediators.[54]

Historian William Hart has described "go-betweens" on the New York frontier where "ethnic identity was cultural and thus subject to appropriation and mutability." Hart's description of cultural mediators like Madame Montour and Sun Fish, a " 'free Negro [Mulatto]' " who lived among the Seneca is equally appropriate for Marie Madeleine.

> Those individuals who successfully borrowed from, negotiated with, and maneuvered within multiple cultures were truly multicultural. They engaged in acts of cultural innovation . . . Cultural borrowers often practiced cultural habits that were specific to particular situations. Anthropologists have referred to this practice as constructing "situational ethnicity." Those who employ two or more identities typically live in biracial, bicultural, or bilingual households and at different times practice both a private and a public cultural identity. In order for their repertoire of identities to work, however, they must conform to the learned cultural habits of the ethnic groups with which they are identifying.[55]

The loyalty that Native people retained toward their "French father" was nurtured by Catholic kin networks that fictively linked the French as godparents to their Indian godchildren.[56] In a world structured by complicated indigenous systems of kinship, these relationships became increasingly more complex as frontier Catholicism took root.[57] When greater numbers of mixed-ancestry offspring migrated to larger fur trade communities, such as Michilimackinac, Green Bay, and St. Louis, they intermarried among themselves at an increasing rate. These intermarriages eventually resulted in the emergence of distinctive Métis communities. Mixed-heredity offspring also appeared with greater frequency as the spouses of French fur traders, but even these preferred brides usually had extensive kin networks.

Most eighteenth-century women became involved in the fur trade when they married Frenchmen, but there were also women who functioned as independent traders. These women appeared in the 1720s, after the fur trade posts were reopened. In 1727, the wife of Louis Hamlin traded at the Menominee post of Folle Avoine, and Charlotte Petit received a license for Green Bay. Hamlin family members could be found among the Catholic godparents at Fort St. Joseph and Michilimackinac, and some had settled among L'archevêque and Chevalier offspring at Cahokia. In 1730, Jean Marie Cardinal was licensed for Green Bay, while Catherine Trotter traded at Michilimackinac. Each woman was granted a license in her own name and, thus, traveled with her boatmen from Montreal. Both Cardinal and Hamlin became lifelong residents of the western Great Lakes.[58]

Without the security of kin networks, these women could not have traded in the west. Although their names appear on fur trade licenses, scant further documentation survives. Unfortunately, kinship's complexity has masked their identities. Only Jean Marie Cardinal has escaped from history's shadows, as many tales have been repeated and reinvented about this Frenchwoman who married her Indian slave and who claimed to be over a hundred years old. Nineteenth-century storytellers kept her memory alive, although in greatly altered form, as historical societies began to collect and publish the "reminiscences" of "pioneer settlers."[59]

Most of the Native women involved in the trade never received the notoriety Jean Marie Cardinal enjoyed. Most probably behaved like Marie Madeleine and acquired new husbands when they were left widowed. Within the parameters of the fur trade, marriage was a kinship marker in which a widow's remarriage represented a further expansion and incorporation of new kin and allies. We can find few eighteenth-century women involved in the fur trade who, when left widows, did not remarry.

Kin networks were so complex and far-reaching that the disruption of fur trade activities at St. Joseph simultaneously threatened the interests of people who lived in Cahokia and St. Louis. After the conquest of Canada, when the French surrendered at Montreal, the English unsuccessfully attempted to send fur traders to the St. Joseph River valley.[60] These Englishmen ignored or dismissed Native women and their fur trade husbands. They did so at their own peril, as we shall see in the next chapter. England lacked a sufficient presence to govern through force, and, in the end, those English officers who understood the nature of kinship in the western Great Lakes governed most effectively. Nevertheless, such men proved insufficient in number, and, as a result, it is not surprising that England lost so large a part of its empire so quickly.

4

British Governance in the Western Great Lakes

CATHOLIC KIN networks shaped French imperial governance in the western Great Lakes in the seventeenth and eighteenth centuries. The importance of kinship was increasingly apparent when the English wrested control of the *pays d'en haut* from the French, following the conquest of Canada in 1763. Kin networks could not be ignored; when the English did so, the results proved disastrous.

The occupation and regarrisoning of France's former forts failed to establish effective British control over the western Great Lakes. Although these fortifications spanned important riverways and were manned by British troops, Indians and French traders canoed silently past the forts during dark evening hours. Even the largest forts, Detroit and Michilimackinac, relied on the cooperation of nearby Native American communities.[1]

Most forts functioned primarily as trading posts and many, like Fort St. Joseph, were never heavily garrisoned.[2] There is nothing to suggest that the French Fort St. Joseph had any purpose other than trade.[3] Indeed, post commandants reaped tremendous profits from trade.[4] Most of these forts were ineffective defensive structures, even though French propaganda had lauded them as a bulwark against English incursion.[5] Although they rimmed the boundary of New France's interior lands or stood adjacent to important river junctions, French claims to authority over this region were belied by the physical insignificance of most of these military installations. Father Charlevoix, whose travels included a visit to the area, was appalled by the lackluster military appearance of these Great Lakes forts. He considered Fort St. Joseph nothing more than the commandant's house, surrounded by a "wretched palisade."[6] Although several small cannons might rebuff surprise attacks, Charlevoix's description shows that the fort's continued existence depended entirely on the surrounding Native American community. The commandant's house stood adjacent to the Potawatomi village, and directly across the river bank was a Miami village. Not even the Jesuit mission was surrounded by a palisade.

In communities like Fort St. Joseph, there were no barracks for military personnel and, consequently, soldiers resided in nearby houses. Fort St. Joseph not only lacked military structures, but its buildings offered no reliable clues to the ethnicity of their occupants. Extended French families lived together in one house; some inhabited *poteaux-en-terre* buildings (vertical log houses with the posts set directly in the ground), while others lived in log cabins or indigenous-style longhouses. At Fort St. Joseph, one Potawatomi headman lived in a timber-frame house, constructed by a French carpenter.[7] Residence patterns often separated the French from the Potawatomi, but even this division was blurred at Fort St. Joseph. The French and Indians frequently lived with or next to each other. Mixed-ancestry descendants, adopted and integrated into clans, lived among the Indians. Native Americans, especially the Panis or Indian slaves, often lived in French households.[8]

During the course of its hundred-year existence Fort St. Joseph had served primarily as a supply outpost for the fur trade.[9] It produced an agricultural surplus sufficient to feed transient traders. The long-distance canoes that traveled from Montreal devoted most of their space to trade goods. Voyageurs ate dried peas, biscuit, and pork until they reached the forts of the *pays d'en haut,* where corn and fresh food supplies were purchased.[10] These men purchased not only Indian corn but also wheat, barley, oats, and goods handcrafted for the trade, such as snowshoes and canoes.[11]

St. Joseph, like other western posts, had a settled agricultural appearance, with the cultivated fields usually managed by matrifocal households of Native women. Fields were plowed with oxen, and French carts carried hay for dairy and beef cattle. There were chickens, pigs, and even fruit orchards that supplemented more common sources of food. Indian ponies roamed the nearby woodlots and carried people and peltry overland. Although tending horses and trapping furs were primarily male pursuits, processing furs and controlling agricultural resources remained female responsibilities.

When the Seven Years' War began in 1756, the Potawatomi actively supported their French allies. Seventy warriors fought on behalf of the French king at Fort William Henry, but they carried smallpox back to their villages. The epidemic that broke out in the St. Joseph River valley devastated the population. France offered no subsequent assistance and then even failed to supply adequate trade goods. For the remainder of the war, most St. Joseph communities devoted their energies to food production rather than warfare. This was the last major epidemic to strike the St. Joseph River valley, and the population levels, fortified by a bountiful harvest, soon rebounded.[12]

Following the French defeat, the Potawatomi allied with Pontiac. The English general, Lord Jeffery Amherst, created a receptive audience for Pontiac by limiting presents to the Indians and imposing more intrusive methods of control at the western posts of Michilimackinac, St. Joseph, La Baye, and Detroit. Reestablished or regarrisoned forts attracted English fur traders, who accompanied the soldiers west. English officers violated the behaviors Indians had long associated with friends and allies when they failed to provide gifts and did not curtail the activities of unscrupulous traders.[13] French traders, infuriated by the appearance of English rivals, first, surreptitiously and, then, blatantly undermined English authority.[14] Although England defeated France, Pontiac's Rebellion demonstrated that Indians and not Englishmen controlled the lands west of the Allegheny Mountains.[15]

The British quickly discovered that highly visible, overt forms of control in the Great Lakes were impractical. They were more interested in the fur trade than in colonization, however, and, therefore, they acceded to Native demands and established the Proclamation Line of 1763, which prohibited immigration west of the Appalachian Mountains. The proclamation, although often ineffective, demonstrated English awareness that this was an indigenous world. Unfortunately, however, the English failed to appreciate that this was a settled landscape with communities established through a century-long process of intermarriage between Frenchmen and Indian women. Fur trade communities were linked by kin networks, relationships so complex that they baffled outsiders and often transformed Frenchmen into Indians. As one Michilimackinac officer remarked, "They have been in these upper Countrys for these twelve, twenty, or thirty years, [and] have adopted the very principles and ideas of Indians, and differ little from them only a little in colour."[16]

British officers focused much of their hostility over Pontiac's Rebellion on French fur traders, whom they disparagingly called the Interior French. The Indian rebellion as well as the attacks on English traders were viewed as French handiwork. Such hasty judgments complicated Britain's ability to govern the western Great Lakes; certainly, Frenchmen might influence but they did not control their Indian allies.

Symbiotic kin networks situated French traders, not as masters, but as codependent partners of the Indians. Kinship ensured trader accountability to Indian people. For example, neither Madeleine nor Louis Chevalier, despite their prominence, controlled the behavior of their indigenous kin and neighbors. Louis Chevalier might prove influential in the consensual process of decision making, but he was incapable of assuring the outcome. Kinship bridged disparate worlds, but it was also an accountable bridge that controlled the behaviors of the French who married and lived among Indian people.

Cultural misunderstanding led many English officers not only to distrust the French but to misunderstand the source of their rival's influence. English patriarchal notions of authority obscured Marie Madeleine's role in the fur trade and her successful integration of Louis Chevalier into the kin networks of the St. Joseph River valley. To the English, Marie Madeleine appeared an inconsequential "squaw wife," and thus, they focused on Louis Chevalier. To the English, the fur trade was a man's world and, obligingly, Louis came to the fore as the intermediary and spokesman for Fort St. Joseph. But Louis' authority derived in large measure from his wife's resources: Her relatives procured and processed the furs, produced goods for the trade, grew sufficient agricultural produce to feed indigenous households and itinerant traders, and produced a marketable surplus. When the British eventually removed Marie Madeleine and Louis, Madeleine's kin network, her daughters, their husbands, and their Indian kin and allies arrived from Illinois Country and forced the British to retreat permanently from the St. Joseph River valley.

In contrast, other English officers successfully solicited Indian support, but they relied on the Interior French to communicate with the Indians. Frenchmen, like Louis Chevalier, if they had access to English trade goods and distributed gifts, might influence some Indians. Such behaviors initially flew in the face of British imperial policy, but effective governance would require flexibility.

The events that transpired in the St. Joseph River valley prior to and during the American Revolution angered and frustrated English officers. But those events were effective evidence of long-term social processes at work, of how kinship served as a strategy of indigenous accommodation, resistance, and persistence. English traders who were not kin were not welcome in the St. Joseph villages. Perhaps the English offered a more varied and richer assortment of trade goods than did the French, but exchange at an impersonal level remained problematic and risky for the trader. When Native people and their French kin overtly and covertly resisted English efforts to gain hegemony in the region, their behaviors presaged the resistance strategies that were later applied by Indians against nineteenth-century U.S. incursions.

ON CHRISTMAS EVE in 1772, Henry Bassett, the Detroit commandant, focused all his frustrations and hostility on one villain, Louis Chevalier at Fort St. Joseph. Just before midnight, Bassett sent a hastily penned, angry letter to General Thomas Gage seeking permission to attack Fort St. Joseph, almost two hundred miles to the west. Bassett was outraged by the way the Potawatomi had treated Cornelius Van Slyck, who had Bassett's permission to trade at Fort St. Joseph. Earlier that evening a frightened and weary Van Slyck had arrived in Detroit, after a perilous weeklong journey along frozen Indian trails. A last-second escape had saved Van Slyck's life, although several of his men had been less fortunate—they were killed by the St. Joseph Potawatomi.

> Mr. Van Slyck, a considerable trader of this place, is just arrived from St. Joseph, the Potawatomi Indians attempted murdering him and three servants about Ten Days since. He had one killed and another wounded so ill that he left him in the house and of course is put to death, the third was a Frenchman who made his escape to the fort. One Indian is killed and two he thinks dangerously wounded. Mr. Van Slyck had received a slight wound in his face and with utmost difficulty had got here, he tells me that it was the fault of some French traders that are settled there. I'm informed there's a certain (Louison Chevalier) a very bad man, that is married to a Squaw and encourages these murders. I'm told that this is the third time within three years.[17]

To the British commandant this incident, with its ominous cast of characters, erupted into a predictable crisis. The French became the villains and the Indians their aggressive, willing pawns. Bassett shaped his telling of the tale into a highly emotional eighteenth-century melodrama in which those Frenchmen who took up with "squaw women" incited the Indians to plunder "young men of good character."

By the spring, Gage had not responded to Bassett's request for permission to march on St. Joseph and "root out these villains." Bassett again wrote Gage and attached Potawatomi testimony affirming the truth of Louis Chevalier's villainy. Bassett even appended to his letter "a true copy of the Indian signatures."

> *Major Bassett:* I am well convinced that there are bad birds among you, and I know some of them too, tell me the Truth, the Master of Life hears

> you and will punish you if you Lie. When Mr. Van Slyck's two men were murdered and his goods plundered was not Louison Chevalier at the Head of that mischief? I know already a great deal of this affair so take care and do not lie.
>
> *Pitchbaon:* Father, I know the Master of Life hears me and I call him to witness that I shall tell the truth, you are not mistaken with respect to Louison Chevalier, for immediately after the bad Indians had struck the blow, and Mr. Van Slycke was fled he encouraged the Indians to go back and plunder, they said they were afraid as they had seen Mr. Van Slycke loading his guns (Louison Chevalier) then told them that he was fled and that they must go and plunder, that there were a great deal of rum and goods left. We secured twenty blankets, three barrels of powder, three bags of ball, and one barrel of rum, etc., and etc.: all which we kept for Mr. Van Slycke and delivered them to him when he returned. But Louison Chevalier and all the French people there plundered as well as the Indians, but he was the worst of them and could have saved all the goods if he would as there were two bateaux lying close by the House to carry them away, and we have reason to believe for his behavior that he encouraged the Indians to strike the blow, he nor the rest of the French have not returned the things they plundered for they sold us of the rum this spring.[18]

Not surprisingly, Bassett never received permission to attack Fort St. Joseph.[19] This fort was actually under the jurisdiction of the Michilimackinac commandant. Bassett supported Van Slyck and dismissed the man with the French name, because Bassett believed that the Great Lakes French were "the outcasts of all Nations, and the refuse of Mankind."[20]

The ethnic, national, and racial diversity of this region complicated hasty judgments about "good and bad" characters. It was difficult to discern friends and enemies when kinship determined identity. A further complication was presented by mixed-ancestry offspring who were often adopted and had Indian names, although many were also known by their French names. People of mixed ancestry often blended seamlessly into Native society and were incorporated into village clans. Some became more prominent figures and spoke several Native languages. Most were fluent in French and English, albeit sometimes the pidgin variety of the fur trade. Because of their linguistic skills, they often served as interpreters, first for the French, then for the British, and still later, for the Americans.

The blending of French and Native cultures represented one dimension of the changes initiated by the process of European arrival and expansion. The region was the refuge of diverse Native people being continually pushed west, first by the Fur Trade Wars and, later, by colonial emigrants. There were Abenaki, Sauk, Huron, Neutral, Shawnee, and Delaware, and this diversity was further complicated by the presence of slaves captured from among the western Pawnee. Although the French used *Panis* as synonymous with slavery, the status of Indian slaves was neither lifelong nor racially based. Fur trade communities had also included enslaved and free black populations. Panis were shipped from Montreal to the Caribbean; others were traded at New Orleans for African American slaves. By 1750, Kaskaskia included 1,000 French residents, 300 black slaves, 60 Panis, and 800 Kaskaskia Indians who lived in adjacent villages. A 1762 census for Detroit indicates that 65 of the approximately 900 people living near the fort were African American slaves. Three years later, the nearly equal ratio of male to female slaves had resulted in a doubling of that population.[21]

Ethnicity and nationality had limited meaning in this socially diverse society. Identity was a more complex issue, dependent on kin networks, residential and occupational patterns, and cultural orientations.

Louis Chevalier lived in a household typical of many Great Lakes traders: Catholic, matrifocal, and the type of Native household in which his wife had been raised. Women processed peltry, produced an annual agricultural surplus, and produced such fur trade items as snowshoes.

British officers expected to command military posts and were unprepared for the multi-ethnic, fur trade communities they found on arrival in the *pays d'en haut.* Native acceptance of the British was hindered by General Amherst, governor-general of North America, when he ordered an end to presents to the Indians. Captain Joseph Schlosser, who assumed command of Fort St. Joseph, never quite appreciated the ritual exchange of gifts that had established bonds of friendship with the Native people.[22] Schlosser's fondness for liquor further compromised the already tenuous British presence.

In 1763, when Pontiac and his followers captured Fort St. Joseph as well as the garrisons at Ouiatenon, Miami, Sandusky, La Boeuf, Venango, and Presque Isle, they left unharmed the French who lived in or near Native communities. Many Englishmen, however, lost their lives. At Fort St. Joseph, Schlosser and twelve of his men were killed; two were taken prisoner and later ransomed at Detroit.[23] The rebellion lasted for only six months, but it was clear that English retribution was futile. Sir William Johnson, the superintendent for Indian Affairs of the Northern Department, wrote to General Gage, "Our Misfortune [is] that the Indians know too well their own Strength, and that it is not in the power of the English alone to punish them effectually."[24]

Pontiac's Rebellion led the Commissioners for Trade and Plantations in England to search for ways to foster the fur trade by minimizing intrusion on Indian lands:

> It does appear to us that the extension of the fur trade depends entirely upon the Indians being undisturbed in possession of their hunting ground, and that all colonizing does in its nature, and must in all consequences, operate to the prejudice of that branch of commerce. . . . let the savages enjoy their deserts in quiet. Were they driven from their forests their peltry-trade would decrease.[25]

More important, English policy then restricted land sales to fur traders at the larger posts, such as Detroit and Michilimackinac, and terminated the kind of large land grants that caused continuing havoc in the Ohio River valley.

Pontiac, unfortunately, also exacerbated the Francophobia of English officers and, following the revolt, even the highest levels of the English command reflected a growing hatred for the Interior French. Major Gladwin, under siege at Detroit, displaced blame for the uprising on the greed of the French traders: "The French are at the bottom of this affair, in order to ruin . . . British merchants, and engross the trade to themselves."[26] Even Thomas Gage believed that the French behaved "in a scandalous and seditious manner."[27] It was the attitudes and behaviors of British traders and the presence of the British military on Native lands that Pontiac and his followers found unacceptable. The traders who came west with the military in 1760 merely magnified the English threat.

Pontiac's short but effective uprising dramatically reversed the direction of English fur trade policy in the western Great Lakes. It set in motion new imperial policies by which the English unintentionally left the western Great Lakes in the hands of Native Americans and their French kin. The Johnson Plan, drafted in response to the uprising, restricted the movement of English fur traders into the Indian villages of the *pays d'en haut.* This plan envisioned the western Great Lakes fur trade operating as it did along the eastern seaboard where Native people transported furs to the posts. In New York, for instance, the trade was confined to the Albany and Oswego forts. The English planned to apply the model of the eastern fur trade to the west, with the major forts central to the exchange process, and, consequently, legal trade would be permissible only at Michilimackinac and Detroit.[28]

Indians had not journeyed long distances to sell their peltry since the early eighteenth century. French fur traders lived in the villages, while others arrived when trade goods were sent upcountry by the Montreal merchants.[29] Because the Johnson Plan restricted trade to Michilimackinac and Detroit, English traders who journeyed to wintering grounds, or to Native villages, were thus engaged in illegal activity. Many English traders ignored the ban, as their seventeenth-century French predecessors had done in 1696 through 1714, but these men were in a precarious position. Those who poached risked their lives, and fort commandants were unable to extend them protection legally. At places like Miami, Ouiatenon, or Fort St. Joseph, kin networks controlled the exchange process, and English traders simply lacked the crucial connections and were not welcome. In the spring of 1766, two English traders were murdered near the River Rouge. Lt. Col. John Campbell, then commanding at Detroit, reported to Gage that

> it was the Potawatomis of St. Joseph that committed the Murder, and that two of them were the Chief's sons of that tribe. . . . I have since put a stop to any trade with that nation, until they deliver up the Murderer, though I suspect it will not have the desired effect.[30]

English traders pleaded with Superintendent Johnson to rescind the restrictions on the fur trade and complained that such limitations would lead to "the total ruin of that Valuable Branch of Commerce, the lessening of his Majesty's Revenue and the Consumption of British Manufactures more especially the Woollen; besides depriving the Merchants of the necessary Remittances."[31] Fur exports to England actually declined for the four years that the Johnson Plan remained in effect.[32] In March of 1767, the newly appointed Governor-General in Montreal, Sir Guy Carleton, lobbied for elimination of the Johnson policy and warned the Lords of Trade in London that the fur trade would continue to decline if the restrictions continued. The next year, the policy was rescinded.

The Johnson Plan initially limited British fur traders and bolstered the fortunes of the Interior French. The French continued to engage in an illegal trade, wintered with their indigenous kin, and collected the season's peltry. Four years of British fur trade restrictions only reinforced the fur trade as it had long existed. Native women and their French husbands continued to control the exchange process. Many were supplied by the English at Michilimackinac or Detroit. Other Frenchmen, however, established new merchant connections at St. Louis and New Orleans, which encouraged the export of furs to the south, rather than via the northern route through Michilimackinac and Detroit.[33]

With the dissolution of the Johnson Plan, the Interior French proved willing to carry English trade goods, but they remained unwilling to accommodate intrusion by British traders. Traders who trespassed into Native villages and wintering grounds south of Lake Michigan faced dire consequences. In the fall of 1767, an English trader named Rogers arrived in the Kankakee River valley, where the St. Joseph Potawatomi wintered. He was killed and his merchandise disappeared. The English trader, Frederick Hambach, whom Louis Chevalier hid in the basement of his house during Pontiac's Rebellion, was also murdered. In January of 1768, Hambach attempted to trade in the St. Joseph River valley, but ignored the L'archevêque–Chevalier kin network. His decision resulted in his death. Cornelius Van Slyck would be fortunate to escape with his life.[34]

English traders threatened the exchange processes that had evolved over generations. Traders like Hambach and Van Slyck, who scorned marriage to Native women, threatened an exchange process that was embedded in the social structure of this region.[35]

The English found it difficult to penetrate the kin networks that controlled the western Great Lakes fur trade. Five to six hundred French traders still arrived at Michilimackinac each summer to exchange the peltry for trade goods.[36] They readily accepted British goods, but rarely returned with British traders aboard their *bateaux* and canoes.[37] British trade goods were substituted when they proved less expensive or when the flow of French or Spanish trade goods into the western Great Lakes was interrupted, but the conveyors of those trade goods remained remarkably unchanged. In 1767, four years after the Treaty of Paris ceded French possessions in North America to the British, over 85 percent of the men identified as Michilimackinac traders were French, while British merchants were posting security for over half the canoes. The personnel of the fur trade in the Lake Michigan area and south along the Mississippi River valley was primarily drawn from the Interior French and their Native allies.[38]

Pontiac's Rebellion and the Johnson Plan ensured that the social landscape of indigenous communities was not disrupted by English intrusion. Kin networks remained intact, and those English traders who successfully penetrated the Great Lakes trade secured entrance through intermarriage. For example, John Askin, a Scots-Irish trader seasoned in the New York trade, entered the Michilimackinac trade when he married in "the manner of the country" an Odawa woman at the nearby

Native village of L'Arbre Croche. At Detroit, he also married Marie Archange Barthe, whose father had traded there since the 1740s.[39] For another example, James Sterling entered the trade by marriage to Angélique Cuillerier, who was the daughter of an Indian interpreter. She was considered to be "used to trade from her infancy, and is generally allowed to be the best interpreter of different Indian languages."[40] There are other examples, but, although some Englishmen integrated themselves into the western Great Lakes trade, they remained primarily suppliers, rather than traders. The British proved far more successful in opening the trade of the Canadian Northwest, which was unencumbered by established kin networks of Frenchmen who had married Native women.[41]

Unfortunately, the English commandants never emulated the marital behaviors of their French predecessors in the Great Lakes. Officers came from the upper strata of English society, and their class consciousness not only separated them from their men but also militated against personal involvements with Native women.[42] For these Protestant officers, there was no religious bridge through which fictive kin networks could be constructed. By the time of the American Revolution, those English officers who remained confused by the diversity and complexity of the western Great Lakes elected what were often disastrous and highly disruptive solutions. Increasingly Francophobic, they advocated forced removal of the Interior French. Their prejudices were inflamed, first, by the English inability to readily discern obdurate enemies from potential allies in this diverse social landscape and, later, by their belief that both Pontiac's Rebellion and the ill treatment that English traders received were the fault of the Interior French. Detroit's Major Gladwin believed that "those vile inhabitants at the outposts ought to be removed, and sent where they can't return."[43] The same remedy was proposed by George Turnbull, who told Gage, "As to removing the French inhabitants between this [place] and the Mississippi, it would be a very great, and necessary piece of service."[44] The military failed to act, but in part that was because English merchants had achieved their objectives in the western Great Lakes: an expanded market for British manufactured goods.

British distrust of the Interior French proved increasingly problematic as the eastern colonies headed toward rebellion. In 1774, when Bassett left Detroit, he was replaced by men who characterized the Interior French as "the most worthless and abandoned Fellows in the Provinces," without education, honesty, or sentiment. When the American

Revolution broke out, Rogers called the Interior French "ignorant Bigots and busy Rebels"; and Capt. Richard Beringer Lernoult, Bassett's immediate successor, condemned them as "Rebels to a man."[45]

During the American Revolution, English officers, blinded by prejudice, disdained many of the Interior French, who were potentially an influential resource for recruiting military manpower. The enlistment of Native warriors on behalf of the British required the diplomatic management of the Interior French, and some English officers who viewed the Interior French more favorably worked through them to secure Native American support.[46] Major Arent Schuyler De Peyster, the commandant at Michilimackinac, exerted considerable influence in this face-to-face world when he relied on Louis Chevalier as his intermediary. De Peyster made no attempt to regarrison the St. Joseph post, but relied on Chevalier to relay messages, secure allegiances, and raise warriors. To do this, De Peyster assigned English trade goods to Chevalier, who then redistributed those goods in established rituals to solidify alliances and successfully solicit Potawatomi warriors.[47]

De Peyster appreciated the social complexity of these fur trade communities and believed that the Interior French, such as Louis Chevalier, were important allies. De Peyster proved amazingly more open to the Interior French than his colleagues, but he, too, overlooked the intermediary role that the Native wives of these traders exercised in their communities. From the patriarchal perspective of the English officer, fur trade wives were invisible, and it was the French traders who appeared to exercise sole and absolute control over the St. Joseph River valley. De Peyster wrote to General Haldimand that, "Mr. Chevalier at St. Josephs holds the pass to Detroit and . . . [t]his gentleman is so connected with the Potawatomis that he can now do anything with them having lived upwards of thirty years at that Place."[48] De Peyster cultivated Chevalier's friendship and increasingly relied on him to meet with the Potawatomi. De Peyster relied on Chevalier to distribute presents as far west as the Sioux and as far north as the Winnebago.[49] Through Chevalier, De Peyster curtailed Native support for the American rebels in Illinois Country, following George Rogers Clark's conquest of Cahokia.[50] Chevalier raised warriors from both the Potawatomi and the Miami to fight on behalf of the British.[51] When Henry Hamilton sought warriors to recapture Vincennes, Chevalier arranged for him to meet with the Potawatomi at St. Joseph.[52] De Peyster also understood the social constraints that structured the obligations of those who lived in kin-based societies. Thus, De Peyster requested that General Haldimand entertain Chevalier's Odawa son when he was in Montreal. De Peyster wrote Gage that "[a] Young Indian named Aimable at present at Montreal is his son" and encouraged him to provide "some mark of distinction."[53] Chevalier thanked Haldimand, "The marks of distinction which you have shown to Amable, give me confidence and confirm me in the resolution which I have already taken. . . . I do my best to give my opinion conformable to the good of the state and acknowledge the great honor you have heaped upon me."[54] Eventually, De Peyster enlisted Amable as a lieutenant in England's Indian forces. De Peyster clearly understood the ways in which the treatment of Chevalier's Odawa son entailed reciprocal behavior.[55]

De Peyster's successful handling of the Fort St. Joseph community was sharply curtailed when he was appointed to the Detroit post in 1779. Patrick Sinclair replaced him as commandant at Michilimackinac. The social obligations that linked Chevalier and the Potawatomi to De Peyster meant that Indian loyalty was transferred from Michilimackinac to Detroit. This angered Sinclair, who viewed this behavior as an affront to his authority. Anxious to retain Potawatomi loyalty and aware of its tenuous nature, De Peyster attempted to maintain communications with Chevalier and wrote to Haldimand.

> The St. Joseph's Indians have a constant intercourse with this place, they come here on horseback, in four or five days, sometimes in great numbers, whereas they seldom, or ever, go [to] the Post of Michilimackinac, except when sent for. . . . If Captain Sinclair thinks I encroach upon his Government I will freely give him up one half of my command, provided Your Excellency thinks it will be for the good of His Majesty's Service—which is the sole object I have to view.[56]

It was not only difficult to maintain Indian loyalty toward the English, but, once at Detroit, De Peyster also discovered the grave extent to which his predecessors had alienated the French residents, which made it difficult to raise support for the English cause. At the time of De Peyster's arrival, almost five hundred French settlers, or one-fourth of the population, were under arrest as suspicious persons.[57] Those arrests had effectively alienated most of the remaining French populace.

The events that transpired in the St. Joseph River valley, then, epitomized the kinds of problems the English encountered in the Great Lakes. Those problems often stemmed from the behaviors of Francophobic English officers, such as Sinclair, who were determined to use forced removal to frustrate the influence of the Interior French. Sinclair relied on the pretense of Haldimand's order, which banished fur traders with questionable loyalty, to forcibly remove the Chevaliers.[58]

Patrick Sinclair never fully appreciated the highly complex and intertwined allegiances of Native American and French kin networks and he failed to understand the ways in which such kinship loyalties could frustrate even the clearest directive. In 1779, Sinclair relied on a Michilimackinac trader, Louis Ainssé, to transport the French from St. Joseph to Michilimackinac. But Ainssé was Louis Chevalier's nephew, his sister's son, and although he followed Sinclair's directive and removed the French, his behavior was ultimately defined by his kinship loyalties. He boarded Louis Chevalier and his French neighbors in six canoes and led the convoy to Michilimackinac.[59] Ainssé did not remove the Indian offspring of Louis and Madeleine Chevalier nor any members of their indigenous kin network. Consequently, Ainssé left the community firmly in the control of Marie Madeleine's kin network.

Sinclair implemented the removal policy long espoused by many English officers, eventually destabilized the region, and turned the Potawatomi against the British. Violence again erupted with the arrival of English traders. The events that transpired following the forced removal demonstrate the political as well as the social power of kinship networks. Shortly after British traders arrived in the St. Joseph River valley, in the fall of 1780, they were attacked by an invading force from Illinois Country. It was composed of Madeleine's kin network. The first unsuccessful raid with thirty Cahokia men was led by Jean Baptiste Hamelin and Tom Brady, the American husband of Madeleine's recently widowed daughter.[60] In December of 1780, the invaders overpowered the British traders, loaded contraband on packhorses, burnt what they could not carry, and set fire to British storehouses and buildings. Lieutenant de Quindre, the British Indian agent for St. Joseph, arrived shortly after the Cahokian departure. He pursued and overtook them, killed four, wounded two others, and captured seven Cahokians.[61]

Several months later a larger, more efficient force was again launched from Illinois Country, but under the Spanish flag. Madeleine and Louis' Indian son, thirty-year-old Louison Chevalier, was the expedition's guide and interpreter. The Potawatomi reckoned the force at "one hundred white people and eighty Indians led by Sequinack and Nakewine."[62] Historians' estimates are lower: perhaps sixty-five men, some from St. Louis and others from Cahokia, and a large Indian contingent. Louis Chevalier's negotiations with the Indians allowed them to surprise the British traders effectively. On February 12, 1781, St. Joseph was plundered anew. Chevalier seized the British trade goods and divided them among his Potawatomi kin. This devastatingly thorough attack included burning a large supply of corn. The invaders were gone before Lieutenant de Quindre arrived, but the Potawatomi, on this occasion, refused to join him in pursuit of the raiders.[63]

De Peyster, anxious to correct the problems caused by removal, summoned the St. Joseph Potawatomi to council in March 1781. They provided plausible explanations of why they had been unable to prevent the attack on the British traders. De Peyster was told, "They came to St. Josephs at a time that all the Indians were yet at their hunt, excepting a few young men who were not sufficient to oppose one hundred white people and eighty Indians." De Peyster made no mention of Louis Chevalier's role in the attack; he was either uninformed or discreetly diplomatic. De Peyster cautioned the Potawatomi strenuously against alliances with the Spanish and the Americans. He repeatedly warned them of the American greed for land, but accomplished little. De Peyster knew that the St. Joseph Potawatomi had received presents from the Spanish from the silver that they wore: bracelets and gorgets decorated with southwestern turquoise.[64]

Even the most lavish quantity of presents failed to regain the loyalty of the St. Joseph Potawatomi to the British. Councils were held throughout the Great Lakes to no avail. Many of the Interior French, rudely treated by British army officers, relied on their kin networks to relocate to other more friendly Native villages and fur trade settlements. With their loyalty continually called into question by men like Patrick Sinclair, many Interior French settled on the west side of Lake Michigan in Green Bay.

De Peyster proved unable to "delicately manage" the Native people of the western Great Lakes without the aid of the Interior French. The warriors previously provided by the Potawatomi dwindled to insignificance, and the English found themselves being lectured by Native people about the folly of warfare. The St. Joseph Potawatomi openly admonished English officers and urged them to lay down their weapons against the Americans.

> I am surprised my father, that you are come to disturb the peace which reigns in our lands. I am pleased to see you with the pipe of peace which you offer us today instead of the tomahawk. . . . I confess to you that the red pipe presented to a party of my nation has been a poison to them as fatal as that of a venomous animal, this smoke has obscured the beautiful light and painted the shadow of death. . . . I have the same thing to say to [you] my father, change thy plans, renounce thy projects which have

> been formed with neither prudence nor wisdom, if you are stubborn and despise my councils you will perhaps repent, believe me my father and go no farther.[65]

Insensitive treatment rendered the Interior French unwilling allies and the Potawatomi a neutral nation. De Peyster found that the numerous councils held directly with the Indians proved futile.[66] By 1782, De Peyster reported to Haldimand that Great Lakes people were fickle allies in the war against the colonials.

> I have wrought hard to endeavor to bring them to it [better discipline], but, I find it impossible to change their natures. I assemble them, get fair promises, and send them out, but once out of sight the turning of a Straw may divert them from the original plan. If too severe with them, upon such occasions they tell us we are well off that there are no Virginians in this Quarter, but such as they bring here against their inclinations.[67]

In the western Great Lakes many Native people found it advantageous to remain neutral in the conflict between the British and the rebel colonies. Over time and because of the fur trade, many Native communities became increasingly agricultural. Most English officers failed to see Indians as more sedentary than nomadic. The houses, orchards, cultivated fields, and livestock of the St. Joseph Potawatomi were irrelevant to the English. Consequently, English officers often failed to realize that the Potawatomi had much to lose if they sided with the British and the colonials burned their fields. There were no means to protect agricultural villages left vulnerable by the departure of warriors.

The agricultural surplus that women produced fed fur traders, and, subsequently, the British and the Revolution created supply problems. Henry Hamilton's expedition against Clark took so many oxen from Detroit that they could not be purchased even at 1,000 livres per head, and the lack of men made it impossible to thresh the grain.[68] The inflation of grain prices became so dramatic in Detroit that, in 1778, attempts were made to regulate the price of wheat, flour, pease, and corn.[69]

The English also failed to appreciate the social obligations required to secure Indian agricultural goods. Louis Chevalier arranged a meeting in 1778 between the Potawatomi and Detroit's Lieutenant Governor Henry Hamilton to use the agricultural surplus at St. Joseph to supply military operations in the western Great Lakes. Hamilton failed to bring the necessary presents and liquor to seal the bonds of friendship. News of the British grain shortage had apparently reached one of the river valley's more prominent Native Americans, Gros Loup, who honored Hamilton with an appropriate gift. In his journal, Hamilton recorded that Gros Loup gave him "[three] large baskets of young corn, dried pumpkin and kidney beans, saying that such coarse fare might serve my cattle if I could not eat it myself."[70]

By the time of the American Revolution, many Native communities produced abundant harvests that fed both residential and transient fur trade populations. Agricultural produce, as well as furs, played an important role in the exchange process. Boatloads of corn and barrels of maple sugar, in addition to furs, were shipped from the St. Joseph region to Michilimackinac, Detroit, and St. Louis.

The tendency toward Native neutrality resulted from England's failure to assess accurately the consequences that warfare entailed for Potawatomi society. Strategic events for the colonials, such as the Revolution, were nonevents for many Indian villages in the St. Joseph River valley, because the Potawatomi often chose to remain neutral. Despite the best efforts of the combatants, Native people were neither cajoled nor bullied into supplying substantial numbers of warriors to either the English or the American forces. Many neutral Potawatomi villages were unaffected by the war and retained their prosperity when the American Revolution concluded.

The English never sufficiently expended the human and financial resources required to win Native support following the French and Indian War. England's military force was dwarfed by the sheer size of the Great Lakes region. Effective military control was established over the St. Lawrence River valley, but Whitehall refused to provide the resources necessary to establish control of the Mississippi River valley. This longer and wider waterway from the Great Lakes to New Orleans would have required a tremendous financial and military outlay. Even climate worked against British control: Most of the Mississippi was navigable twelve months of the year, while freezing temperatures closed the St. Lawrence River during the winter.

English governance in the western Great Lakes was further compromised by Spanish control of New Orleans. This strategically important city was the communications center and market outlet for both the Lower and Upper Mississippi River. Its importance was enhanced by the eighteenth-century founding of St. Louis and its emergence as a collection point for furs.[71] The Mississippi proved a viable fur trade highway, because short portages at the Fox, St. Joseph, and Miami Rivers drew the western Great Lakes into its confluence. The river's southward flow facilitated the transportation of furs. At the conclusion of the French and Indian War, Gage had acknowledged the increased importance of New Orleans as a fur trade market.[72] The trade, he said, would "always go with the stream . . . either down the Mississippi or the St. Lawrence."[73] New Orleans proved problematic for the British when, as Gage pointed out, higher peltry prices drew furs in that direction.[74]

England established forts on the eastern shores of the Mississippi, as their French predecessors had done, but they were of limited value. Many forts were similar to St. Joseph, but others, more martial in appearance, lacked an adequate military presence. Indebtedness from the Seven Years' War limited British expenditures and enforced policies of economy and entrenchment on colonial administrators.

Spain, which also claimed sovereignty over a large North American empire, faced equally severe financial limitations. Both countries found it advantageous to avoid military confrontations.[75] Both knew their territories were defensibly vulnerable. British officers resented, but understood, the necessity of peaceful coexistence with Spain. In 1767, Frederick Haldimand wrote to General Gage,

> It does not seem that it would benefit the Spaniards to ever undertake anything against us on these banks. . . . It is true, however, that our posts on the Mississippi, very badly constructed, perhaps badly situated and dependent on New Orleans for their subsistence, are in a very hazardous position today.[76]

The British failed to surmount the hurdles posed by geography and limited military resources because they were unable effectively to enlist the support of the Interior French. Sinclair's forced removal of the L'archevêque–Chevalier kin network demonstrated his naïveté about the complicated way in which kinship structured Great Lakes society. English officers often distrusted the Interior French and simultaneously misunderstood the complex kin-related world in which they lived. Kin networks proved increasingly important to imperial control when expenses were reduced and posts were staffed minimally or closed. Kin networks maintained order across the continent's vast interior landscape. The evolution of these networks gave the Interior French an established presence that it was foolhardy to ignore. Obviously, Major Arent Schuyler De Peyster, Sinclair's predecessor at Michilimackinac, came to understand the power of these networks, for he commented,

"The Canadians I fear are of great disservice to the Government but the Indians are perfect Free Masons when intrusted with a secret by a Canadian most of them being much connected by marriage." It was unfortunate for the British that Sinclair, like other officers, allowed his paranoid distrust to interfere with the effective utilization of the Interior French.[77]

English control over the western Great Lakes was far from effective. Those officers willing to function within the established social system proved the most successful, while ignorance of or blatant disregard for social processes produced disastrous results. Kin networks enhanced or hindered governance and were indicative of the way in which encounter had promoted not only change but also social stability. The St. Joseph Potawatomi and the L'archevêque–Chevalier kin demonstrate that a common ground had evolved from the intermarriage of Frenchmen and Native women and that power and human agency were exhibited in ways often misunderstood by the English.

5

Agriculture, Warfare, and Neutrality

THE AMERICAN REVOLUTION has been routinely interpreted as a turning point, as "a disaster for Indians," and this was certainly true for eastern Indians, such as the Iroquois.[1] Along the St. Joseph River, however, many Potawatomi remained neutral and refused to take up arms on behalf of the British or the colonials. Even when the Potawatomi became allies, Britain frequently discovered that Native support was halfhearted. Groups of warriors who were aligned with either the British or Americans may have been encouraged to move from the St. Joseph River valley and establish separate villages along less traveled, more distant river pathways. Remote, isolated villages created viable alternatives for young men who chose warfare over neutrality and transformed the American Revolution into a nonevent for many villages in the St. Joseph River valley.

The Seven Years' War had marked a turning point in Great Lakes history when conflicts between the French and English were no longer routinely transferred to North America. Indians were freed from longstanding alliances and, for the first time since encounter, population levels began to recover. In the past, warfare had been equated with the outbreak of disease. Returning Indian warriors often carried smallpox to their villages, and these epidemic outbreaks led to dramatic population declines.[2] Among the St. Joseph Potawatomi, the last and one of the worst smallpox outbreaks occurred during the Seven Years' War.[3] Many Indian communities experienced less turmoil from warfare and disease during the last half of the eighteenth century than during their previous century-long involvement with the French.

The conquest of Canada ushered in a period of peace and prosperity for many Indian communities in the western Great Lakes. Imperial conflict was muted. The financial burdens of the fighting forced the English to find ways to coexist peacefully with the Spaniards.

Despite Britain's defeat in the American Revolution, many fur trade communities in the western Great Lakes were protected from an United States incursion when Britain refused to relinquish control of Detroit and Michilimackinac. These forts, rebuilt during the war, served as more effective fortifications, were less vulnerable to attack, and guarded waterway access into the lakes. In addition, the British constructed a new fort on the Maumee, near present-day Fort Wayne, on United States territory. The profitability of the fur trade reinforced Britain's determination to ignore the terms of the Treaty of Paris, Montreal and Quebec's fur exports amounted to £200,000 annually, with half of all revenues coming from the Great Lakes and the Upper Mississippi River valley. In the early 1790s, the English fur trade lobby even persuaded the government to support the concept of an Indian barrier state in the West, with boundaries drawn to include the fur trade basin of the Great Lakes and the American West. The idea was rejected by the United States and, consequently, dropped by British diplomats.[4]

During the American Revolution, the St. Lawrence riverway remained open and the Michilimackinac trade flourished. The fur trade operated much as it had done in the past and even appeared to be entering an expansionary phase when St. Louis and New Orleans emerged as alternative markets. Even prior to the Revolution, St. Joseph villages accepted gifts from the Spanish at St. Louis.[5] The relocation of Marie Madeleine L'archevêque Chevalier's daughters at or near St. Louis increased the market alternatives for the St. Joseph River valley Potawatomi.

Increased market competition for Great Lakes furs and for agricultural goods ensured the viability of many fur trade communities. Demand for agricultural produce was fueled by Britain's need to supply its troops. Market-based agriculture provided an economic safety network that facilitated Indian neutrality. When warfare threatened their villages, the St. Joseph Potawatomi ignored seasonal hunting routines and thus angered fur traders. In neutral villages, women's labor both fed the households and produced a marketable surplus.

The agricultural orientation of villages in the St. Joseph River valley discouraged their involvement in war. These farming communities stretched along the river banks from Michigan into Indiana and Illinois. Their agricultural prosperity was part of a long-term process of accommodation and change, partially triggered by the encounter, necessitated by the demographic dislocations of the Fur Trade Wars, and fostered by Indian involvement in the fur trade.[6]

The demand for food dramatically increased during the Fur Trade

Wars, when Great Lakes peoples were pushed west by the Iroquois. Available hunting territory decreased when thousands of Natives clustered together in the Green Bay refugee area. Survival required expanded agricultural production. The Potawatomi, for instance, transformed all of Washington Island into cornfields and vegetable plots and established a trading center on nearby Rock Island.[7] Food was produced in larger quantities, and agricultural fields were expanded to meet the demand of several villages as well as to supply newly arriving or transient refugees.

The agricultural surplus produced by Indian women fed an increasingly large refugee population and also the influx of Frenchmen. Fur traders in the western Great Lakes found it impossible to transport sufficient produce from Montreal to feed either themselves or their voyageurs. Both distance and the small size of those early canoes mitigated against the transportation of large quantities of foodstuffs.[8] Nor were transient traders proficient hunters; they were ignorant of both the landscape and animal behavioral patterns.

Food was as central to the exchange process as furs; and, although New France officials attempted to end fur trader dependence on this indigenous food supply, they were unsuccessful. In 1681, for instance, Robert La Salle planted "French grain, Indian corn, peas, cabbages and other vegetables," when he established Fort St. Joseph.[9] These behaviors were encouraged by Governor Louis de Buade Frontenac, who believed that commandants could be less dependent on Native Americans through proper management of the voyageurs. Frontenac contended that Frenchmen should collect wood, catch fish, and plant crops. Despite Frontenac's encouragement, the French became more, rather than less, reliant on Native American women for their food supply. French fur traders were too mobile to tend crops, and fur profits were enhanced by voyageurs engaged in the trade, rather than in farming.[10]

Those traders who married Native women never worried about how to feed themselves; that remained a female responsibility. Indigenous divisions of labor proved beneficial to French fur traders. Indians regarded agriculture as women's work, and women controlled productive resources.[11]

When the Fur Trade Wars ended, women in reestablished or newly founded fur trade and river portage villages began producing a surplus specifically for the trade. Agriculture evolved as integral to the exchange process. Thus, at Wagansgisi, also known as L'Arbre Croche, or Crooked Tree, along the northern shoreline of Michigan's Lower Peninsula and near Michilimackinac, an unusually long growing season, coupled with increased viability of the fur trade, encouraged many Odawa people to remain in or near their villages during the long, cold winters of Michigan's Upper Peninsula.[12] Farther south, at portages, where fur trade routes crossed from Lake Michigan to the Mississippi River valley, equally important agricultural villages were established.[13]

Areas like the St. Joseph River valley were well suited to meet the increased agricultural demand. The Jesuits compared this fertile land favorably to France with its pheasants, quail, and vineyards.

> 'Tis a spot the best adapted of any to be seen for purposes of living and as regards the soil. There are pheasants as in France; quails and perroquets; the finest vines in the world, which produce a vast quantity of very excellent grapes, both white and black, the berry very large and juicy, and the bunch very long. It is the richest district in all that country.[14]

Native women in the St. Joseph River valley raised the grain crops of French farms. Marie Madeleine Réaume L'archevêque Chevalier, for instance, grew wheat, barley, and oats as well as corn, beans, and squash. French fur traders may have been reluctant farmers, but they proved very able instructors.[15] Grains were ground at mills in Indian villages.[16] In Illinois Country there were gristmills as well as mills driven by horses and powered by the wind.[17]

By the mid–eighteenth century, the rhythm of daily life had changed dramatically in areas such as the St. Joseph River valley. The agricultural abundance produced by Indian women fed both residential and transient populations and was exported to other posts. There were local and export markets for chickens, cattle, oxen, and horses.[18]

The agricultural surplus produced by Native women also supported military operations in the western Great Lakes. Native women were paid to feed French soldiers and Indian warriors and to feed the families of those warriors temporarily garrisoned at Fort St. Joseph. For example, before she married Louis Chevalier, Madeleine Réaume L'archevêque can be traced in the official reimbursement records of the fort. Madeleine supplied the wheats, oats, and corn needed by the St. Joseph commandant in the fight against the Chickasaw.[19] Even American troops garrisoned at Detroit were supplied with cattle by the Indians.[20] Traders were now brokers of foodstuffs as well as furs. They shipped corn and maple sugar, as well as furs, to Michilimackinac, Detroit, and St. Louis.[21] The agricultural orientation of fur trade communities such as Fort St. Joseph can be further confirmed by the reimbursement claims filed by Louis and Madeleine Chevalier, following their forced removal. Their claim describes a settled community with cultivated fields, orchards, and domestic livestock. Removal had deprived them of "ten houses, good lands, orchards, gardens, cattle, furniture, utensils and [of course], debts." The fur trade constituted only a part of their annual endeavors.[22]

What little we know about eighteenth-century Indian agriculture derives from the commandant's records at the western posts, such as Fort St. Joseph, where French troops and Indian allies were mustered and fed. Ledger books for eighteenth-century traders like Madeleine and Louis Chevalier do not exist—or have not yet been uncovered. We are unable to ascertain or, more important, fully analyze the extent to which women's agricultural work was involved in the exchange process of the trade.

By the late eighteenth-century, the extent to which women's labor was central to the fur trade becomes apparent in the ledgers of individual traders. The trade in agricultural produce was central to the success of the local trader who replaced the L'archevêque–Chevalier family, William Burnett. When he entered the St. Joseph trade is unknown, although his biographer contends that it was in the late 1770s. He married a prominent, full-blood Potawatomi woman, Kakima. Burnett's personal correspondence and fur trade ledgers indicate that he traded in both agricultural products and peltry. Thus, in May 1786, Burnett's letters indicate that he had both a surplus of corn on hand and the prospect of another good summer harvest. He requested that a boat from Michilimackinac pick up 220 bushels of corn from his St. Joseph post. Later that month, when he hired four winterers from Michilimackinac to accompany him to the Kankakee, Burnett made additional arrangements to ship more Indian corn. "As I have an opportunity of making a good deal of Indian corn, I wish you could contract with somebody at Makina to furnish them two or three hundred bushels."[23]

Wheat also played an important role in Burnett's fur trade transactions. "I had a very fine harvest last fall, among which I have had a hundred bushels of wheat. I leave tomorrow, for Detroit with an expectation of getting a mill."[24] Wheat required more intensive soil cultivation than corn, and Burnett's correspondence included orders for the necessary agricultural equipment. Although heavier American plows were available, Burnett wanted the smaller and lighter French variety, the type that women might use. "If possible, I must desire you will get me a plough shear, as the french call it, *en bardeau,* about five and twenty pounds weight."[25]

Despite Burnett's enthusiasm for wheat, corn remained the agricultural staple of the fur trade. Corn was a reliable commodity, an especially crucial factor when the harvest of peltry proved insufficient to meet trade goods expenditures. Burnett was at his Kankakee post when he wrote to his English partner describing that year's gloomy fur trade prospects. "The Indians will make but a very poor hunt this year." But as soon as he returned to St. Joseph, he promised to "send off a Canoe for Makina, loaded with Corn."[26]

When the Potawatomi did not go on their winter hunt, but remained near their villages, agricultural produce paid for Burnett's trade goods. Maple sugar, like corn, was a saleable and highly reliable product. During the late winter and early spring months, Indian women produced considerable amounts of maple sugar. The sugar was packed in mokucks, baskets woven expressly for this purpose, while sugar produced nearest the trading posts was shipped in casks.

A shipping invoice of May 26, 1801, shows that aboard the *General Hunter*, bound for Detroit, Burnett shipped five casks and eight mokucks of sugar. Each cask weighed close to 300 pounds; the mokucks generally weighed 40 to 50 pounds. Burnett's shipment included more than 1,700 pounds of sugar. Despite complaints about a "bad hunt," he also sent 11,570 skins and pelts—the fur trade remained a profitable venture in the nineteenth-century St. Joseph River valley.[27]

Although Burnett's written records provide partial evidence for this increased agricultural orientation, the natural landscape tells an even more dramatic story of how Indian people transformed these fertile river basin lands to meet their needs. They left an imprint of extensive agricultural activity that, as we shall see, was at least partially extant until the end of the nineteenth century.

Remnants of thousands of acres of cultivated Indian fields remained visible in southwest Michigan until after the Civil War (see figs. 5 to 8). Most fields ranged in size from 20 to 100 acres, but others were more extensive and encompassed as many as 300 acres. Most of these fields were appropriated by nineteenth-century settlers as their farmland. Many cities founded in nineteenth-century Michigan, such as Kalamazoo and Marshall, were located on former Indian agricultural tracts. Many were elaborate fields, cultivated in curvilinear fashion or laid out as extensive vegetable gardens. One nineteenth-century Michigan historian, Bela Hubbard, assumed the Potawatomi were nomadic and took these fields as evidence of a lost civilization. The search for evidence of a precontact landscape that rivaled those of antiquity led writers to transform the

FIGURE 5. *Ancient garden beds, rectangular, St. Joseph River valley, Michigan.* The diagram at the top is drawn from Bela Hubbard's "Ancient Garden Beds of Michigan," in *Michigan Pioneer and Historical Collections,* 2, 30. The artist's rendering depicts how these fields might have been configured. Illustration by Kathryn Darnell.

FIGURE 6. *Ancient garden beds, patchwork, St. Joseph River valley, Michigan.* The top diagram is drawn from Hubbard's "Ancient Garden Beds of Michigan," 2, 31. The artist's rendering depicts how these fields were configured in a patchwork pattern. Illustration by Kathryn Darnell.

FIGURE 7. *Ancient garden beds, circular, Prairie Ronde, St. Joseph River valley, Michigan.* The diagram is drawn from Hubbard's "Ancient Garden Beds of Michigan," 2, 32. The circular shape is illustrative of one of the more unusual shapes. Illustration by Kathryn Darnell.

FIGURE 8. *Ancient garden beds, arrowhead, St. Joseph River valley, Michigan.* The diagram is drawn from Hubbard's "Ancient Garden Beds of Michigan," 2, 32. The garden, near present-day Galesburg, suggests that gardens were laid out to accommodate different types of terrain. Illustration by Kathryn Darnell.

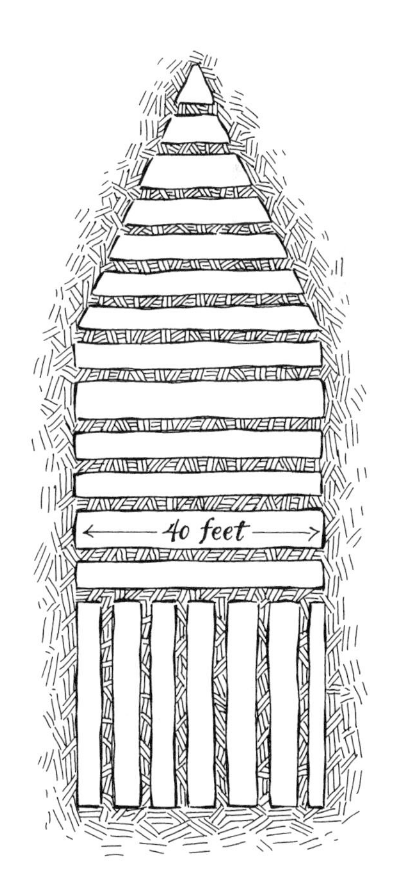

evidence of Indian agriculture into an American version of the Gardens of Babylon. Hubbard's written evidence and his sketches of abandoned fields, read for alternative purposes, offers dramatic proof of the extensive acreage cultivated by Potawatomi women. The multiplicity and complexity of the fields defied simple description and attests to the agricultural creativity of Native women. Hubbard, confused by the enormous size and variety of the fields, developed descriptive categories to catalogue his evidence. Unfortunately, his classification system did not include all the visual evidence he recorded in his sketchbook.

1. Wide convex beds, in parallel rows, without paths, composing independent plats. (Width of beds 12 feet, paths none, length 74 to 115 feet.)
2. Wide convex beds, in parallel rows, separated by paths of same width, in independent plats. (Width of beds 12 to 16 feet; paths same; length, 74 to 132 feet.)
3. Wide and parallel beds, separated by narrow paths, arranged in a series of plats longitudinal to each other. (Width of beds 14 feet; paths, 2 feet; length, 100 feet.)
4. Long and narrow beds, separated by narrower paths and arranged in a series of longitudinal plats, each plat divided from the next by semicircular heads. (Widths of beds 5 feet; paths, 1 1/2 feet; length, 100 feet; height, 18 inches.)
5. Parallel beds, arranged in plats similar to class 4, but divided by circular heads. (Width of beds, 6 feet; length, 12 to 40 feet; height, 18 inches.)
6. Parallel beds, of varying widths and lengths, separated by narrow paths, and arranged in plats of two or more at right angles N. and S., E. and W., to the plats adjacent. (Width of beds, 5 to 14 feet; paths, 1 to 2 feet; length, 12 to 30 feet; height, 8 inches.)
7. Parallel beds, of uniform width and length, with narrow paths, arranged in plats or blocks, and single beds, at varying angles. (Width of beds, 6 feet; paths, 2 feet; length, about 30 feet; height, 10 to 12 inches.)
8. Wheel-shaped plats, consisting of a circular bed, with beds of uniform shape and size radiating therefrom, all separated by narrow paths. (Width of beds, 6 to 20 feet; paths, 1 foot; length, 14 to 20 feet.)[28]

Hubbard's descriptions and diagrams demonstrate that indigenous agriculture had advanced beyond the traditional practices generally attributed to Indians. For instance, these fields were furrowed by plows. French plows, such as the *en bardeau* variety purchased by William Burnett, were probably used to cultivate these fields. Each field of a 100 or more acres consisted of individual, rectangularly shaped beds 5 to 16 feet in width and more than 100 feet in length. Paths separated the rows of vegetable gardens. Rows formed rectangular blocks divided by avenues.[29] The configuration was similar to that of the large common fields of seventeenth-century New England towns.

The size and extent of these fields suggest that the villages of the St. Joseph River valley were permanent as well as large. These fields were not unusual; there were others in North America. In eighteenth-century North Dakota, along the Missouri River, there were fields over 100 feet in length. There, as in other villages, "the size of the garden was determined chiefly by . . . the number of mouths that must be fed." The landscape evidence of such agricultural practices has not been incorporated into Great Lakes Indian history. Instead, historians have relied on the rather scornful letters of settlers and territorial officials who conveyed the impression that agriculture was a part-time endeavor, with Indian women tending small household gardens rather than cultivated fields.

Michigan's Potawatomi women also created elaborately configured fields. They farmed in triangular and square-rigged patterns as well as more traditional forms. These differences suggest variations in soil, terrain, and crops or that these fields had a dual function. At St. Joseph, there were circular garden beds—each had 25 to 30 foot beds radiating from the center (see fig. 7). The beds were separated by wide avenues, suggesting walkways, along the garden paths. Henry Schoolcraft, who traveled through nineteenth-century Michigan, also described Indian fields with "various fanciful shapes combined in a fantastic manner" and "parterres and scalloped work, with alleys between, and apparently ample walks leading in different directions." Schoolcraft, like Hubbard, attributed this landscape evidence to "an industrious population" that had long since disappeared. Prejudice obscured the vision of Henry Schoolcraft, "How a work of this kind could exist in a country that has hitherto (according to received general opinion) been the seat of war to untutored Indians alone . . . I know not." This future Indian agent went on collecting evidence because he believed that his notes might lead "to a more perfect investigation . . . and give us a very different ideas of the ancient state of realms that we at present believe to have been from the earliest period only the habitations of savages."[30]

Michigan gazetteers, the travel guides of the 1830s, as well as county histories written shortly after the Civil War, were written from direct observation and provided elaborate descriptions of former Indian fields. This physical evidence was later destroyed by those farmers who appropriated Indian fields as part of their lands. In the northern part of Wright Township, one Potawatomi village had fields, or gardens, extending over 15 acres.[31] Two early Kalamazoo farmers, Henry Little and A. T. Prout, described several circular garden beds as well as numerous other cultivated fields.[32] Indian fields were described as plowed and fenced and contained rows of "corn, beans, pumpkins and other vegetables."[33] Early histories also commented on the fruit-bearing orchards that existed when settlers arrived.[34]

The increased dependence on agriculture encouraged neutrality. Many St. Joseph Potawatomi refused to side with one particular nation and engaged in conversations with the Spanish at St. Louis, traded with the English at Detroit and Michilimackinac, visited Clark at Kaskaskia, and signed letters of friendship with the Americans.[35] Rather than view this as a manipulative tactic that allowed Indians to play one foreign power against another, we might more realistically see this as a defensive strategy designed to protect prosperous agricultural communities. Native villages with agricultural fields, productive orchards, and herds of livestock had much to lose when they left their villages unprotected. It is not surprising that the Potawatomi were condemned as being "very inconsistent in its friendships."[36] When forced to favor one aggressor over the other, they did so with halfhearted enthusiasm. Thus, in October of 1778, only a few St. Joseph Potawatomi joined Henry Hamilton's attack on Vincennes. They steadfastly refused to provide more than fifteen warriors.[37] Within three months, those few warriors returned home. This strategic support and neutral behavior allowed the St. Joseph Potawatomi to emerge from the American Revolution relatively unscathed.

At the end of the Revolutionary War, the St. Joseph Potawatomi were well fed, wore English woolens, cottons, and silks, and adorned their clothes and themselves with trade silver. Agricultural surpluses enabled the men to remain in their villages when warfare interrupted their seasonal rounds of hunting and trapping.

Historians have been reluctant to replace the image of the nomadic Indian with the agricultural Indian, just as it has proven difficult to convince people that the appropriation of the Indian as a symbol of savagery is at best insensitive and, at worst, incorrect. Historians themselves are partially to blame for this distortion. We are not immune to the myths of popular culture and we are too fond of telling war stories. History remains constrained by popular images that depict Indians as warriors and by a narrative time frame that continues to rely on warfare as the chronological markers of history. Alternative narratives about Indian persistence are difficult to construct, because mainstream history remains framed by events that have limited relevance for Indians.

THE OHIO River valley offered the St. Joseph Potawatomi dramatic evidence of what Indians had to lose from warfare. Those communities that supported the English during the American Revolution lost all claim to their lands. Initially, the United States government declared that the Native allies of the British forfeited their lands when England lost the war.[38] That defeat transformed Indians into refugees, and those who did not flee to Canada fled north and west into the lands that lay between Lakes Huron and Michigan. The St. Joseph River Potawatomi incorporated many of those refugees. By the end of the eighteenth century, ethnically diverse refugee villages extended along the banks of the St. Joseph, down along the Kankakee, and south into Miami lands, along the Wabash and Elkhart Rivers of present-day Indiana. Despite the influx of many Delaware and Shawnee, the Potawatomi and Miami retained their distinctive identities and assimilated these newcomers, just as they had in the past.[39]

The multitude of lesser tributaries, small streams, and intermittent swamps of Michigan's southern borderlands were safe havens. Continued British control of the forts on the Great Lakes and the construction of Fort Miami on the Maumee River encouraged this influx of refugees to settle in and abandon their northern and western migrations. A disjointed Indian alliance was formed between villages in the Ohio River valley and the refugee communities from eastern Lake Erie. The St. Joseph Potawatomi maintained a wary distance from it. This newly expanding Pan-Indian alliance defeated Josiah Harmar's and Arthur St. Clair's American forces in 1790 and 1791, but the St. Joseph Potawatomi remained reluctant allies.

Victory over Harmar's poorly organized troops instilled a false sense of confidence in the Indians. The United States simultaneously overreacted to this evidence of renewed Indian militancy.[40] At the Battle of Fallen Timbers, three thousand American soldiers under Anthony Wayne's leadership defeated four hundred to thirteen hundred Indians. Wayne initiated a scorch-and-burn policy that forced Indians north and west, exiled remaining Indians from their homelands, and reduced most refugees to starvation. Wayne leveled and torched Native dwellings, hauled away the winter stores of Indian grain to American markets, and burned agricultural fields. Before the Battle of Fallen Timbers, cornfields had extended from four to five miles along the Au Glaize. There were over a thousand acres of corn, large vegetable patches, and orchards. Wayne, himself, had vividly described the river valley's agricultural abundance:

> The margins of these beautiful rivers, the Miamis of the Lake (Maumee), and the Au Glaize (A southern tributary), appear like one continuous village for a number of miles, both above and below this place, Grand Glaize, nor have I ever beheld such immense fields of corn in any other part of America, from Canada to Florida.[41]

Anthony Wayne transformed these fertile farmlands into charred, fire-scarred wastelands. Starvation transformed agricultural Indians into nomads.

At the Battle of Fallen Timbers, when the English abandoned their Indian allies, the Indians learned a bitter lesson about trusting the British, especially the Detroit Potawatomi, who had provided many of the warriors.[42] The British became untrustworthy allies.[43] Indians who fled Wayne's forces were denied sanctuary when Major William Campbell closed the gates of Fort Miami, and an Indian defeat was transformed into a massacre. In the final crush of defeat, the western Potawatomi had few warriors—probably no more than seventy-five men participated.[44] The St. Joseph Potawatomi were never wholehearted supporters of their eastern kin, nor were they overly receptive to the plight of Native people in the Ohio River valley. Prior to Fallen Timbers, the Americans attempted to use the western Potawatomi to allay Indian unrest in the Ohio River valley. At a 1792 peace conference, La Gesse, who had aided Siggenauk in the 1780 attack on Fort St. Joseph, assured United States negotiators of their willingness to participate in any peace conference on the Wabash, as friends of the Americans.[45]

Fallen Timbers was a tragic reminder of the vulnerability of an agricultural lifestyle. Wayne's victory transformed the St. Joseph Potawatomi into halfhearted supporters of any future Pan-Indian confederacy directed against the United States.[46]

Wayne's decisive victory also encouraged British withdrawal and thus resulted in the successful negotiation of Jay's Treaty. This 1794 treaty had a far greater impact on Great Lakes villages than the 1783 Treaty of Paris, which concluded the American Revolution. English troops were withdrawn and the twelve-year occupation of U.S. territory by British troops ended; Detroit, Michilimackinac, and Maumee were turned over to the United States.

British withdrawal heightened Native fears about increased American intrusion and simultaneously fueled the growing nativist insurgency. The St. Joseph Potawatomi confronted a new century complicated by a Pan-Indianism that rejected European ways and people and was hostile to accommodation and change. The nontraditionalist Indians, like those of the St. Joseph River valley, were anathema to the Shawnee brothers Tecumseh and Tenskwatawa, the Prophet. Neutrality emerged as the only viable pathway and, unfortunately, many young men condemned their "neutral" elders as cowards. The Potawatomi faced new pressures to accommodate an emerging generation of warriors, inspired by a reactionary, spreading Pan-Indianism. Rather than reject and dismiss these militant young men, new villages were again established, and the Potawatomi expanded south and west into former Ilini lands. Main Poc and Chebanse, both Potawatomi, were ardent advocates of Tenskwatawa's nativist crusade and they established villages along the Kankakee. Other militant communities also evolved along the Wabash and Elkhart Rivers. Young Potawatomi warriors who abhorred the appeasement-oriented approach of their village elders joined these communities.

The westward expansion into former Ilini lands included not only this nativist contingent but also ardent pro-American Potawatomi. Black Partridge, Gomo, his younger brother Senajiwan, and Swift Current were all pro-American and established villages near Lake Peoria's northeastern shore. They traded with the Americans at Fort Dearborn and the French at St. Louis. Later, they moved their villages back to the vicinity of Peoria, following the completion of Fort Clark.[47]

Most St. Joseph villages relied on physical distance to separate themselves from both nativist and pro-American factions. Tenskwatawa in his prophetic role openly and personally attacked leaders involved in "civilizing missions."[48] Although the sedentary fur trade villages of the St. Joseph River valley professed interest in the Prophet's teaching they remained noncommittal. Their own lifestyle mitigated against a return to imagined norms and stereotypes of traditional Indian behavior. Unfortunately, Potawatomi neutrality proved an increasingly difficult path to follow when the Shawnee Prophet settled among the nearby Miami in 1808. Then, Main Poc, a Tenskwatawa supporter, resettled his followers on lands directly south of the St. Joseph. The St. Joseph Potawatomi completely separated themselves from the nativist crusade when Main Poc, along with Chebanse, began raiding American settlements in southern Illinois, as well as Osage villages across the Mississippi River.

Increased nativist militancy encouraged the neutrality of the St. Joseph Potawatomi. Neutrality proved a judicious choice, again reinforced by the way in which the Americans retaliated against the Shawnee Prophet's allies. Following the Battle of Tippecanoe in 1811, Americans confiscated large quantities of beans, peas, and corn and burned what had not been harvested.[49]

Defeat at the Battle of Tippecanoe led the followers of Tenskwatawa and his brother Tecumseh to side with the English in the War of 1812. Again, most of the St. Joseph Potawatomi remained neutral. Chebanse, Main Poc, Moran, and Mad Sturgeon worked to keep the Potawatomi warlike, but the St. Joseph River Potawatomi remained focused on how best to protect their villages from the scorch-and-burn policy of the Americans. Potawatomi fears were well grounded. Like Ninian Edwards in Illinois, territorial governors planned incendiary raids against those Indian villages that sent warriors to fight on behalf of the English in 1812.

> The absence of warriors will enable [them] to make great destruction upon the village's corn fields and some will escape to carry the news to their friends at Malden who you will know could not be withheld from returning to the relief of their families the moment they should become alarmed for their safety. . . . The movement would operate equally upon all and might produce a general defection of the Indians, while it should take the British at equal surprise and greatly disconcert them by being so suddenly deprived of a force on which they will make great calculations.[50]

The pro-English Miami, nearby neighbors of the St. Joseph Potawatomi, suffered the consequences of such aggressively destructive behaviors. In July 1813, three empty villages were attacked and destroyed by the Americans: one village on the Eel, another on the Wabash, and a third on the Mississinewa River.[51] In September, the deserted Potawatomi village at Chillicothe and two others were also burned by Americans.[52]

During the War of 1812, American fears about Indian involvement were exacerbated by British attempts to secure Potawatomi allegiance. English commanders recognized that "the Indians were divided in their loyalty to the U.S." and they attempted to win support of the St. Joseph Potawatomi through the fur trade. Joseph Cadot, a well-known Michilimackinac trader employed by the British Indian Department, presented gifts to neutral villages in the Grand and St. Joseph River valleys. On behalf of the British, Cadot distributed much needed supplies, cloth, awls, hats, and other valued trade items.[53] His presence was problematic but his announcement that others traders would arrive shortly with additional supplies represented a serious threat to Indian neutrality. British traders would provide a ready excuse for an American incursion.[54] Consequently, the new arrivals were captured and delivered to the Americans, an action that proved sufficiently instructive so that "in consequence, no others [British traders] would venture among them."[55] The English failed again to draw the villages of the Grand and St. Joseph River valleys to their side. Most British support came from northern Indians rather than the Indians of the villages in the southern Great Lakes. Even pro-British Potawatomi, such as Chebanse and his supporters, headed north, where they found more compatible allies.

In September of 1815, at Spring Wells, near Detroit, the United States officially ended the war with the Native people. There was a large group of Potawatomi as well as Wyandot, Delaware, Shawnee, and Seneca who gathered to sign the treaty. Among the signatories was Louison Chevalier, who at the age of sixty-five had continued to live and to fight among the Native people.[56] Chevalier had disappeared from the pages of history for almost forty years, but he had remained a trader among the Potawatomi. His kin network at St. Louis provided an alternative market for the fur trade communities in southwest Michigan.

The decisions that most St. Joseph villages made to remain neutral may seem surprising, but not if we view men such as Chebanse and Main Poc as the leaders of separate, militant villages. Most St. Joseph villages consistently and consciously avoided warfare. However difficult it was, the St. Joseph Potawatomi steadfastly maintained their relationship with dissident relatives in other villages. Kinship was often strained by outbreaks of fighting, but relationships were routinely reaffirmed through the exchange of trade goods for peltry. To understand how that process worked requires a closer understanding of how and why the fur trade fulfilled a mediatory function in a divisive landscape.

By the late eighteenth century, involvement in the fur trade had shaped new social identities and solidarities. Indian communities in the southern Great Lakes were engaged in a wider process of expansive social transformation that differentiated villages by religious and political orientation and by lifestyle. A Potawatomi village might contain an ethnically diverse population, Shawnee, Ojibway, or even white captives, but villages rarely mixed Catholic Indians with those who were religious traditionalists, or who were pro-British or pro-American.

Customs and behaviors that bridged disparate ways of life were invented on the middle ground and, once established as accepted and expected behaviors, shaped the process of cultural redefinition. The middle ground initially evolved as an arena of compromise between the Indians and the French, but, by the end of the eighteenth century, the middle ground had evolved as an arena for the negotiation of different or opposing perspectives aggravated by the potentially disruptive political alliances of adjacent Indian communities.

Successful fur traders relied on their wives to mediate the potentially explosive alliances of neighboring villages. Burnett married Kakima, one of the most prominent Potawatomi women in the St. Joseph River valley. At the time of her marriage, in Detroit by a Catholic priest, Kakima was already a baptized Catholic,[57] but it was neither religion nor Catholic kin networks that mediated the political differences apparent within her family and village. Kakima was related to important men who at any moment might disrupt the river valley tranquility. One brother was the militant, pro-British leader, Chebanse; another brother, Topenabe, was pro-American; while a third brother, Pokagon, was a headman of neutral persuasion and probably Catholic. Chebanse, the Duckling, was a rabid anti-American, pledged to Tecumseh and the Prophet. During the War of 1812, he sided with Tecumseh in support of the English. It was Chebanse who helped defend Michilimackinac against American attack.[58] Kakima's pro-American brother, Topenabe, used Tenskwatawa's defeat at Prophetstown to publicly declare his support for the Americans. He signed the Greenville Treaty, which granted peace to "the bands of the Putawatamies, which adhere to the Grand Sachem Topinipee, and to the Chief Onoxa." Topenabe promised to aid the Americans in any future war against the English.[59]

Kakima negotiated the potentially explosive positions of her relatives through her husband's access to trade goods and his need for peltry. Kakima's intermediary role became obvious during the War of 1812, when many of her relatives moved into oppositional villages. Kakima exchanged furs for trade goods with all of her brothers' villages, regardless of political allegiance. "Anti-American Potawatomi continued to receive goods by way of the St. Joseph River and the South Bend portage to the upper Kankakee." Even the militant Main Poc, whose village was located at a sequestered site on the Yellow River in the swampy headwaters of the Kankakee, had access to St. Joseph River trade goods.[60]

For the St. Joseph Potawatomi, the potential dangers of being too visible or too closely allied with the losing side entailed disastrous outcomes. Kakima facilitated an exchange process that allowed the Potawatomi to avoid a disastrous path of being unwaveringly pro-British or pro-American. Unfortunately, Kakima's involvement in the trade has been masked by the historical attention focused on her husband. Fur trade historians have described the St. Joseph River valley fur trade as the almost-exclusive province of one American frontiersman, William Burnett.[61] Popular historians have ignored his Scots–Irish origins, and he has been inappropriately characterized as the first "American" pioneer. He has also been lauded for audaciously and blatantly thumbing his nose at the English and continuing to trade. But these exaggerations and notions of American cleverness both mask Kakima's role in the fur trade and neglect Burnett's forced removal from the Great Lakes by the British.[62] His prominence as a St. Joseph trader resulted from his marriage to Kakima and from her active involvement in the trade.[63]

Burnett's influence had little to do with wily behavior. In fact, his blatant support of the Americans probably led to his death. William Burnett lived and traded in a far more impersonal world than that of Marie Madeleine and Louis Chevalier. Kakima was a full-blood Potawatomi, and her kin network extended only to her people. She had neither familial nor fictive kin at other trading posts in the western Great Lakes. Nineteenth-century fur traders operated in an interpersonal world, with a market economy that demanded payment in furs for goods extended the previous season on credit. Burnett's supplies were British and came from Detroit, Michilimackinac, and Montreal. In each place, he was dependent on established merchants to obtain trade goods and to sell his furs; there were no Catholic kin networks to ensure alternative markets for his furs or to provide him access to trade goods.

Burnett's success in this increasingly competitive market economy depended on his wife's kin network and her own skills as a trader. Good-quality furs were the best insurance policy in an increasingly competitive market, and Kakima's indigenous kin network ensured him access to those furs. While her husband wintered in the pro-American Potawatomi villages of the Kankakee River valley, Kakima remained in the St. Joseph River valley community. Kakima's role in the trade is apparent from Burnett's correspondence. He wrote to his Michilimackinac partner, Charles Patterson, "I took with me eight pieces of Shrouds and the Assortment and the rest I left here with my Indian woman and she had done on her part in the trading very, very well."[64]

William Burnett's dependence on Kakima extended beyond trading skills. He also relied on the agricultural prowess of his wife's household to produce sufficient corn, wheat, and maple sugar to feed their own household and to export as a marketable surplus at both Michilimackinac and Detroit. Burnett was increasingly dependent on an agricultural landscape when warfare threatened to disrupt seasonal hunts. As Burnett's correspondence indicates, Potawatomi men neither routinely nor regularly left for their wintering grounds. They refused to leave either communities or fields unguarded.

> There is no appearance of doing anything here this year, as fear keeps the Indians from hunting. They continually imagine that the Americans are coming upon them. . . . Let me know if provision will be scarce this year at Detroit and in particular if Indian corn will be worth anything. When I left Makina last fall there was no great appearance of any crop at L'Arbre Croche.[65]

Burnett's economic woes, although troublesome, often proved less problematic for him than his own vocal displays of political allegiance.[66] Burnett's fur trade activity spanned the period from 1780 to 1812, when the English controlled both Detroit and Michilimackinac and when the most desirable trade goods came from England. Whenever Burnett displayed too prominent an American presence, he found himself in trouble with the British. Once, the English commandant at Michilimackinac required Burnett to take on English partners from the firm of McBeth and Grant. Another time, when his boisterous American boosterism overwhelmed his better judgment, Burnett found himself forcibly removed by the English from the western Great Lakes. He was placed under arrest at Michilimackinac, returned on board ship to Detroit, and was sent to Montreal. Refused a pass to return to St. Joseph by the English, he eventually returned to New York and Philadelphia, and from there returned to his post.[67]

Burnett relied on entrepreneurial strategies to counteract his problematic relationship with English traders. He turned westward to Fort Dearborn, to the fledgling American fur trade community evolving at present-day Chicago.[68] Burnett had close fur trade ties with Fort Dearborn's Jean Baptiste Pointe Du Sable, who was initially a Lake Peoria trader supplied by Burnett. Du Sable was married to a Potawatomi woman, and she, like Burnett's wife, supervised an extensive agricultural household. There were cultivated fields of corn, barley, and wheat; a full complement of livestock that included cows, pigs, horses, and chickens; a millhouse that ground wheat into flour and a bakery to convert flour into bread. There was even a smokehouse in which to cure meats.

Long-standing fur trade ties to Du Sable allowed William Burnett to expand westward and establish a warehouse for storing furs near Fort Dearborn (now Chicago). At the end of the eighteenth century, Du Sable sold his fur trade interests, William Burnett stood surety for one of his own clerks to purchase Du Sable's holdings. Sympathetic political allegiance further cemented the friendship of these two men, for Du Sable, like Burnett, reportedly became an American partisan during the War of 1812.[69]

Du Sable is frequently identified as the African American founder of Chicago, and, like Burnett, is cast as an American pioneer, the trailblazer for later settlement. However, both men owed their prominence and success to the kin networks of the indigenous communities into which they had married. Theirs was an indigenous universe where economic success depended on the role that their Potawatomi wives played in the fur trade. The extensive kin networks and agricultural and trading skills of these Native women allowed both Du Sable and Burnett to winter among the Potawatomi, to acquire the choicest furs, and to be absent from their trading posts for prolonged periods of time.[70]

Burnett's vociferous allegiance to the American cause during the War of 1812 increased friction between him and the neutral, as well as the pro-British, Potawatomi. St. Joseph Potawatomi were consciously inconsistent allies who also could avoid Burnett and rely on alternative fur trade partners, such as the L'archevêque–Chevalier kin network at St. Louis.[71]

Kinship networks drew the peltry trade westward to St. Louis. Burnett countered this competitive threat by hiring Michilimackinac winterers with kinship ties to the St. Joseph Potawatomi. For instance, he hired Pierre Lasaliere who was married to Thérèse, an Odawa woman born into the L'archevêque–Chevalier kin network at Fort St. Joseph, prior to the 1780 removal. Her parents had been forcibly removed from Fort St. Joseph, and she was raised among her mother's people, the Grand River Odawa.

Burnett increasingly relied on traders from the L'archevêque–Chevalier kin network and, ironically, these actions reestablished an exchange process long familiar to the St. Joseph River valley Potawatomi. Catholic kin networks were permanently reestablished when Joseph Bertrand arrived in the St. Joseph River valley, sometime between 1803 and 1806.[72] Bertrand, like Burnett, married a Potawatomi woman, Mouto, whose baptismal name was Madeleine.[73] Although her ancestral lineage, remains unconfirmed, she may have been related to Kakima and may have been a sister to Topenabe.[74]

Bertrand became central to the story of Potawatomi persistence because, unlike Burnett, he and his wife worked to reestablish a Catholic kin network in the St. Joseph River valley. He was also a more agreeable fur trade partner for the Potawatomi because he possessed none of Burnett's nationalistic fervor and established a neutral stance toward entangling alliances with either the Americans or the British. Perhaps Bertrand's allegiance was only more clandestine, for, after the war, he claimed he had been an American spy. During the War of 1812, however, he avoided public support for either the English or the Americans. Unlike Burnett, Bertrand lived in the midst of the Potawatomi villages clustered near the former Fort St. Joseph, about four miles south of present-day Niles.[75]

Bertrand's newly established post drew on the associations of the pre-nineteenth-century fur trade world. His house was constructed of logs from the old Fort St. Joseph mission. His wife actively promoted Catholicism and reestablished the Catholic kin networks that had long forged the social links in the exchange process. Bertrand emerged as independent of Burnett and was able to offer the Potawatomi better-quality goods that he acquired through John Jacob Astor's American Fur Company.

The return of an exchange process mediated by Catholic kin networks was ensured by Burnett's disappearance during the War of 1812. Burnett's vociferous support of the American cause alienated the neutral Potawatomi. He then intervened in the Indian attack on Fort Dearborn, thus openly aligning himself with the Americans. Shortly after that event, he disappeared, reportedly the victim of an irate, pro-British Indian.[76]

Despite the volatility of oppositional loyalties during the war, Potawatomi kin networks remained intact. Refugees returned to the St. Joseph River valley, drawn by kinship loyalty.[77] Kinship mitigated personal conflicts. Even though her husband was probably murdered, Kakima never demanded revenge and, indeed, she reaffirmed the importance of kinship and repaired the social damage done by competing political alliances. One of Kakima's sons, Abram Burnett, adopted the son of the pro-British Chebanse. Chebanse was Kakima's brother and, although he initially fled to Canada, he later returned and lived with Kakima's daughter. Chebanse's young son took the name of his father, Abram Burnett, and thus a full-blood Potawatomi become the son of a mixed-ancestry father.[78]

The Burnett family gradually lost control of the St. Joseph fur trade. Kakima moved to Indiana to head the household of her son, Abram Burnett, who became an Indiana trader.[79] The St. Joseph post was left in the hands of Burnett's two eldest sons, and their share of the trade spiraled ever downward. Both were educated in Detroit, among Americans rather than among Kakima's people, and although both married Potawatomi women, their marriages proved temporary. Their wives left them and migrated west with the Potawatomi.[80]

From 1812 to 1832, the Indians allied with Burnett were increasingly drawn to Bertrand as the Catholic kin networks regained control over the fur trade. Catholicism again took root in the St. Joseph River valley, and it would prove central to Potawatomi persistence. It would come as no surprise to either Bertrand or his Potawatomi kin that the Chicago Treaty negotiated in 1832 contained an important clause that exempted Catholic Potawatomi from removal. Only forced removal threatened the future of the Potawatomi Indians, and, even then, kinship became an effective means of combating removal and ensuring persistence.

The fur trade as a social process has remained submerged beneath a more familiar myth: the illusion that Indians were nomadic, the notion that the fur trader was an independent male adventurer, and the rarely questioned view that the fur trade led to indigenous demise. Most historians, as Richard White has pointed out, have too long believed that "Indians may diminish and decline, but they never change."[81]

The Old Northwest is not depicted as an agricultural landscape inhabited by sedentary Indians. Rather, the view that this land was vacant has perpetuated stereotypical images of Indians who engaged in seasonal rounds of hunting and minimalist agriculture. The next chapter demonstrates that the St. Joseph Potawatomi were both willing and able to live in the midst of an increasingly agricultural society. When the chance to do so was threatened, they again turned to Catholicism to thwart removal effectively.

6

Being Indian and Becoming Catholic

THE POPULAR nineteenth-century perception that Indians were agriculturally unskilled was promoted by the desire to appropriate Indian lands. Politicians such as Lewis Cass constructed the myth of the primitive Indian, often in direct contradiction to their own observations. As Daniel Richter has pointed out, there were other groups who were better intentioned and planned to "civilize" Indians but, unfortunately, they also described Indians as primitive. Direct observations and contradictory evidence did not affect these descriptions, and such observers continued to promote preconceived notions about Indian demise. For instance, Gerald L. Hopkins, a Quaker missionary who visited the Potawatomi in 1804, "relied less on what he had actually seen than on what he thought before he began his journey." Hopkins visited the more prosperous Potawatomi villages of the Fort Wayne area and, as historian Daniel K. Richter has pointed out, Hopkins's insistence "that these people were ill-fed and ill-clad was a remarkable triumph of ideological construction over visual and gastronomical evidence."[1]

Although British defeat in the War of 1812 opened the western Great Lakes to American emigrants, the Potawatomi possessed sufficient agricultural skills to support themselves in the midst of American farming communities. It was not surprising that the Potawatomi wished to remain in the St. Joseph River valley nor that they requested agricultural supplies and assistance. These people had lived among a variety of Euro-Americans: French, British, Spanish, and even Americans. Eastern emigrants were a continuation of an ever-flowing migratory stream. These Indian communities were willing to cede land to these new arrivals but they also intended to keep sufficient land to support their own families and villages.

During the 1820s, when American negotiators arrived in the St. Joseph River valley, they assumed that there were few Indians remaining and that there would be few objections to the remaining land cessions. They encountered an unexpectedly large number of Potawatomi. In several locations, population levels had actually increased. There were four new villages, settled primarily by Indiana Potawatomi, who had relocated to Michigan. Three additional villages were established near the Notawaseppe Prairie, adjacent to the Huron and St. Joseph Rivers. One village was established in 1821 and then enlarged in 1827, when the Potawatomi ceded lands closer to Detroit. On the Kalamazoo River, there were nine newly established Potawatomi villages near Gull Prairie. On the Elkhart, there were two Potawatomi villages as well as three others on the nearby Kankakee River. In 1830, there were thirty-six Potawatomi communities with almost two thousand five hundred Potawatomi, and there were twenty-three Miami communities with about a thousand people. About fifteen thousand Indians lived in Michigan's Lower Peninsula and approximately twenty-five hundred were Potawatomi.[2]

The large number of sedentary villages surprised and disturbed the government negotiators. The observer sent by Lewis Cass, a man identified as Reed, believed that higher than anticipated Native American population levels would complicate the treaty negotiation process.

> The estimate of Indians living at each village is far too low. I have put down the number estimated when I visited there. I am assured that there are not less than four to five hundred on this tract. That is, who raise their corn here and call it their home.

The Potawatomi's desire to remain in the river valley also surprised the Americans, and their agricultural demands were such as would ensure their continued presence: cattle, farm implements, and hired laborers to cultivate their fields. Treaty negotiations represented an opportunity for them to replace the provisions, implements, and livestock lost during the War of 1812 and to supply the increasing population. Reed again informed Cass that the Indians wished to remain:

> From the 8th to the 16th of July, I was engaged in performing a tour along the St. Joseph. . . . The Indians uniformly said they wished to keep small reservations for each family, to have provisions made in the treaty for supplying them with cattle, farming implements and a certain number of days labor in ploughing and fencing.[3]

The Americans sought to control the lands that bordered the St. Joseph–Kankakee River portage but they acquired only a portion of those lands. The Potawatomi accepted some land concessions, because the Americans had complied with their agricultural demands.

Lewis Cass was infuriated by the large tracts of land retained by the Potawatomi, and the American negotiators blamed the unexpectedly higher population levels for their failure to extinguish the Indian land claims. Reed was both to pressure the Indians westward and to force Indian land cessions. Reed was initially encouraged by the Potawatomi request that the St. Joseph fur trader, Joseph Bertrand, speak for them. Reed described Bertrand as the only person who had any influence with the St. Joseph Potawatomi and anticipated that Bertrand would help him with the obstinate Indians, in exchange for treaty lands.

Joseph and Madeleine Bertrand were the river valley's most prominent fur trade family. They had lived near the old St. Joseph mission, not far from present-day Niles, since 1804. They filled the trader vacuum created by the death of William Burnett during the War of 1812 and the departure of Kakima Burnett to Fort Wayne.[4] Joseph and Madeleine Bertrand reestablished the type of Catholic fur trade community that had existed during the lifetime of Marie Madeleine L'archevêque Chevalier, with kinship, Catholicism, and trade inextricably intertwined.

Reed encouraged Bertrand to initiate meetings that brought together the various Potawatomi villages, but, increasingly, found Bertrand's actions hostile to the national interests. Reed was excluded from the meetings and was unable to break the confidentiality of the Potawatomi meetings. He began to refer to Joseph Bertrand slightingly as the Talleyrand of the West.

Bertrand's efforts helped to thwart, first, the wholesale cession of lands and then, later, helped to shape the final treaty concessions that prohibited the forced removal of Catholic Indians. With Bertrand in attendance, Potawatomi village councils began to meet repeatedly and formulate a uniform set of demands. Like Reed, official American observers resented the secrecy surrounding these meetings and they were frustrated, like Reed, by an inability to learn anything about these conversations. Reed blamed Bertrand, "I have no doubt that Bertrand charged them to be silent respecting it." Reed did not understand the kin networks that generationally linked fur traders such as Joseph Bertrand and the Potawatomi. Nor did men like Reed appreciate the ability of the Potawatomi to act in a concerted manner. Instead, Reed blamed the continually delayed treaty negotiations on Bertrand, who was thought to be holding out "for a great price and to do the best he can for himself and family in the way of getting reservations." Reed disparaged Bertrand as "a sinister half-breed." Such racial slurs discredited the motivations of Potawatomi spokespeople such as Bertrand.[5]

Joseph Bertrand encouraged Potawatomi firmness during the negotiations. As a result, the Potawatomi received higher prices for ceded lands and, more important, retained title to selected sections. Surprisingly enough, the Potawatomi had also received similar advice from some of the early emigrants. This, of course, infuriated Cass's representatives. Reed told Cass that "the Indians have got a wild notion of asking a large sum for this tract . . . that the American settlers here, have persuaded them of the great value of this tract, and advised them to hold out for a high price." But Reed's displeasure focused primarily on Bertrand, whom Reed now described as an outsider with no claim to the land. To men like Reed the presence of any Indian on saleable land was unacceptable.

> It will be a misfortune to the country if any reservation is made at this place and Bertrand has no color of a claim. Were the government to divide this point into townlots and sell it judiciously in five years, it would pay more than double the expense of the treaty, including a liberal annuity for thirty years.[6]

Indian persistence has been obscured by American negotiators, like Reed, who promoted land cessions and assumed that Bertrand spoke only for himself. Reed equated Bertrand's behavior with self-interest, and this unjustified, biased viewpoint was accepted by later writers and historians. But Bertrand's behavior was defined by kinship and what he said and did was bounded and constrained by his role as spokesperson. Reed misunderstood the interdependence of fur traders and Indians.

In the end, the 1828 Treaty negotiated at Carey Mission made a surprising number of concessions to the Potawatomi who wished to remain in the river valley. Land was set aside for nineteen reservations.[7] The government agreed to clear and fence additional lands and to provide both livestock and agricultural tools.[8]

By 1832, the Potawatomi estate, although greatly reduced, still included more than 5 million acres. In southwest Michigan, the Potawatomi retained control over an extensive domain. One reservation at Notawaseppe contained over 10,000 acres; another, south of present-day Niles and near the lands granted to Bertrand's family, contained 32,000 acres. The size of these reservations led to a renewed call for additional land cessions. Unfortunately, both the Bertrands and the Potawatomi controlled some of the most fertile areas in the river valley. Known as Parc aux Vaches—cow pasture or cowpens—this had been the grazing area for wild buffalo. This rich, lowland area extended over 3,000 acres, and the early spring floods continued to create lush grazing pastures.[9] The lands were also located at the crossing of the great Sauk Trail and thus provided a safe, central respite for Indian travel and trade.[10]

Men such as Lewis Cass, Michigan's territorial governor, refused to leave this rich, fertile land under Potawatomi control. Despite treaty assurances to the Indians, Cass wanted all land east of the Mississippi available for public purchase, but repeated attempts to persuade the Potawatomi to sell were unsuccessful. At a Notawaseppe council meeting, Red Bird described not only the Indians' desire to remain, but also described the support his village received from their American neighbors.

> We have held our consultation . . . and what you said yesterday did not please us at all. You told us that we must go west of the Mississippi. In our former councils we have always said we would not go, and our minds have not changed. At the council at Niles the same question was put to us and we said we would not go. . . . Now, there are a great many whites that want us to stay here. They hunt with us and we divide the game, and when we hunt together and get tired we can go to the white man's house and stay. We wish to stay among the whites, and we wish to be connected with them, and therefore we will not go.[11]

American treaty negotiators were equally intent on prying control of these lands from the Indians. Despite the 1828 Treaty assurances, it was increasingly clear that the government was refusing to tolerate even a limited Indian presence. Many Indian communities that also wished to remain in Michigan Territory relocated close to the Bertrand settlement. Their villages were clustered along the banks, streams, and tributaries of the St. Joseph River valley. This geographic proximity of like-minded communities facilitated communication and coordinated resistive behaviors.

The Potawatomi also would require assistance from outside the St. Joseph community if they were to oppose successfully someone as powerful as Lewis Cass, who was then territorial governor and later the federal official responsible for forced removal. The Potawatomi turned first to Isaac McCoy, who had established the nearby Carey Mission, but this proved to be an unwise decision. When McCoy and Topenabe's village endorsed a program of civilization through removal, Potawatomi interest in Catholicism became more pronounced.[12] Most St. Joseph Potawatomi terminated their relationship with the McCoy Mission in the spring of 1823.[13]

The Potawatomi turned next to missionary priests. Two years after the 1828 Carey Mission Treaty and McCoy's departure, the Potawatomi sought and received the support of the Catholic Church—initiated by a meeting with Father Richard in Detroit.[14] Pokagon was a Catholic Potowatomi and an effective speaker who publicly pleaded with Father Richard for a missionary priest to live among the St. Joseph Potawatomi:

> "I implore you," said Pokagon, "to send us a priest to instruct us in the Word of God. If you have no care for old men, at least have pity on our poor children who are growing up in ignorance and vice. We still preserve the manner of praying as taught our ancestors by the black robes at St. Joseph. Morning and evening with my wife and children, we pray together before the crucifix in the chapel. Sunday we pray together often. On Fridays, we fast until evening, men and children, according to the traditions handed down to us by our fathers, for we ourselves have never seen a black-robe. Listen to the prayers we say, and see if I have learned them correctly."[15]

To convince Father Richard of his sincerity, Pokagon fell down on his knees and recited a litany of Catholic prayers. Father Richard believed that Pokagon had never seen a priest and was convinced that the Potawatomi had kept alive the Catholic faith of their ancestors.[16]

Pokagon's astounding recitation bore the visible traces of the influence that Native female converts exerted among their Potawatomi kin.[17] Pokagon claimed that his daily behavior included the "manner of praying as taught our ancestors by the black robes at St. Joseph." Pokagon probably never met a Jesuit, although priests from Vincennes may have traveled through the area. His behavior testifies to the presence of a Catholicism fashioned by Native converts. There were numerous Catholic women, such as Madeleine L'archevêque Chevalier, Kakima Burnett, and Madeleine Bertrand, from whom he could have learned Catholicism's ritual prayers.[18] Madeleine Bertrand was the most obvious source, but there were other possibilities. For instance, Kakima was a Catholic convert and the sister of the headman, Topenabe, whose daughter Pokagon married.[19] Like many residents of the St. Joseph River valley, Pokagon was adopted and then married into the family of Topenabe.

Catholicism became embedded in the broader dynamics of social change and shaped resistance strategies. By the time Americans arrived in significant numbers, Catholicism had an institutional structure that it had lacked during the Franco-Anglo period. The St. Joseph River valley resistance involved the reestablishment of Catholic kin networks, the presence of missionary priests, and the construction of mission churches, as well as Indian schools.

CATHOLICISM BECAME an important refuge for those Indians who opposed removal westward. These converts turned to Catholicism because it was a means of accommodation rather than transformation. The Bertrands helped forge the Catholic community that figured prominently in the resistance effort. Their efforts were neither radical nor innovative but, rather, followed the patterns established by generations of Catholic fur traders. Madeleine Bertrand functioned in the catechizing role established by Marie Rouensa and Madeleine L'archevêque Chevalier in serving as baptismal sponsors. Madeleine's daughter, Thérèse and her son's wife, Théotés, were frequent godparents for Indian converts.[20]

Kin networks facilitated conversion and this was evident when the Bertrands became baptismal sponsors for the various members of Pokagon's village. Pokagon, his wife, Elizabeth, their children, numerous Potawatomi, as well as Bertrand family members were baptized by Father Rese, when he traveled through Michigan in 1830. Father Stephen Badin, assigned to the Potawatomi by Father Richard, later transcribed the names into his register from Father Rese's records.[21] Rese baptized not only the fifty-five-year-old Simon Pokagon and his wife, but an assemblage of people indicative of the extensive intermarriage between the Bertrand family and Pokagon's village. The eight children of Daniel and "Théotès, sauvagesse" were baptized, the oldest of whom was nineteen. The priest had also delivered the marriage blessing to Marguerite Bertrand and Daniel Bourassa, Laurent Bertrand and his wife Thérèse, as well as to the newly baptized Simon and Elizabeth Pokagon.

In the nineteenth century, the efforts of village headmen supplemented and eventually supplanted female catechizers. These headmen converted entire villages. Kinship and Catholicism became inextricably intertwined. In southwest Michigan, there were at least six Catholic Potawatomi villages, headed by Pokagon, Wesaw, Shavehead, Wakimanido [White Spirit], Mkogo, and Pepiya.

These Indian communities were confirmed as Catholic, but they remained Indian regardless of how they were viewed by outsiders. Headmen influenced conversion and perpetuated the religious syncretism of a loosely structured Catholicism. That process is best illustrated by Leopold Pokagon, who was born when Roman Catholic priests were occasional visitors or, perhaps, nonpresent. When nineteenth-century priests arrived at Pokagon's village they lacked the strenuous missionary preparation of the early Jesuits, and therefore Pokagon emerged as an ideal proselytizer. He was verbally skilled, supplied an attentive audience, and appeared to be a sincere and devout Catholic. Most of these later missionaries spoke no Indian languages. Pokagon's position was comparable to that of eighteenth-century lay Catholic women, and like the efforts of those converts, Pokagon's behaviors were also encouraged by the priests.

Fortunately, for Leopold Pokagon, many traditional Potawatomi practices paralleled those of nineteenth-century Catholicism. Europe's new wave of Catholic piety encouraged Catholics to find their way to the sacred through an increased emphasis on ritual and on the intercession of saintly spirits. Three of the priests who ministered to the Potawatomi, Fathers De Seille, Petit, and Baroux, left Europe in the midst of the Devotional Revolution. Adoration of the Holy Family, and particularly of the Virgin Mary, had reshaped Catholic piety. Believers venerated sacramental objects and sacred sites. Devotion to the Holy Family and the saints encouraged a Catholic generosity, community, obedience, and respect for family that also characterized traditional Potawatomi society. Innumerable feast days, fasts, and the appeal to saints highlighted the Catholic ritual.[22]

Many of Pokagon's behaviors could be construed as evidence of his being either a devout Catholic or a traditional Potawatomi. For instance, fasting was as much Potawatomi as Catholic. The priests described Pokagon's fasts as more lengthy and disciplined than those of the clergy and, clearly, they exceeded Catholic notions of abstinence. Pokagon's fasts were also indicative of Potawatomi vision quests and they perpetuated his reliance on traditional behaviors to acquire both the power and guidance for the changes that occurred in his village.[23]

Other actions of Pokagon, however, were difficult to interpret as Christian. For example, he acquired three additional wives, all widows with children, and they lived with him in traditional Potawatomi fashion. The priests described his behavior as acts of Christian charity and they referred to the widows as having been adopted into his family.[24]

Pokagon's ability to integrate western religious traditions with his own indigenous lifestyle emerged because of the interpretative role played by Native women and the fur traders. These lay Catholics minimized difference and strove for compatibility. The Native American view of the natural world permeated Catholicism, as the Catholic God of the heavens became a Manitou and simultaneously assumed a place in the Native American pantheon.

Biblical stories were reshaped so that they resonated with indigenous beliefs. A nearby French trader named Joseph Bailly, who lived in the nearby Kankakee River valley, left a record of his missionary efforts among the Indians.[25] For instance, he popularized Catholicism by transcribing its parables into more culturally acceptable notions of Native American spirituality.[26]

Joseph Bailly entertained both his Potawatomi and Odawa visitors with Christian parables and with Christ as the Gitche Manitou. In the evening, Native Americans crowded into the living room to hear his Christian stories, according to his granddaughter, Frances Howe.

> They enjoyed hearing the whole connected story of Man's relation toward his Creator and his Savior. . . . When the time came for them to go Northward, a deputation came to the house to give formal thanks for this great kindness. A woman was the spokesperson. Her words were never forgotten.
>
> "We thank you, our friend and brother, for the great satisfaction that you have given us in our Spirit, by telling to us the whole story of all that Gitche Manito has done for His children among men, and for having taught us what He wills we shall do. We thank you, and it shall always be remembered."[27]

The Christian God was transformed into a manitou, one of the many spirits that pervaded the sacred natural landscape.[28] Manitous were capable of taking manifold physical forms, and this compatible Christian God possessed similar powers. He was triune: three distinct beings with three different names.[29] In deference to his purported power, he became Gitche Manitou, the Great Manitou.

In sacramental rites such as baptism, the use of water had a spiritual significance that resonated with Native American practices. Water was used for purification and to transport Native American prayers to the spirit world. Water was thus symbolically important, although not congruent in purpose, with Christian ritual.[30]

Two rather disparate religious traditions transformed the baptismal sacrament into a ritual designed to appease the Christian manitou and to ensure a safe journey to heaven. A Potawatomi who sprinkled tobacco on the water to appease the manitou and to ensure a safe canoe journey understood a baptismal rite that sprinkled water on a sickly, newborn child to ensure a safe journey to heaven. For this reason, Native women called on their Native kin to baptize their children when they believed death to be imminent. Joseph Bailly had married a L'Arbre Croche Odawa woman whose Catholicism was emblematic of the way in which Native people often reconciled western religious beliefs with indigenous practices. This convergence of disparate but often sympathetic religious behaviors was epitomized by the baptism of her son. After his birth, she found herself stranded in Menominee country in northern Wisconsin, where there was neither a priest nor a fellow Catholic to baptize her dying baby. An unconverted Menominee came to her aid and baptized the child.

> He knew that anyone, even a pagan, might baptize an infant at the point of death, provided he sincerely wished to perform the ceremony in accord with Christian faith. He remembered the ceremony, but the words, "Father, Son, and Holy Ghost," had slipped from his memory. The Christian God, he said, though one, was threefold, and had three names, which must be spoken while the water was poured on the child's head, but he had forgotten them. . . . Then taking water, he poured it on the head of the babe, saying: "I baptize thee in the names of the threefold God, in whom thy father believes and whom he serves.[31]

During the nineteenth century, Indians offered visual proof of their Catholic faith in their dress and trade goods. The crucifix became a prominent part of nineteenth-century trader inventories. There were several hundred large and small crucifixes listed in Burnett's fur trade ledgers for 1800.[32] Even the American Fur Company traded crucifixes for furs. An 1820 invoice shows that seventy-eight large double crucifixes were shipped to John Kinzie, a former St. Joseph trader relocated in Chicago.[33] Through the crosses that the Potawatomi wore affixed to their clothing, they proclaimed their Catholicism. Crosses decorated the silk turbans that men wound around their heads and were attached to the buttons of their shirts. One Native woman's clothing resembled the habit of a Roman Catholic nun. Miss En Nash Go Gwah wore both a saint's medal and a large silver crucifix (see plate 1). Her dress purposefully displayed her Catholic faith.

DESPITE POTAWATOMI protestations, Cass cajoled, threatened, and bribed the Potawatomi to Chicago for another council meeting. His goal was to terminate the remaining Indian title to all lands east of the Mississippi. His efforts were directed at those villages in Michigan, Indiana, and Illinois that had resisted removal. Lewis Cass chose Chicago because he believed that "the sense of attachment to, and reluctance to part with things and places long dear to them would be less strong when those things and places were at a distance than if directly in view."[34] Before departing for Chicago, however, the St. Joseph headmen, opposed to further land concessions, met and issued the warning that any headman who signed a treaty ceding land faced physical harm.

The St. Joseph Potawatomi distanced themselves from the negotiations by camping on lands adjacent to the village where the Chicago meetings took place.[35] Their opposition was so strong that the government was forced to negotiate a separate treaty with them later. Ultimately, the government, through threats of force and increased annuity payments, was victorious. Cass's victory remained clouded by the provision that the Potawatomi might remain on their land until two years after the treaty's ratification by the U.S. Senate. But even more significant for Potawatomi resistance was a clause inserted during the final treaty negotiations that allowed Catholic Potawatomi to remain in the Great Lakes region "on account of their religion." The negotiators understood that these "Catholic Indians" would move to northern Michigan.

By December 1832, all the St. Joseph River headmen as well as 360 adults and 160 children were baptized. There were more than 600 baptized St. Joseph Potawatomi, and there was also a daily increase in the number of Catholic conversions among other Michigan Indians. Farther north at New Arbre Croche, now Harbor Springs, Father De Jean baptized 97 Odawa. In the later 1820s, the Odawa at L'Arbre Croche had appealed for a priest or a teacher, and, in 1829, Father Peter De Jean was sent north by the Bishop of Cincinnati.[36]

The 1832/33 treaty stipulation that Catholic Indians move to the Upper Peninsula was frustrated by a lack of available land. Pokagon's village vacated their Indiana lands, but moved only slightly north, to lands adjacent to those granted to Madeleine Bertrand by the Chicago Treaty. Following the Chicago negotiations, many Potawatomi returned to their Michigan villages and then routinely ignored repeated government suggestions to move westward.

Leopold Pokagon acquired legal title to Michigan land, following its admission as a state. He purchased 874 acres in the vicinity of Silver Creek from the Kalamazoo land office,[37] and this became the land of the Pokagon Potawatomi (see fig. 9). Other Catholic Potawatomi villages moved from the southern banks of the St. Joseph in Indiana north toward Silver Creek.[38]

In 1840, the U.S. government made one last concerted effort to

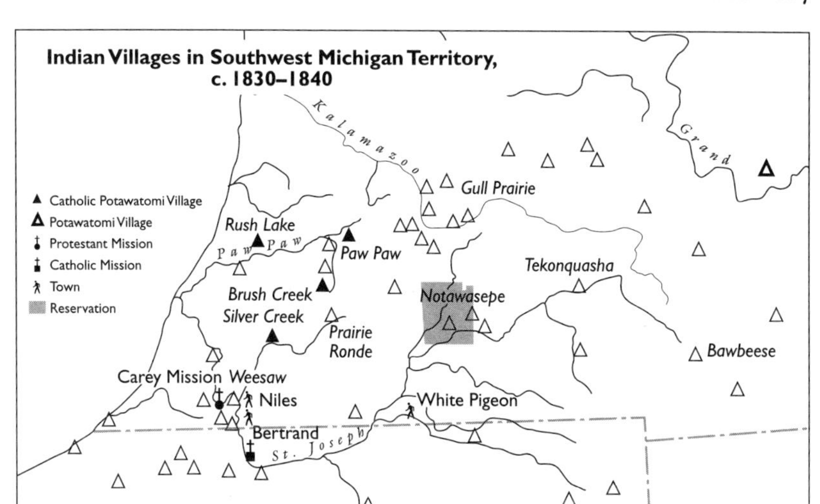

FIGURE 9. *Indian villages in Southwest Michigan Territory, c. 1830–1840.*

remove Michigan's Catholic Indians. The government believed that removal had been too long delayed, and the Secretary of War ordered Hugh Brady, Commanding General of the Seventh Military District based at Detroit, to remove forcibly all remaining Potawatomi from Michigan and northern Indiana. Civilian contractors, reinforced by troops, focused on the St. Joseph Potawatomi, and these villages immediately turned to the Catholic Church for assistance.

The Pokagon Potawatomi effectively thwarted the government's deportation efforts. Aided by the community's Catholic priest, Pokagon sought and received legal advice from a Detroit lawyer, Epaphroditus Ransom, who was an associate justice of the Michigan Supreme Court. Ransom contacted the Secretary of War and informed General Brady that Catholic Potawatomi detained for forcible removal would be released with a writ of habeas corpus.[39]

Although Brady abandoned his effort to remove the Catholic Potawatomi, other Indians were less fortunate and were brutally forced westward. In August 1840, General Brady met with the Potawatomi of Pokagon's village and granted them written permission to remain in Michigan. He supplied a written pass which identified, by name, the Catholic Potawatomi exempt from removal. Ironically, the list included Joseph Bertrand. It is unclear whether Bertrand lived among the Potawatomi, had been adopted, or simply feared for his own removal.

Potawatomi persistence can be tied directly to the Catholic conversion of many St. Joseph villages. Religion had political ramifications. Resistance and Catholicism became inextricably intertwined. But Catholicism also took root through institution building in the nearby town of Bertrand, made possible by Madeleine Bertrand. She built St. Mary's Church and then provided a house for a convent and land for a Catholic school.

Although such magnanimity is usually considered reflective of great piety, this was not the source for Madeleine Bertrand's gift. Indeed, she was little remembered for her religiosity. Like many Catholic Potawatomi, she was not a devout Catholic. She attended mass at the small Catholic church in Bertrand, but the sisters remembered very little about her except that she was "a good singer during mass," who enthusiastically sang her two favorite hymns, "Hail, Heavenly Queen" and "Bright Mother of Our Maker, Hail."[40]

Unfortunately, Madeleine's life attracted little attention. Bertrand was not a town fondly remembered by nineteenth-century emigrants. Nor did the Catholic sisters wish to sentimentalize a founder who lacked religious devotion.

Despite Madeleine's less than enthusiastic Christian demeanor, she transformed Bertrand, Michigan, into a Catholic community. The intent was to thwart the forced removal of Madeleine's Catholic Potawatomi kin and to preserve Indian culture, not to transform it. Catholic priests were an integral part of these missions and they were highly literate men. Those who lived among the St. Joseph Potawatomi were educated and trained in France and Belgium.[41] These men provided Indian communities the literary and legal expertise necessary to thwart removal. Government Indian agents, such as Abel C. Pepper, vociferously denounced these priests and their Catholic Indian congregations. In reports to his Washington superior, Colonel Pepper condemned the priests and referred to southwest Michigan as the home of the "Catholic party." Quite rightfully, Pepper believed that Catholic priests had countered Indian removal. Father De Seille, who had supported Menominee's resistance efforts in Indiana, proved equally supportive of the Pokagon Potawatomi.[42] Pokagon's access to legal assistance was facilitated by priests who frequently traveled to Detroit, the center for the Michigan Diocese. A Detroit lawyer had opined that the Catholic Pokagons were exempt from removal.[43]

Priests thus proved crucial to the persistence of "Catholic" Indian villages in southwestern Michigan.[44] Pokagon's village is well known among them, although others remain obscure. In Paw Paw, another Potawatomi clan was ministered to by the Holy Cross Brothers.[45]

Catholicism's integration into resistance strategies was facilitated by the transformation of Bertrand Village into a Catholic community. That process took place following the Panic of 1837, after the Bertrand Real Estate Company went bankrupt and land speculation ended. Bertrand was no longer considered a prosperous community. There were few new arrivals and those that did come were Catholic—they were attracted by the presence of priests and by a building process that institutionalized the community as Catholic. Directly across the St. Joseph River from Bertrand was Notre Dame. Father Sorin, Notre Dame's founder, had precipitated a housing crisis when he recruited Holy Cross Sisters from France to serve as domestic workers for his school. They were to "cook, wash, mend, nurse, [and] even milk the cows," but their presence caused overcrowding in Notre Dame's one small building that housed a school, chapel, students, and twenty-two priests. The Catholic diocese in which Notre Dame was located turned down Father Sorin's request to locate a Holy Cross convent in Indiana.[46] Consequently, Madeleine Bertrand brought the Holy Cross Sisters to Bertrand. She moved them into her house and gave them land for additional buildings. Father Richard in Detroit readily approved the founding of the Order of the Holy Cross in Michigan. The sisters immediately took up residence in Madeleine Bertrand's house, and within a year the newly established convent had twelve members.[47]

The Bertrand location proved fortuitous and the convent flourished; within a decade, the sisters had established a Catholic academy for women, an orphanage, and an Indian school, in Pokagon's village. The Holy Cross Order, twenty years after its American foundation, consisted of twenty-four sisters and postulants. Twenty orphan children were under the sisters' care, and there were thirty-one young women enrolled in St. Mary's Academy in Bertrand.

The Sisters of the Holy Cross played an important role in Potawatomi persistence, following their arrival at Bertrand.[48] They established a mission school at Silver Creek, among the Pokagon Potawatomi. Here two sisters lived and worked as teachers.[49] They brought a communal dimension to Catholicism that was familiar to Native people. They lived together in a household setting and were engaged in behaviors that resembled those of Native women: They cared for children, sewed, and tended vegetable gardens. Although Father Sorin described the sisters as the domestic labor force at Notre Dame, they came to America to work with Native people. Their immigration from France had been inspired by reports from other sisters who worked among the Potawatomi. Sister Euphrosine, for example, described a priest who

> spoke so enthusiastically of the good done by two Sisters of the Holy Cross in Pokagon, Michigan, that I was fired with a desire to labor among the Indians also. . . . Four of us were chosen. All of us were certain we were going to labor among the Indians. Sister Arisen was even provided with baby outfits to which were pinned cards with names to be given to the children she would baptize.[50]

The Holy Cross Sisters taught at the Pokagon school, and were reportedly more popular than the missionary priests.[51] Unlike the fathers who had difficulty with the Potawatomi language and relied on interpreters,[52] the sisters not only learned the language but taught lessons in Potawatomi. They translated Catholic hymn books into Potawatomi, and "when the sisters came home for the summer months they often entertained the other religious by singing the Indian hymns."[53]

The sisters also actively financed their mission work among the Potawatomi by returning to France to solicit funds. For instance, Sister Mary of the Five Wounds raised money for the Pokagon school in France in 1845. She shipped a large crate filled with the handwork of Native American women and displayed the pieces as a traveling museum to which she charged admission. She later used these items to accompany her talks and eventually sold the pieces at auction. She wrote Father Sorin, "I will consult my brother to find out in what city I should show these museum pieces; it will probably be La Rochelle. First, the curious will be invited to see them, . . . buy[ing] a one-franc ticket of admission; and then afterwards we will have a sale." Several highly ornate embroideries were sold, one of which she described as a pouch or bag embroidered with porcupine quills as "the most perfect work I had ever seen, both for the beauty of the design and the perfection of the work."[54]

The obvious success of Catholic Bertrand provided a focus for Nativist hysteria. Intolerance found fertile soil in the St. Joseph River valley, and, from 1844 to 1855, the small village was the scene of local anti-Catholic protests. These demonstrations began when the first nuns took their vows in the Bertrand church. The sisters' procession to the church was greeted with angry protests from an assembled mob.[55] Elizabeth Godfroy, frightened by the protests, later took her vows in France. The church was even robbed of its communion service, following the first communion of the young girls of the school.[56] This was followed by a

Plate 1. *Miss En Nash Go Gwah* by George Winter. Tippecanoe County Historical Association, Lafayette, Indiana. Gift of Mrs. Cable G. Ball.

Plate 2. *Nan-Matches-Sin-A-Wa, 1839, Chief Godfroy's Home* by George Winter. Tippecanoe County Historical Association, Lafayette, Indiana. Gift of Mrs. Cable G. Ball.

Plate 3. *The Deaf Man's Village* by George Winter. Tippecanoe County Historical Association, Lafayette, Indiana. Gift of Mrs. Cable G. Ball.

Plate 4. *D-Mouche-kee-kee-awh* by George Winter. Tippecanoe County Historical Association, Lafayette, Indiana. Gift of Mrs. Cable G. Ball. She was the wife of the Potawatomi Abram Burnett, who had been adopted by his mixed-ancestry uncle, Abraham Burnett.

Plate 5. *Mas-Sa* by George Winter. Tippecanoe County Historical Association, Lafayette, Indiana. Gift of Mrs. Cable G. Ball.

Plate 6. *Te-quoc-yaw* or *Bouriette—Indian Interpreter* by George Winter. Tippecanoe County Historical Association, Lafayette, Indiana. Gift of Mrs. Cable G. Ball. He was married to a daughter of Frances Slocum.

Plate 7. *Pot-Ta-Wat-Ta-Mie Chief, I-O-Wah* by George Winter. Tippecanoe County Historical Association, Lafayette, Indiana. Gift of Mrs. Cable G. Ball.

Plate 8. *Wewissa* by George Winter. Tippecanoe County Historical Association, Lafayette, Indiana. Gift of Mrs. Cable G. Ball.

Plate 9. *Kee-waw-nay Village* by George Winter. Tippecanoe County Historical Association, Lafayette, Indiana. Gift of Mrs. Cable G. Ball.

Plate 10. *Rescue Group* by Horatio Greenough, commissioned in 1837, placed in the East Portico of the Capitol, Washington, D.C., 1853.

Plate 11. *Frances Slocum* (with her daughters) by George Winter. Tippecanoe County Historical Association, Lafayette, Indiana. Gift of Mrs. Cable G. Ball.

Plate 12. *Frances Slocum* by George Winter. Tippecanoe County Historical Association, Lafayette, Indiana. Gift of Mrs. Cable G. Ball.

fire in the Bertrand building where the Notre Dame washing was done. The laundry was not rebuilt, and, instead, several sisters moved to the college campus.

In 1854, Bertrand's reputation was further blemished by a cholera outbreak. A dam, constructed adjacent to South Bend, intensified the stagnant conditions of the marshes at Notre Dame. The disease proved particularly virulent along the St. Joseph and it triggered renewed anti-Catholic hysteria.[57] That summer, five sisters at the Bertrand convent died and three postulants left. Two other nuns returned to their mother houses, one sister to France and another to Canada.[58] At Notre Dame, death came to five brothers and three postulants.

> "Father Sorin tried to keep them in the dark. The Dead were taken to the cemetery at night and buried without any religious solemnity. In South Bend, and in surrounding towns, they were saying openly that there must be something about Notre Dame itself that was causing all this sickness. . . . There was the bitter insinuation of the Know-Nothings that the Notre Dame cholera was brought on by the Catholic religion."[59]

Father Sorin relocated Notre Dame inland to higher ground close to South Bend. The sisters' convent and school were saved by the intervention of the Rush family, who had lost a daughter at Bertrand and a son at Notre Dame during the epidemic. St. Mary's moved to its present, more secluded location on donated South Bend land, and Father Sorin blessed the cornerstone of the new St. Mary's Academy on April 24, 1855.[60]

INVISIBILITY WAS part of a conscious strategy. It protected Catholics from outbursts of religious hysteria. This purposeful obscurity has unfortunately increased the difficulty of establishing a historically more inclusive narrative about cultural interaction and persistence. For instance, there were Native women who joined the Holy Cross convent. One postulant named Elizabeth Godfroy was probably an Indiana Miami, but there has been no definite proof of her identity (Elizabeth Godfroy may have been related to Francis Godfroy, see plate 2). Many of these early records, still extant, do not provide background information on the sisters, as did the later records.

Many Catholic Indians in and near Bertrand also found migration preferable to hostile Protestants. In May 1851, when Nativist hysteria was at its height in Bertrand, Benjamin Bertrand, one of Joseph and Madeleine's sons, led 660 Catholic Potawatomi Indians to St. Mary's in Kansas to live in an already established Catholic mission community of former

St. Joseph River valley Potawatomi. His elder brother, Joseph, Jr., had left several years ahead of him and was living in St. Mary's with his wife, Elizabeth Ann Jackson, a former sister in the convent of the Sisters of the Holy Cross at Bertrand.[61]

Bertrand, with its town square dominated by Catholic buildings, had become an obvious target for Nativist hysteria. The Sisters of the Holy Cross had been a highly visible presence from the time of their arrival in Bertrand. They wore long, flowing dark robes and white-winged hats. The brick school that they built in 1846 was the largest and most impressive structure in the small community. It was located next to St. Mary's Catholic Church, the small but elegant brick structure built by the Bertrands. Protestant hysteria was intensified by the area's ministers. One Protestant minister referred to Bertrand as the "cinque of iniquity."[62]

When the Sisters of the Holy Cross left Bertrand, their Protestant former neighbors rampaged through Bertrand. They vandalized the Catholic cemetery and threw its headstones in the nearby St. Joseph River, they dug up the convent cellar floor to search for kidnapped and murdered Protestant babies, and they vandalized the school building.[63]

Increasingly, the Pokagon Potawatomi withdrew into their own separate community—they became publicly more Indian and less Catholic. Ironically, it was probably that withdrawal from the larger Catholic community and from the institutional structure of the Catholic Church that preserved their distinctive Potawatomi traditions and rituals.

THE POKAGON Potawatomi remained Catholic, but their version of Christianity bore only faint resemblance to either the institutional presence or hierarchical nature of mainstream American Catholicism. Catholicism had attracted a large number of Indian followers. Most of these converts were more than mere opportunists. For most, Catholicism represented familiar behaviors, shaped by generations of Native practitioners. Pokagon's religious behavior was not unique, but was rather evocative of similar behaviors that had been practiced by a long line of earlier Native converts.

Encoded in Indian Catholicism were familiar behaviors of adaptation and accommodation. Although Richard White has shown how the British departure signaled the collapse of a diplomatically negotiated middle ground, the negotiating of disparate religious traditions produced a new middle ground and created many of the cultural practices associated with Catholic Indians. For instance, kin-based communities were the locus of most Potawatomi congregations. Most Catholic villages lacked even a mission church. This was a loosely structured Catholicism that drew its identity from the community and not from the buildings erected to establish its presence. This kind of Catholicism was repudiated by migrating Catholics, especially the Irish Catholics. They pushed for reforms to restore what they believed was religious orthodoxy.

The less formally structured nature of frontier Catholicism provoked Irish immigrants. These men had come to southwest Michigan to work on the canals and they were drawn to Bertrand by the presence of a priest. When the Irish attempted to reshape the Catholic Church along lines that were familiar to them, they demanded the construction of their own church. This annoyed both Indian and mixed-ancestry Catholic women who complained bitterly and openly about the newly arrived Irish immigrants. It is not surprising that they did so, for their authority was threatened by the new arrivals. These women were not a silent majority but openly criticized the Irish propensity for building.[64] "Immigrant Catholics never understood pioneer Catholics. . . . They demanded as the one sole evidence of piety and zeal the erection of buildings for ecclesiastical purposes."[65]

Irish Catholics also rejected the idea of mission stations in the homes of Catholic Potawatomi or the houses of fur traders where occasional priests conducted services, heard confessions, and said mass.[66] These immigrants disapproved of the usurpation of the priests' sacramental functions by fur traders and Indians, especially the rite of baptism. Equally abhorrent was the animistic dimension of the Christian parables and biblical narratives as related by the Potawatomi.

Irish arrival brought an invasive institutional presence that the Potawatomi had never intended, nor associated with Catholicism. During the 1830s and 1840s, Catholicism had allowed the Potawatomi to resist American hegemony and to survive the extinction of title to their homelands. But the Potawatomi rejected Irish hegemony, which was increasingly being fostered by nearby priests such as Notre Dame's founder, Father Sorin, who favored institution building. The Pokagon Potawatomi refused to defer to the larger Catholic community of immigrant Irish.

The withdrawal by the Potawatomi from the larger Catholic community took place not just because of the increasingly rabid level of anti-Catholic hysteria, but because the nature and structure of Catholicism had changed. The conversion of entire Potawatomi villages had been fostered by the absence of priests and by the Catholic kin networks of fur trade society. As cultural mediators, Native women merged the tenets of Western religion and indigenous beliefs into a synthetic belief system as intertwined and complicated as the kinship networks of the fur trade. This syncretic, frontier Catholicism was then further reshaped by Potawatomi headmen to accommodate the animistic orientation of their villages. Adaptation, change, and persistence all took place beneath this umbrella of frontier Catholicism.

THIS UNANTICIPATED Catholic presence often surprised and frequently challenged American notions about the nature of community formation. In the mid-1830s, when easterners streamed in and purchased St. Joseph lands, they were surprised to find that Indians also lived in the river valley and that the town's founders were mixed-ancestry descendants of Indians. The emigrants found it difficult to distinguish Madeleine and Joseph Bertrand and their children from their Indian neighbors. Increasingly, being Indian was being constructed by race. Physical identifiers, such as skin color, were increasingly important determinants of who was white and who was Indian. Emigrants as well as Indians used physical characteristics to describe Joseph Bertrand's appearance and those descriptions demonstrate the growing relationship between race and skin color. Joseph Bertrand's "skin was dark for an Indian, notwithstanding he claimed to be one-quarter French." Bertrand possessed other physical identifiers of being Indian: "uncommon" strength, superb hunting, fishing, and trapping skills, and a "hearty laugh" that attracted people to his trading post. He spoke little English, and his rather abortive attempts earned him the reputation of "the 'Injun' who murders the English language." The Potawatomi described Bertrand in much the same way that the American emigrants might have described the Indians they encountered:

> as of medium height, uncommonly broad shouldered, and well developed in body and limb. When laughing or excited in talking, he opened his mouth so wide that his great double teeth could be plainly seen. He always appeared in the best of spirits. . . . As old as I am now I would walk twenty miles to hear such a laugh.[67]

The Bertrands had helped ensure Potawatomi persistence, but their lives marked a turning point in the nineteenth century. They became half-breeds rather than French or Canadian or Métis. Indian identity when constructed by race problematized their ability to resist removal. Midwestern Indians who farmed, lived in log cabins, dressed in tradecloth garments, and rode horses now faced a new obstacle: race. Legally enforceable categories, such as being Catholic, proved an important avenue of protection for many Michigan communities. Even being Catholic acquired some physical identifiers. These Indians were distinguished by wearing elaborate crucifixes, religious rings, and saints' medals.

Indians also developed other strategies to resist white racism and thwart removal. In Indiana, they erected "facades of whiteness" to mask their indigenous identity. The next chapter shows how racism allowed them to hide in plain view.

7

Hiding in Plain View

Persistence on the Indiana Frontier

Potawatomi and Miami villages in Indiana's river valleys who successfully resisted removal were initially supported by recent eastern emigrants and established fur traders. Indians met the criteria of "civilized" because they farmed, raised livestock, and lived in log cabins.[1] But these criteria changed radically when Indian agricultural villages attempted to establish legally enforceable land titles. Indians found themselves increasingly defined as the uncivilized, racialized other, and skin color took precedence over "civilized" behaviors.[2] The attitudes of fur traders toward Indians also changed dramatically. In 1840, the government transformed traders from allies into removal advocates by restricting the future distribution of annuity payments to Indian villages that removed west of the Mississippi. Fur traders would no longer be able to collect their Indian debts from annuity payments unless their debtors deserted their Indiana homelands.[3]

Like the St. Joseph Potawatomi, many Indiana villages also devised successful resistance strategies, but in their efforts religion played a minor role. Instead, Indian villages there focused on the construction of white facades that effectively masked their identity. Indian spokesmen were chosen who resembled their white emigrant neighbors. Ethnically and racially diverse Indian villages usually had residents who could readily pass as "white." These mixed-ancestry villagers were usually men with Indian mothers and Euro-American fathers. They served as translators and even as headmen in the nineteenth century. Indians who possessed none of the "acceptable" physical attributes became increasingly invisible.

This "construction of whiteness" consigned successive generations to hiding in plain view and thus reinforced the concept of the antebellum frontier as a relatively empty stage on which the nation's emerging middle class set about building communities, unhindered by Indian neighbors.[4] The remaining visible Indians were depicted as stragglers, enshrouded in a world of alcohol dependency and reduced to starvation and poverty. We as a nation have omitted from the historical record the evolution of an increasingly agricultural Native population that at the same time engaged in a highly profitable fur trade.

The facile stereotype of the uniformity of Indian demise continues to shape midwestern frontier history.[5] Historians have located the Indian decline as consequent to American sovereignty, British departure, and an absence of national rivalries that had enabled Indians to play one rival power against another. Reportedly, the War of 1812 rendered Indians inconsequential.

> The imperial contest over the *pays d'en haut* ended with the War of 1812, and politically the consequence of Indians faded. They could no longer pose a major threat or be a major asset to an empire or a republic, and even their economic consequence declined with the fur trade. Tecumseh's death was a merciful one. He would not live to see the years of exile and the legacy of defeat and domination.[6]

Reduced to insignificance, the remaining Indians of the Old Northwest were supposedly eliminated by the Removal Act of 1830. With President Andrew Jackson's blessings and Lewis Cass's assistance, Native people were escorted west in a series of removals between 1830 and 1838. A final forcible removal, in 1840, purportedly eliminated the few remaining Potawatomi and Miami. In these circumstances, Indian decline would be inevitable, and their seminomadic existence untenable amid an agriculturally oriented society.[7]

> Since the fur trade had diminished and most of the Potawatomis had no interest in becoming farmers, they no longer had any economic base in their former homelands. Although the Potawatomis received government annuities, the funds were insufficient to support the many members of the tribe. Moreover, an agriculturally oriented society would not tolerate large numbers of semi-nomadic hunters in its midst.[8]

These conclusions are problematic for several reasons. First, as the previous chapters have shown, this characterization of all Great Lakes Indians as seminomadic is inaccurate and requires that we dismiss the agricultural evidence of thousands of acres of cultivated fields as nothing more than the seasonal occupation of Indian women or, even more improbably, the remnants of a lost civilization. Second, Indians had accommodated both a French and a British presence. Historians have often focused on the negative impact of cultural interaction and tend to view the fur trade as a demoralizing process that transformed Indians into efficient fur trappers, rather than agriculturalists. This dismisses fur trade villages as simultaneous sites of agricultural production. Repeated Indian demands for private reservations, the construction of houses and mills, for seed and plowing assistance were central to land-cession treaties in the Old Northwest and crucial to persistence. They are misinterpreted as the verbal posturing of Indians or as evidence of the civilizing goals of the larger society. Third, contrary to prevailing stereotypes, the fur trade did not dramatically decline in the nineteenth century. Instead, the beaver trade was replaced by the black raccoon trade, and the records of fur trade companies depict a struggle to control this increasingly profitable trade. The black raccoon was available only in the river valleys south of Lake Michigan, especially in the Kankakee River valley, which was the wintering ground of the St. Joseph River Potawatomi and Indiana Miami.

Centuries of interaction with Euro-Americans changed the social, economic, and political behaviors of many Native villages. Here, these broad-based changes are examined to demonstrate that the St. Joseph Potawatomi were not an aberrant Catholic clan whose resistive behavior was without parallel. Historical evidence suggests that resistance behaviors were widespread and were expressed through a variety of strategies. When successful resistive behaviors jeopardized the cession of large tracts of Indian lands, those lands were appropriated through forced removal.

Decline and demise are neither appropriate nor uniform descriptors of nineteenth-century Indians in the Old Northwest. Although these Native people were less politically powerful than their eighteenth-century predecessors, they were not all impoverished and on the brink of starvation—many even lived in relative affluence. Lands granted as private reservations, annuity payments made in specie, the continued viability of the fur trade, and productive farming were responsible for prosperous Indian households and communities. Although, the Indians were defended by humanitarian emigrants, they simultaneously faced a larger number of hostile emigrants, who resented both their presence on adjacent fertile lands and their material affluence. Consequently, Indians were routinely trapped in a paradoxical universe: victimized by white neighbors but protected by the alternative groups of Americans who often covertly, rather than overtly, frustrated their removal.

In this chapter, the focus shifts from the Michigan to the Indiana frontier with two objectives: First, to demonstrate that Indiana Native villages frustrated removal in an increasingly hostile, white, agricultural society. Second, to examine the ways in which their accommodation and change were masked by popular depictions of Indians as primitive, a convenient, but misinterpreted facade that then allowed Indiana Natives to identify themselves as white and thus resist removal.

IN THE EARLY years of the nineteenth century, when the Potawatomi dominated southwest Michigan, five thousand also lived in Indiana, and still others in Illinois and Wisconsin.[9] In 1828, Indian population levels remained stable.[10] Most Indians south of the Great Lakes were not nomadic, and the land was visibly marked by their presence. Timber-framed houses as well as log cabins characterized most Indian settlements.[11] These permanent Indian dwellings were the architectural markers in an otherwise confusing landscape. They were the directional markers for an unmarked maze of Indian trails. One traveler remarked that without such landmarks, "There were nothing but blind roads and Indian trails for our guidance."[12] One well-known landmark, on the way to Prairie Ronde in the St. Joseph River valley, was the old chief's house. Charlotte Copley noted in her diary that it was "a large brick house" surrounded by "a large farm, [with] a great many horses they dress in the Indian fashion."[13] In 1826, the government built a brick house for Papakeecchi, or Flatbelly. As a Miami headman, he had been granted a reservation that protected not only his village but the adjoining agricultural fields. The perimeter of this reservation measured 24 miles in length.[14] Flatbelly's village, near Lake Wawasee, eventually relocated among the Catholic Potawatomi at Silver Creek, Michigan.[15]

Another prominent Miami village, Nan-Matches-Sin-A-Wa, was situated along the Mississinewa River. Here Pa-Lonz-Wa, or Francis Godfroy, a Miami chief, had a large two-story house adjacent to five or six two-story houses in which members of his immediate family lived.[16] They were built in a traditional village pattern within a square enclosure, with visitors admitted through a gate. It was this house that the recently arrived English artist, George Winter, depicted in 1839 (see plate 2). Godfroy's other house, farther south on the Wabash, was referred to as Mount Pleasant.[17] Winter's painting of Godfroy's Mississinewa home, depicts a spacious timber-framed house. Notes recorded at treaty negotiations often provide a window on this long obscure world and describe the houses of the people in this village, the fence that surrounded that community, the entry gates, and even the adjacent millhouse. Treaty council notes confirm the presence of adjacent buildings, which do not appear in Winter's work.

This agricultural village existed before the adjacent white communities were established. Although treaties were used to deprive Indian people of their lands, Indians also relied on land concessions to improve the material well-being of individual communities. Treaty provisions remodeled buildings in established villages and also constructed houses in new Indian villages. Land cessions that involved village relocation required the government to clear new lands, build houses, and supply farming implements and domestic animals. To fulfill the terms of the 1828 Treaty with the Indiana Potawatomi, the government spent $5,000 and hired a variety of workmen to meet such provisions (see table 1). The Indian agent responsible for supervision of this work described not only the date on which the work was completed but also the names of the laborers and the type of work for which they were engaged. Thus, the government itself, unintentionally, fostered Indian persistence in Indiana.

Persistence necessitated permanent housing, and this was often achieved as a consequence of treaty negotiations. Along the Wabash, the government built log houses for the Indians, which were clustered together in traditional village settlement patterns. Ten one-story log cabins, as well as two one-and-a half-story log houses were built of hewn logs. Each building had a brick chimney (see table 2). The Indians also insisted that brick chimneys be added to their existing structures. Thus, the government paid two masons to construct an additional twenty brick chimneys with interior hearths. Again, the Indian agent John Tipton paid the workmen after they completed the work. He submitted the requisite information, as proof that these claims were not fraudulent.

These treaty provisions offer dramatic evidence that the Miami and Potawatomi villages intended to remain in Indiana. Even Indians who relinquished their lands intended to remain resident. There was a substantial Indian presence in the river valleys, well after government reports placed all Indians west of the Mississippi.

Embedded in the treaty language is the evidence of a preexisting agricultural landscape and proof that Indians sought to retain possession of their improved lands. For example, Godfroy's children received lands inclusive of "the improvements where he (she) now lives." Lands given directly to Miami women contain the same kind of descriptive evidence, such as, "to the wife of Benjamin Ah-mac-kou-zee-quah, one section of land where she now lives near the prairie, and to include her

Table 1. Abstract of payments made by John Tipton for clearing land, building houses, etc. for Potawatomi Indians, 1829

Abstract of payments made by John Tipton Indian Agent for clearing Land, building houses, and for the purchase of farming Utensils and domestic animals for the Potawattimie Indians agreeably to the provisions of a Treaty with that tribe on the St. Joseph of Lake Michigan on the 20 september 1828.

No.	Date 1829	To whom paid	Nature of payment	Amount Dlls.Cts
1	June 3d	Joseph Barron	Horses & plough	244.00
2	June 3	Cyrus Taber	Horses &c.	120.00
3	June 3	John Smith	Farming Utensils	180.00
4	July 14	David Gray	Horses	200.00
5	July 22	John Smith Jr.	Clearing Land &c.	331.00
6	July 22	Moses H. Scott	Building houses &c.	392.25
7	July 22	William Scott	Clearing Land	647.55
8	July 22	Robert Scott	Clearing Land	280.80
9	July 22	Nathan Rose	Clearing Land	165.50
10	July 22	Joseph Douglass	Clearing Land	287.00
11	July 22	Harris Barnett	Clearing Land	367.50
12	July 22	Moses Barnett	Clearing Land	361.00
13	July 22	Jacob R. Hall	Clearing Land	166.25
14	Aug. 10	Jordan Vigus	Horses	190.00
15	Aug. 14	Thomas J. Matlock	Horses	225.00
16	Aug. 17	Moses Scott	Building Houses	150.00
17	Sep. 3	Andrew Motter	Clearing Land	213.60
18	Oct. 3	Andrew Waymire	Horses &c.	110.00
19	Oct. 8	Joseph Barron	Horses	58.00
20	Oct. 10	William Scott	Clearing Land &c.	310.55
			Dlls	5000.00

Source: The John Tipton Papers, in *Indiana Historical Collections* (Indianapolis: Indiana Historical Bureau), part 2, 25: 237. Filed with the Tipton Papers of October 10, 1829.

improvements." These individual land grants, such as Seek's Reserve, ensured Indian claims to improvements as well as to adjacent orchards. Many of these lands were then joined together and held as extended private reservations.

A well-organized political framework linked individual villages and facilitated the presentation of uniform Miami demands. The Indian agent, John Tipton, in 1831, wrote Secretary of War John Eaton, "The Miamis are reduced to a small number,—but well organized in their kind of government, with one of the most shrewd men in North America at their head."[18]

Table 2. Payments made by John Tipton in fulfillment of treaty with Thorntown Indians, October 31, 1828

Abstract of payments made by John Tipton Indian Agent On the Wabash, for building houses, clearing Land, and performing other labour for the Thorntown Indians in pursuance of the Treaty of 11th of February 1828.

Date 1828	No. of Vouchers	To whom paid	For what purpose	Amount Dlls.Cts.
Oct. 31	1	Samuel McGeorge	For erecting one house of hewn logs of 1½ stories high with brick chimneys	300.00
Oct. 31	2	Morgan Shortridge	For erecting one house of hewn logs of 1½ stories high with brick chimneys	300.00
Oct. 31	3	Henry Robinson	For erecting one house of hewn logs on Eel River	190.00
Oct. 31	4	John Odle	For erecting one house of hewn logs on Eel River	190.00
Oct. 31	5	H. B. Milroy	For erecting one house of hewn logs on Eel River	180.00
Oct. 31	6	Alex. McAlester	For erecting one house of hewn logs on Eel River	180.00
Oct. 31	7	Robert Scott	For erecting one house of hewn logs on Eel River	180.00
Oct. 31	8	John Smith	For erecting one house of hewn logs on Eel River	180.00
Oct. 31	9	John McGregor	For erecting one house of hewn logs on Eel River	180.00
Oct. 31	10	Lewis Rodgers	For erecting one house of hewn logs on Eel River	180.00
Oct. 31	11	Champion Henley	For erecting one house of hewn logs on Eel River	180.00
Oct. 31	12	Abner Gerrard	For erecting one house of hewn logs on Eel River	180.00

Source: The John Tipton Papers, in *Indiana Historical Collections* (Indianapolis: Indiana Historical Bureau), part 2, 25: 111. Receipts for the payments are among the Tipton Papers of October 11 and 31, 1828.

The Miami recognized that significant land parcels with their extensive improvements also attracted avaricious and dishonest land speculators. They inserted legally protective devices into the treaties to secure against alienation of their lands. The 1838 Wabash Treaty details some of the protections that Indians secured to prevent loss of their annuities and lands.

> And the said Miami tribe of Indians, through this public instrument, proclaim to all concerned that no debt or debts that any Indian or Indians of said tribe may contract with any persons, shall operate as a lien on the annuity or annuities, nor on the land of the said tribe, for legal enforcement; nor shall any person or persons other than the members of said Miami tribe, who may by sufferance live on the land of, or intermarry in, said tribe, have any right to the land or any interest in the annuities of said tribe, until such person or persons shall have been granted by general council adopted into their tribe.[19]

In 1839, Winter sketched and transferred to canvas two of these Indian villages. Both were along the Mississinewa, several miles from the Godfroy village. Unfortunately, Winter's romanticized depiction of Deaf Man's Village minimized both the extent of the village and the substantial nature of the residential structures (see plate 3). But, Winter's journal entries as well as the written descriptions of other visitors provide substantial evidence of a nonmigratory, well-established agricultural village. Mo-con-no-qua, the widow of the Miami headman, Deaf Man, lived in a double log, cabin with

> two or three cabins of lesser pretensions . . . attached. . . . A good-sized log stable stood diagonally back from the main building; and a tall corncrib stood farther back to the left, separated by some fifty yards distance. . . . It was one of the substantial old-fashioned quadrangular "forest mansions"—such as the thrifty farmer builds, when his interests expand and his family becomes enlarged.[20]

The interior of her cabin, although sparsely furnished, was described by another visitor as

> well supplied with all the necessaries, if not with luxuries. They had six beds, principally composed of blankets and other goods folded together; one room contained cooking utensils, the other the table and dishes. . . . They have a looking glass and several split bottom chairs. A great many trinkets hang about the house, beads and chains of silver and polished steel. Some of their dresses are richly embroidered with silver broaches; seven and eight rows of broaches as closely as they can be put together. They have many silver earrings.[21]

The exterior landscape, like the household interiors, attested to permanence and persistence and presented clear evidence of their agriculturally oriented communities. Indians lived in double log cabins, raised livestock, particularly horses and cattle, which they housed in barns adjacent to fodder-filled corncribs. Housed in the stables and barns of Deaf Man's Village were between "fifty and sixty horses, one hundred hogs, seventeen head of cattle, also geese and chickens." Not only were there livestock, but "they have saddles and bridles of the most costly kind; six men saddles and one side saddle."[22]

Winter's interest in Deaf Man's Village was the result of a commission he received from the Slocum family to paint a portrait of Ma-con-no-qua, a white captive raised as an Indian. Born Frances Slocum, she was abducted from her family's Pennsylvania farm when she was five years old. Frances Slocum first lived and married among the Delaware and then subsequently married Deaf Man, a Miami warrior. Following the War of 1812, the Miami relocated to the Mississinewa River valley. When George Winter sketched her village, she was almost seventy years old. Her entire household lived in her double log cabin, and it included her two daughters, Kick-ke-ne-che-qua (or Cut Finger), O-saw-she-quah (or Yellow Leaf), their children, Kip-peno-uah (Corn Tassel), Wap-pa-no-se-a (or Blue Corn), Kim-on-tak-quah (or Young Panther), and one daughter's husband, as well as an elderly relative.

Over time, Ma-con-no-qua was transformed into "Frances Slocum the lost sister," and the material prosperity of her village was attributed to her presence and her influence as a white woman. But eyewitness accounts from the period refute such reinventions. The people of Deaf Man's village did not speak English, were not Christian, shared a ritual calendar of Miami feasts and ceremonies, followed traditional indigenous burial practices, lived as extended families in single households, and slept together in the same room.

The failure to recognize this as an indigenous agricultural landscape resulted from persistent stereotypes of Indians as hunters and warriors.[23] Propaganda, during the American Revolution and the War of 1812, had reinforced the image of the "savage" who was "infinitely violent, inconstant, treacherous, and degraded"—an effective propaganda tool for eliciting popular support for the American cause.[24] Antebellum America had constructed a romanticized depiction of the Indian as a noble denizen of the forest or as a plains buffalo hunter. Although these images countered the notion of a treacherous, violent Indian, they also reinforced prevailing notions about the inevitable demise of Indians. "Primitive" dress indicated a lack of agricultural prowess, a distinctive handicap in a nation that associated agriculture with progress. Indians were depicted as half-naked, or clad in animal skins; men had shaved heads and sported scalp locks; women were more fully clad in leather-fringed dresses with papooses strapped to their backs. Such images were usually the work of artists who remained carefully ensconced in their eastern studios and hired models—sometimes Native Americans—to pose for them. Other artists who sought to capture this "primitive" Indian, clothed in furs and decorated with paint and feathers, went west of the Mississippi.

Popular artists, like George Catlin and George Bird King, ignored the Indians of Michigan and Indiana because they did not dress in the romanticized manner that the artists believed represented the "genuine" Indian.[25] Eighteenth-century trade goods had dramatically transformed the appearance of Great Lakes people. Although they wore furs during the cold weather, Potawatomi women found the woolen and cotton cloth woven on European looms highly durable and transformed it into wearable items. Cloth represented well over half of all the goods traded at Great Lakes fur trade posts. At Detroit, that figure increased to over 75 percent (see table 3). Guns were not integral to the eighteenth-century exchange process, even at more distant posts such as Nipigon and Rainy Lake, where they constituted less than 1 percent of all trade goods.[26]

Clothing was the work of skilled female artisans, and it was fashioned from trade cloth. Early in the eighteenth century, for instance, matchcoats became a standard part of Indian attire. These elegant garments, worn by both men and women, were of Indian fabrication. Burdeners, those man who carried the beaver packets, were paid in cloth, which women transformed into wearable attire. This part of the exchange process was long entrenched, and a 1716 fur trader paid his twenty-one Indian burdeners, "that brought down the Bever . . . one Yard and a Half of Blew Duffields for Match-coats, and a quarter Yard Strouds, for Flaps."[27]

Indians did not, as we so stereotypically suppose, sling a trade blanket over their shoulders and consider themselves dressed. Women transformed trade cloth into distinctive clothing styles: dress even distinguished one people from another. For example, cutwork, or cloth cut into small pieces and stitched together, was a notable feature of Miami and Potawatomi clothing. Their beadwork was also highly refined and reflected the curvilinear patterns of the woodlands landscape. Women and men wore cloth leggings, winged with multiple silk ribbons and then lavishly embroidered.[28]

George Winter's paintings captured the dramatically striking appearance of Indian people in the southern Great Lakes. His work differed radically from that of his more popular contemporaries, George Catlin and Charles Bird King, and he readily dismissed their more popular fictional representations. For Winter, "The more 'poetic Indian,' that is

Table 3. European trade goods in the western Great Lakes, 1715–1760, compiled from invoice data in the Montreal Merchants' Records [ranked by trader expenditure]

Ranking	*% all Invoices*
Detroit	
1. Clothing	75.58
2. Hunting	11.91
3. Alcohol use	4.83
4. Cooking & eating	4.28
5. Adornment	1.73
6. Grooming	.54
7. Tobacco use	.50
8. Woodworking	.46
9. Digging/cultivation	.09
10. Maintenance	.07
11. Amusements	.02
12. Weapons	—
13. Fishing	—
Ouiatenon	
1. Clothing	55.04
2. Hunting	20.28
3. Cooking & eating	7.22
4. Alcohol	6.95
5. Adornment	5.62
6. Woodworking	2.25
7. Grooming	1.24
8. Tobacco use	1.20
9. Digging/cultivation	.10
10. Amusements	.08
11. Weapons	.02
12. Fishing	.01
13. Maintenance	—
Green Bay	
1. Clothing	65.08
2. Hunting	18.09
3. Cooking & eating	4.59
4. Alcohol	4.37
5. Adornment	2.95
6. Woodworking	2.39
7. Tobacco use	1.61
8. Grooming	.87
9. Weapons	.19
10. Digging/cultivation	.07
11. Maintenance	.06
12. Fishing	.03
13. Amusements	.01

Source: Dean L. Anderson, "The Flow of European Trade Goods into the Western Great Lakes Region, 1715–1760," in *The Fur Trade Revisited,* ed. Jennifer S. H. Brown, W. J. Eccles, and Donald P. Heldman (East Lansing: Michigan State University Press, 1994), 107.

represented always in nudity, with a fine roman nose, shaven head—with the scalp lock decorated with tufts of feathers . . . never [came] within my observations."[29]

Nineteenth-century Great Lakes fur traders routinely carried silk and the best of woven cloth. The choicest peltry was exchanged only for the finest trade goods. Trade cloth transformed Indian dress and created a highly visible dress style that was in marked contrast to the homespun of their white neighbors. Pale pastel silks and fine cottons were used by men for frock coats. Vividly colored cloth was wound elaborately into head turbans. Heavy silver ear bobs hung down to the shoulders of both women and men. Women sewed elaborate trade-silver medallions to their silk blouses. Vast quantities of iridescent trade beads in dramatic floral patterns decorated skirts, blouses, coats, turbans, necklaces, shoulder bags, knife cases, sashes, and garters. Even their leggings and undergarments were decorated with streamers of ribbon sewn together in rainbow fashion. There are numerous entries in Winter's journal about the styles of leggings worn by women. Winter described how their "nether garments" were "handsomely bordered with many colored ribbons, shaped into singular forms—and wrapped tightly around [their legs]." He even noticed the ornate style of the elaborately decorated women's moccasins and meticulously described how beads, ribbons, or porcupine quills were decoratively incorporated into the floral patterns.[30]

The opulent dress of the Potawatomi and the Miami are apparent from the hundreds of sketches and drawings George Winter completed and from his written observations—he recorded the details of each subject's dress. He relied on his journal entries to transpose his notebook sketches to canvas accurately. His written work parallels his artistic work and forms a literary panorama of prosperous Indian villages and their inhabitants.

Winter's sketches were not published in book form until the twentieth century, first in 1948; today, even after being reprinted in revised form in 1993, they remain relatively unknown. These portraits and sketches demonstrate how the fur trade transformed the lifestyles of Great Lakes Indian communities. Winter's work offers visual evidence of how the goods supplied by generations of traders such as Marie Madeleine and Louis Chevalier, Kakima and William Burnett, and Joseph and Madeleine Bertrand transformed Indian dress. Burnett's ledgers listed such goods as fine woolen, cotton, and silk cloth; scissors, needles, and thread; and ribbons and trade silver. Winter's rich pastel palette reflected the refined and dramatic elegance of trade goods transformed into Native American dress.

George Winter rejected both traditional studio depictions and scorned the somber reds and blacks that characterized popular Native American portraiture. Instead, Winter's portraits glowed with the vibrancy of Indian society. His portrait of Abram Burnett's wife, D-Mouche-kee-kee-awh, was indicative of the elegance of Indian dress (see plate 4). Although she refused to pose for Winter, he had created her portrait later from several notebook sketches and from the written descriptions in his journal. He cautiously pointed out that "it is not overdrawn in the interest of flattery." Adorned in pink silk with a highly ornate trade silver mantle, silver pendants hanging from her ears, and a necklace thick with trade beads, she was a woman who "excited the admiration of white men as well as that of the Indians."[31]

D-Mouche-kee-kee-awh's portrait in Winter's portfolio of Indian portraits confirms both the affluent appearance of nineteenth-century Indians as well as the ways in which persistence, like the fur trade, was facilitated by kin networks that linked traders and Indians. This woman and her husband were both full-blood Potawatomi, but they relied on their Christian surname, Burnett, to identity themselves as part of white society. Abram Burnett was the son of Chebanse, the pro-British, St. Joseph Potawatomi who had assiduously worked to incite his people against the United States, during the War of 1812. Chebanse's sister, Kakima, was the wife of the pro-American trader William Burnett. Following the War of 1812, when Kakima moved to live among the Indiana Potawatomi, her son, Abram Burnett, legally adopted Chebanse's son and gave him the name Abram Burnett, too. Both young Abram Burnett and his wife, D-Mouche-kee-kee-awh, identified themselves as Burnett, despite their obvious Potawatomi appearance and heritage.[32]

Winter's Native American portraits are the visual evidence of the prosperity that characterized indigenous communities in the southern Great Lakes (see plates 4–8). Nor were the more elegant figures in Winter's portfolio dressed for ceremonial occasions; theirs was the dress of daily life. When Winter sketched Te-quoc-yaw, the husband of Mo-con-no-qua's daughter, he was walking along the road to Peru, Indiana. Te-quoc-yaw, like the Burnetts, was known by his Christian name, Jean Baptiste Bouriette (see plate 6). For his half-day walk into Peru, he wore a pastel frock coat lined with blue silk. An apricot silk shirt overhung his cherry-red leggings, which were elegantly winged with embroidered silk ribbons. Bouriette's six-foot-two stature was enhanced by a colorful silk shawl that he wrapped in turban fashion around his head. Heavy silver ear bobs hung to his shoulders.

Winter's recorded descriptions for almost all of his sketches included pages of details—cataloguing the striking beauty of fur trade cloth. He noted the colors of the women's blouses and described the floral embroidery that decorated equally dramatic ankle-length skirts.

Winter's portraits also reflect a more positive, long-range impact of the fur trade. Traders did not simply pawn off cheap cloth on unsuspecting Indian customers.[33] Supply and demand decreed high-quality cloth. The goods that William Burnett supplied to different traders, and that he himself took into the Kankakee River valley, were evidence of a fur trade that had been transformed into a luxury trade. In 1800, William Burnett traded none of the usual items so closely associated with the fur trade: There were no guns, powder, iron kettles, or even awls. Instead, William Burnett exchanged "83 pairs of large ear bobs, 48 pair of small ear bobs, 736 broaches, 6 small wrist bands, 4 large wrist bands, 500 small broaches, and one large cross for beaver pelts." What Burnett took with him was typical of most outfits: Traders were supplied with 700 to 800 large broaches, 500 to 600 small broaches, 80 to 200 large ear bobs, and 50 to 200 small ear bobs. Among the variety of other goods carried, the most common included scissors, thread, needles, thimbles, and looking glasses. Most traders also carried crosses, large as well as small. Most surprising were other unusual items, goods that truly transformed this into the luxury trade: pewter teaspoons, soupspoons, and tins of tea that reveal an affluent Indian lifestyle, which transformed the interior of the Indian cabin. Other equally luxurious products, such as saddles, spurs, and bridles decorated with silver, allowed the Indians to live at a level of luxury that exceeded that of many of their white neighbors.[34]

The fur trade had been and remained a prosperous enterprise for many Great Lakes people. From 1820 to 1890, there was a substantial increase in the total number of furs and skins exported to Britain from the United States.[35] After 1820, the type of peltry being harvested changed, and by the mid-1830s, black raccoon had replaced beaver as the dominant pelt sent to both domestic and foreign markets from the southern Great Lakes. Over 4 million raccoon pelts were exported to England in the 1840s, almost double the number of the previous decade, and over 9 million were exported in the 1850s and 1860s. In addition to the overseas fur market, a substantial number of furs were also provided to eastern markets where they were used for hats, coats, and trim. Unfortunately, while records were kept on exports, there were no measures of the domestic market, albeit it was undoubtedly large.[36]

Raccoon's displacement of beaver remains unacknowledged, and most historians remain unaware that the southern Great Lakes produced the only marketable black raccoon pelts in the nation. Most valuable were the Indian-processed peltry from the Indiana, Ohio, and Illinois River valleys. The finest pelts came from the Kankakee and White River basins in Indiana—prized because of their dark, almost black, hue. Almost two-thirds of the raccoon pelts sold by the American Fur Company were graded number 1 prime, and most were labeled "Indian-processed." Raccoon pelts dominated the trade until after the Civil War, and, by 1839, Astor's American Fur Company was Indiana's most important fur trading merchant house.[37]

Many of the Indians in George Winter's portraits wore the trade cloth they had received for black raccoon pelts. His depictions contradict the traditional portrayals by more popular artists. Winter sought a government commission to depict these Indiana Potawatomi and Miami, but was unsuccessful because Congress, like the nation it represented, preferred more "primitive" Indians. Winter proposed that Congress install a large canvas or wall mural in which a "very picturesque . . . [and a] splendid group" of Potawatomi and Miami negotiators forcibly argued against removal. Winter's lengthy descriptions of how the figures in his canvas would appear provides a vivid picture of how he intended to refute the received opinions of Indian demise and decline. Winter described each speaker's appearance and included excerpts from the speeches. He began by describing the speaker who stands at the left in this sketch (see plate 9).

> Nas-waw-kay—speaker for the Indians. He is dressed in a white counterpane coat with cape. His figure was erect—though an elderly man. His complexion was very dark. His hair longer than the Indians generally wear it. It fell in flowing locks over shoulder. He wore a red belt across one shoulder–to the side, with a number of tassels attach[ed] in the common style of Indians. A crimson sash around his waist. Red leggings—with wings, as usual. Standing forward from the principal group of Chiefs and Head men. His appearance was very striking & imposing.[38]

Nas-waw-kay's dress was similar to that of several other Native American participants, who appear to Nas-waw-kay's left. George Winter's small individual portraits of two of Nas-waw-kay's companions, I-O-Wah and Wewissa (see plates 7 and 8) allow us to imagine the larger, more vivid canvas that Winter would have created (plate 9). Indians arrayed in their finest attire, who looked more like English nobles than forest denizens, would have stared unabashedly at the Capitol's astonished visitors. Winter even penned a quotation from Nas-waw-kay's speech on the back of his canvas, "My Father, I do not see why it is that we should be requested to go west. . . . Man's life is uncertain; and ere we reach that country, death may overtake us. I see not how our natural existence should be prolonged by going west."

In describing the proposed mural, Winter dismissed popular depictions of "the more 'poetic Indian'" as fictional. He justified his own depictions as more realistic.[39]

> I honestly claim originality with many . . . Indian subjects—and . . . familiarity with Indian life which few in the profession have. . . . Many painters have painted Indians from the imagination . . . I know, until I saw the red man . . . how sorely I was misled.[40]

Congress rejected Winter's proposal and, embracing the theme of the "savage warrior" commissioned Horatio Greenough to provide a large, free-standing sculpture for the East Portico of the Capitol (see plate 10). Greenough, in his *Rescue group,* depicted a woman and her child under savage attack from an Indian being rescued by a white farmer. Greenough placed a tomahawk in a scantily clad Indian's hand and ominously raised it over the helpless woman's head. Obviously, nineteenth-century congressmen, particularly those who supported removal, preferred the "uncivilized" depiction of Indian behavior. As a recent English immigrant, George Winter's work displays his cultural naïveté about the implications of permanent and prosperous Indian communities. To Winter, as an immigrant Englishman, America possessed an overabundance of land, while for land-hungry eastern speculators and emigrants, good land was limited and the Indians possessed highly desirable, fertile landscapes. Winter's work remained consigned to a much smaller, regional Indiana audience.

Winter's journals and sketchbooks suggest that Indians sought a variety of allies in their determined effort to thwart removal. From what we know about the Pokagon Potawatomi, it is not surprising to learn that some of their most effective supporters and spokesmen were Catholic priests. Winter's sketchbooks also demonstrate that this new generation of "black robes" was actively involved in Indiana resistance strategies.

Two Roman Catholic priests attempted to prevent one of the worst tragedies of Indiana's misdirected removal policies, the forced removal of Menominee's village. Menominee was granted twenty-two sections of land as a private reservation by the 1832 Tippecanoe Treaty. When Indiana officials threatened his village with removal and American squatters invaded Indian lands, Menominee and several Potawatomi journeyed to Washington, D.C. Federal officials assured them that they could remain on their land, along the Yellow River near Plymouth. Subsequently, in February, Menominee received the same written assurance from Lewis Cass, then the Secretary of War.[41]

Federal assurances proved worthless when settlers encroached on Potawatomi lands and triggered state-level removal policies. When Menominee's village destroyed several squatters' shacks illegally constructed on their land, violence erupted. It was stereotypically blamed on drunken Indians, and, in retaliation, eight Potawatomi cabins were set ablaze.[42]

Settlers who attempted to preempt the rich agricultural tracts of Menominee's village discovered a willing helpmate in Abel Pepper, the Indiana militia officer in charge of removal. He used settler demands to negotiate a treaty fraudulently with three Potawatomi chiefs, who shared the lands granted to Menominee's village. Menominee protested the treaty proceedings, and it was Father De Seille who recorded the Potawatomi objections and, then, forwarded the protests to Washington. Pepper resented the priest's interference and he silenced further written protests from the Potawatomi by threatening to prosecute the French priest for treason. Father De Seille retreated to the safety of the Potawatomi villages in Michigan's St. Joseph River valley. Menominee had lost a skilled tactician and ardent supporter. Another priest replaced De Seille, but young Father Petit was unskilled in the Realpolitik of removal.

Abel Pepper was a tireless removal advocate who fabricated the evidence necessary to call out the state militia, detain Indians in a removal camp, and then brutally march them westward. Pepper exaggerated the volatility of the events at Menominee's village when he informed Indiana Governor David Wallace that violence would erupt and that white people would be massacred. Wallace hastily authorized Pepper to raise one hundred volunteers and to take the necessary steps to prevent bloodshed. Meanwhile, Pepper used the issue of conflicting Indian land claims to invite Menominee to a meeting to resolve the impasse. In August of 1838, following Menominee's departure for Pepper's camp, the hundred armed volunteers surrounded his village. A removal camp was hastily established, but no provisions had been made for food, housing, or sanitation. Menominee was also taken into custody by Pepper. The Indians were held for almost a month, forced to wait until other Potawatomi were removed from small, remote St. Joseph and Wabash River valley villages and imprisoned at the makeshift camp.[43]

Eight hundred and fifty people were detained at this Indiana camp, and, in September of 1838, the poorly trained but enthusiastic militia bayoneted the Indians westward. Young Father Petit recorded the horror of that death march. Over one-third of the Indians, three hundred people, contracted typhoid fever. Food was so spoiled that the militia refused to eat it, and Native women prostituted themselves to obtain meager provisions for their families. Forty-two people died before reaching Kansas. Others died after their arrival. Father Petit was among the victims; he contracted typhoid during the march.[44]

This brutal march was led by men who felt no remorse over their treatment of their Indian prisoners and the loss of human life that ensued. Instead, the American traders were angered by the hasty departure preparations. One trader, George Ewing, was angry because his regiment had had insufficient time to organize a fife and drum corps. Apparently, he intended staging a victory parade with the Indians being escorted out of Indiana as a defeated army. Although Ewing accompanied the troops for several days, he returned to Logansport to lobby government officials immediately for the payment of his Indian claims. John Tipton supported Ewing's efforts and wrote, "Few men have been more zealous—none more efficient than the members of these firms in effecting the organization of the late emigration of the Pottawatomies." Ewing received particular praise because he personally collected Indians from smaller fur trade villages that otherwise would have escaped official notice.[45]

Like the Ewing Brothers, fur traders profited when the government assumed responsibility for paying Indian debts with their annuity payments. Like the Ewings, other traders enhanced their fur trade profits by marking up their goods by 100 percent before selling them to their Indian customers. These debts, once the Indians were removed, were then paid by the government. The fur trade had long operated on credit. Traditionally, Indians had received goods in the fall and paid their debts subsequently in furs from the winter hunt, but this system now functioned to the advantage of greedy merchants. The government deducted payments due traders before Indian annuity payments were distributed. Many Indian people, devoid of kinship ties to traders, became enmeshed in a cycle of mounting debt.

Treaty negotiations for Indian land cessions further enhanced the profitability of the Ewings' Indian trade. Local merchants supplied the goods that the government distributed as presents to the Indians during the treaty negotiations. Dishonest merchants often dominated these negotiations and, although they transformed the government into a wary consumer, these traders were eventually paid. In 1839, George Ewing submitted claims against the Indians that amounted to $14,500; then, between 1836 and 1838, the Ewings claimed another $30,000 in unpaid Indian debts. Traders not only inflated the price of goods distributed to Indians but also filed fraudulent claims for gifts the Indians had never received. By 1838, the treaty negotiations were so corrupt that the Indian Office inserted provisions in the treaties that mandated investigation of all claims, but it was too late. By 1839, Ewing's system of trade involved inflated prices and government payments that were so profitable that he dedicated himself to the trade and swore off land speculation: "I swear I will have nothing to do with white people, I go for Indian skins—Indian specie, Land, and Treaty allowances in future—Thus my object is singled out. Settled & fixed so I know what to do."[46]

One would like to think that the Indians in the Old Northwest learned a bitter lesson from men like George Washington Ewing. Word of Menominee's brutal removal and Ewing's eager pursuit of Indian stragglers must have spread quickly through the remaining Miami villages. Indians ceased to be Ewing's dedicated trading partners and, more and more, the Ewing Brothers found that, despite hiring the best fur traders, they had lost ground in the trade to Astor's American Fur Company. Only kin-based traders proved consistent allies, and so the Ewing Brothers relinquished the Indiana trade to the American Fur Company. By 1841, the Ewings' small nucleus of trading posts was located on the Mississippi.

IT WAS APPARENT, following the Ewings' betrayal of the Indians, that American fur traders were no longer reliable allies in the struggle against removal. Greedy traders willfully and brutally forced agricultural Indians westward. It was no longer sufficient for Indians to farm and to live in framed or log houses like settlers. A white frontier society, confronted with a settled Indian presence, proved that it would not tolerate Indians in its midst.

Americans in pursuit of an agrarian ideal dismissed all evidence of Indian agriculture. Removal incorporated new exclusionary standards based on race and religion that stripped Indians of their "civilized" status. Protestant missionaries claimed that Indians were impervious to biblical teaching. Indians became "poor, darkened savages," whose lack of Christianity made them unworthy inhabitants of frontier communities.

> How striking the difference between the heart that has been educated and trained under heathenism, and the same heart trained under the light of the Gospel. The sweet sympathies of the heart are not there, and no chords in the bosom respond to the touch of affection and love. . . . The intellectual, immortal part is put into dark subjection to the animal part of man.[47]

From the perspective of eastern clergy, the larger Christian society taking shape in the Old Northwest required Indian removal. The future of the New Republic resided in upwardly mobile, Protestant communities. Indians restricted access to land, widely perceived as crucial to "free labor" and upward mobility. This republican society excluded even educated Indians. Christian ministers believed that Indians inevitably returned to primitive ways and that only white men produced leaders.

> It is remarkable that among all the Indians who have been educated in different parts of the United States—and some of them have been so highly educated that they could speak different languages—few have become distinguished men. Most of them return again to the wilds of the forests—unable to lay aside the habits of nature and of childhood.[48]

These words, written by the Reverend John Todd about the Miami and the Potawatomi of the Indiana frontier, justified an exclusionary Christianity and fostered a racist rationale for their removal. Todd's sermon echoed the tensions underlying community formation in the Old Northwest and forced numerous Potawatomi and Miami communities to devise new strategies to combat this spreading racism. In Indiana, Indians focused on securing legally enforceable title to their lands. Consequently, in the 1840 Treaty at the Forks of the Wabash, most of the 875,000-acre Miami National Reserve east of present-day Kokomo, being nibbled away at by debts to traders, was transformed into private reservations.[49] The Wabash Treaty contained a five-year transition period for villages that agreed to removal.

Despite the betrayal by and corruption of traders, it was racism that proved the most formidable obstacle to Indian persistence. Indian villages began consciously to construct themselves as white in an attempt to remain on their lands. There were mixed-ancestry offspring who credibly represented themselves as white and spoke on behalf of their people. In addition, white people who remained among the Indians provided other, even more obvious, opportunities for communities to construct themselves as white. This was the strategy that a politically savvy Deaf Man's Village pursued when Mo-con-no-qua, the widow of Deaf Man, publicly revealed that she was a white captive. Despite previous opportunities to reveal her white identity, she took no action until the onset of forced removal. There was no response to her rather surprising 1835 announcement, and for the next two years people in Logansport probably doubted her claim to whiteness. Frances had dark hair and skin, dressed in Indian fashion, spoke Miami, did not understand English, and could not remember her English name. In 1837, a brother and sister arrived from Pennsylvania to substantiate Frances' claim of captivity. Had her white relatives' arrival been further delayed, they would have found their sister and her village west of the Mississippi. Subsequently, she would became a well-known public figure, but without Frances Slocum, Deaf Man's Village would have ceased to exist.

With her white identity confirmed, Frances was publicly mythologized as a tragic figure. Her story was revealed in captivity narratives, and it inspired sympathy for her life. With strong public support for keeping Frances in Indiana, her lawyer presented a petition to Congress to prevent her removal. That petition not only guaranteed Frances's continued presence but also became the means to ensure her entire village protection from forced removal. The petition referred to Mo-con-no-qua as Frances Slocum and imaginatively depicted her as an elderly, frail white woman who had survived the horrors of sixty years of Indian captivity. Frances requested that Congress allow her to live out the remainder of her tragic life in Indiana, close to her white people. The play on public sympathy for this elderly woman disguised a more important request, that she be given title to a section of public land, one that incorporated her homestead, and that she receive her treaty annuities at Fort Wayne, not in the west. Frances's petition carried the names of what she claimed were members of her immediate Indian family. Their presence was to be her comfort in her old age. Because Frances did not speak English, she dictated the list of her family members in Miami. When translated, the list reveals the names of her entire village: her daughters, their present and former husbands, the brothers of their former husbands, the sister of her dead husband, all their children, husbands, and even a miscellany of other names that included the children of Francis Godfroy and a young boy adopted by Mo-con-no-qua. The untranslated Miami names on these petitions, approved by both the House and the Senate, ensured this Miami village legal protection against forced removal.

In the Senate, the chairman of the Committee on Indian Affairs made it exceptionally clear that removal and the payment of annuities were of crucial concern to Frances Slocum. She would be "embarrassed" and required "to go west of the Mississippi" if her annuities were not paid at Fort Wayne. Vociferous objections to the bill came from Indiana men in charge of removal, from General Milroy, who expressed the fear that "the adoption of the joint resolution might disincline other Miamis to remove to their new homes." Milroy lost the contest, and Frances Slocum received an entire section of land, 620 acres, and her family was accorded legal immunity from the clutches of the removal militia.[50]

Frances's lawyer garnered political support by exaggerating her attachment to her white Slocum family and then misrepresented her captivity by depicting it as cruel and inhumane.

> She was taken, as she states, I think, by the Shawnee Indians, at the age of about six years, somewhere near Wyoming [Pa.]. Her friends made fruitless search for her for a great number of years, and she likewise for many years made every endeavor to return to them, but without effect. In the progress of time, she was sold and became the wife of one of the head men of the Miamis, known as the deaf man, with whom she removed to the Mississinewa, where she has continued to reside for the last forty years. Her relatives still reside at or near the place where she was captured, and are among the most respectable families in that part of the country. . . . I have no doubt she would willingly meet death, than either to be obliged to remove west of the Mississippi, beyond the reach of her white relatives.

Frances Slocum's petition cast her in a familiar role: a frail flower among the Indians who required the protection of male figures, particularly congressmen and the president.

> She says she has lived a life of hardships, and is now quite old, and wishes to spend the remainder of her days among her children, on their lands here; and she does not see why her great white father should not grant them the . . . privilege to remain here upon their lands, and receive their annuities here.[51]

Lawyers and legal petitions transformed Mo-con-no-qua into a subservient white woman, and George Winter provided the visually creative evidence of that transformation. George Winter was commissioned to paint a picture of the "Lost Sister" by her Pennsylvania relatives. The somber Frances Slocum of the final Winter portrait bore faint resemblance to Mo-con-no-qua's more colorful Indian appearance. Winter carefully recorded in his journal what he observed during his visit to Deaf Man's Village. His journal contains many of the details that Winter did not transfer to canvas.

> Her toute ensemble was unique. She was dressed in a red calico skirt, figured with large showy yellow and green flowers, folded within the up-

per part of a metta coshee, or petticoat of black cloth of excellent quality. Her nether limbs were clothed in red leggings, winged with green ribbons and her feet were moccasinless.

Kick-ke-se-quah, her daughter, seemed not to be without some pride in her mother's appearing to the best advantage, placed a black silk shawl over her shoulders—pinning it in front.

In two hours operation, I had transferred a successful likeness. . . . Frances looked upon her likeness with complacency. Kick-ke-se-quah eyed it approvingly, yet suspiciously. . . . The widowed daughter, O-Shaw-se-Quah would not look at it . . . but turned away from it abruptly. I could feel as by intuition that my absence would be hailed as a joyous relief to the family.[52]

Winter sketched Frances with both her daughters (see plate 11), and each was robed in colorful Indian garments. The portrait for the Slocum family depicted a somber, solitary woman with a lined, weathered face that suggested a long, harsh life. Winter included neither her daughters nor her vivid clothing. Her multicolored calico blouse became a muted red. There was no visual reference to Frances's colorful leggings or her bare feet, for that was unnecessary in an upper body portrait (see plate 12). This became Winter's most widely circulated portrait. It was reprinted in newspapers, magazines, and in the various captivity narratives published by a series of writers who, of course, had never met her.

Few Indian villages had the presence of a Frances Slocum to insure them against removal. Mixed-ancestry residents, however, helped their villages devise equally ingenious ways of constructing whiteness. Francis Godfroy, or Pa-Lonz-Wa, who considered himself an important Miami leader, drew on similar white resistance strategies. Like Frances Slocum, he did not speak English and used an interpreter. Godfroy's village, like that of Deaf Man, was relatively affluent. While Frances Slocum appealed to Congress for a land grant, Francis Godfroy as a headman of the Miami secured his village lands as a personal reservation.

As Francis Godfroy, rather than Pa-Lonz-Wa, he was accorded the positive attributes associated with white blood. From a slovenly, lazy Indian he was transformed into an intelligent man for whom, "Nature has done much." White writers praised Francis Godfroy for his "wealth, and influence, besides a shrewd head on his shoulders." Most writers failed to mention that Francis Godfroy weighed close to 350 pounds and made no attempt to engage in the type of agricultural work that most easterners associated with agricultural success. Many Miami continued to live on the Godfroy Reserve, and it was there that some of those who were once forcibly removed later returned. Godfroy, in time, built cabins to accommodate sixty Miami who came back from Kansas.[53]

IN THE HIGHLY emotional climate of a new nation undergoing its own process of self-identification, the westward movement produced new anxieties when Indians appeared to be more affluent than their white neighbors. George Winter's journal reveals an indigenous world where Indians had ceased to be the primitives by which people judged the opposite—themselves—to be civilized. These Indians did not exist on the edge of demise, and they often lived better than their emigrant neighbors. Winter's journals remained unpublished, in part because antebellum America preferred the more primitive Indian that justified removal. It certainly did not want to hear about Indians who lived in two-story, timber frame houses and double log cabins with fireplaces. There was little to entice easterners West if the frontier was already occupied. Nor was antebellum society interested in either inhabiting or preserving a world in which African American men married Indian women and produced children.[54] In his journal, Winter described a situation common to many Great Lakes Indian villages where African men, either free or escaped slaves, had married Indian women. The African American translator who lived in Deaf Man's Village was

> a man of color [who] had identified himself with the Indians. He had married a squaw, and spoke fluently the tongue of that people. He was a general mechanic in the settlement. At the time I arrived at the village, he was engaged in rebuilding a lathe and plaster chimney for Frances Slocum.[55]

The criterion for removing Indians from the Old Northwest shifted from discussions about civilizing the Indians to policies that categorized Indians as racially inferior. A facade of whiteness protected some Indian villages. Those villages that persisted became more self-sufficient agriculturally, and they continued to hunt and trap. Their prosperity was as time went on threatened by decreasing annuity payments and by their obligation to support growing numbers of refugees who returned from the west.

Although we may applaud the ingenious "white" strategies that many villages devised to prevent removal, we should also be cognizant of the long-range impact of these behaviors. Indian villages on the Old Northwest frontier being forced to hide in "plain view" doomed subsequent generations to invisibility. The Mississinewa Valley Miami thwarted antebellum removal, but, by the end of the century, they paid a high price for that resistance when the federal government revoked their tribal status. In 1897, the federal government administratively terminated recognition of the Indiana Miami. Following this disaster, the State of Indiana revoked their tax-exempt status. When Gabriel Godfroy lost his appeal of the state's actions to the Indiana appellate court his Indiana community was further devastated. The court ruled that being Miami was defined by "degrees of 'whiteness' or acculturation." Only tribal status could justify tax exemption. The court decided that Gabriel Godfroy was no longer an Indian because he sent his children to public schools and dressed like a white person. His behavior "had voluntarily placed [him] within the legal definition of citizen."[56] The Miami, who had learned to negotiate flexible boundaries of identity, paid a high price for their "construction of whiteness." In the years before the Civil War, it had ensured their persistence; by the end of the nineteenth century, the Indiana court had decided that Indians who behaved like white people were no longer Indians.

8

Emigrants and Indians

Michigan's Mythical Frontier

Native villages intent on persistence, when neither Catholicism nor the construction of whiteness proved viable strategies, sought refuge in the marshes and swamplands of the Great Lakes basin. These were the least desirable lands, ignored by speculators and emigrants, and they provided a refuge that thwarted removal.[1] Ironically, Indians often returned to seventeenth-century lands where they had lived prior to the European arrival. The numerous rivers and lakes that formed the Great Lakes drainage system facilitated the harvesting of peltry, but also served as an environmental obstacle course that hindered the arrival and overland travel of eastern emigrants. Michigan's high water tables transformed lowlands into swamplands, discouraged emigration, and even delayed statehood. Ohio entered the Union in 1803, Indiana and Illinois in 1816 and 1818, while Michigan was not admitted until some twenty years later, in 1837.

Just after becoming a state, Michigan was crippled by the Panic of 1837. The severe depression that gripped the nation proved problematic for the new state; land sales plummeted as banks closed and paper money proved worthless. Land speculators went bankrupt and many firms, like the Ewing Brothers, verged on bankruptcy. President Andrew Jackson's Specie Circular required that public lands be paid for in hard currency, but few people could make hard currency payments. Foreclosures and bankruptcies ended Michigan's real estate boom. Speculators and farmers in danger of debtors' prison fled west. To preserve their land investments, many businessmen, like the Ewings, dismissed land speculation and focused on the Indian trade. The Ewings' behavior testified to the way in which Indian land cessions and annuity payments, made in gold and silver, were used by American traders to offset the economic dislocation caused by the depression.[2]

The effects of the 1837 panic were felt until the late 1840s, and by then many Indian villages had resettled into geographically isolated niches. Swamplands and slow-moving shallow rivers, inhospitable to farming, remained an ideal habitat for fur-bearing animals. Settlement patterns before the Civil War were sporadic and often failed to encroach on small riverine Indian communities. Northwestern Indiana and southwestern Michigan lands rarely rivaled the fertility of prairie lands in Illinois, Iowa, and Kansas. Many emigrants bypassed swamp areas for western lands. Limited population intrusion and agriculturally marginal lands thereby facilitated Indian persistence.

This chapter focuses on the Michigan frontier, examining the ways in which geography and the Panic of 1837 reinforced diverse indigenous resistance strategies, but also shows how, in the process of eluding removal, Indians became increasingly invisible. Issues of race and ethnicity forced indigenous communities to construct themselves as white, and this invisibility contributed to the "frontier" myth that depicted the Old Northwest as a land settled by "white pioneers." Nineteenth-century white communities experienced high mobility rates, while Indians, with limited lifestyle options, to a greater and greater extent remained in one place. Indians stood apart from that broader continuous swirl of emigrants perennially in search of better lands. They settled invisibly on the less desirable lands and they persisted, while many of their emigrant neighbors moved westward.[3] The emigrants believed in the inherent virtue of mobility and consequently moved repeatedly from one place to the next.[4] The people who had transformed public lands into private holdings were not good caretakers of place—even before the Civil War, the Old Northwest was replete with abandoned farms, depopulated rural villages, and failed speculative ventures.

THE LANDS of southwest Michigan and northwest Indiana were level, but wet and swampy. In the spring when the snow melted and in the fall when seasonal rains arrived, lowlands became wetlands.[5] Michigan had over fifty portages, all of which were transformed into biannual rivers.[6] The network of rivers, lakes, and streams that crisscrossed southern Michigan and linked it to northwestern Indiana and northeastern Illinois was conducive to travel in shallow boats or canoes, but problematic for wagons.

Fur traders had used this network of rivers to travel throughout Illinois, Indiana, and Michigan. Repeatedly, St. Joseph traders sent goods along such small and relatively unknown Michigan tributaries as the Paw

Paw, Dowagiac, Pipestone, and Galien as well as along the more navigable Kankakee, Wabash, and Illinois Rivers.[7]

Few travelers followed a straight path through Michigan's southern tier, and many preferred a more circuitous and less swampy route north from Fort Wayne, Indiana.[8] Southwest Michigan's earliest emigrants followed the trail along the Elkhart River to Niles.[9] The Copley family's journey along this route in 1833 was dutifully recorded by their eldest daughter Charlotte. It took eight days—they averaged less than seven miles a day and were "continually detained by getting stuck in mud holes." Each morning they rose at dawn and often traveled until well into the evening. Only the Elkhart was bridged; they crossed the St. Joseph in a flat boat.[10]

The difficulty of reaching the southwestern shore of Lake Michigan was complicated by the lack of an east–west road across the territory. Rivers made road construction difficult. In 1825, Congress appropriated $10,000 for the construction of a Territorial Road along the old Potawatomi Trail, but it was not surveyed for another eight years. The road was officially finished in 1836, but completion of the road did not mean efficient transportation.[11] Although early Michigan historians reminisce fondly about the various stage lines that linked towns along the Michigan frontier, closer scrutiny reveals that these stages were usually open lumber wagons and were frequently drawn by oxen rather than horses. People did not travel during Michigan's fall and spring rains because the roads were impassable.

Spring rains transformed the Territorial Road into an intermittent swamp. Many travelers journeyed on foot because horses refused to enter the cold, icy streams. After floundering through the marshes, the Reverend O. C. Thompson's horse "became discouraged and obstinate, so that . . . he utterly refused to plunge down the . . . banks of a stream." Thompson returned his rebellious animal to Jackson, but foot travel proved equally difficult, because "west of Jackson it was next to impossible to distinguish the main road from the Indian trails. . . . I became lost in the openings, and was obliged to make my dinner that day on raw turnips I found growing on a deserted homestead."[12]

Emigrant letters and travel diaries testified to the difficulty of the east–west journey along Michigan's southern tier of counties. When Robert Burdick journeyed to Michigan, with his three sons and their young families, it took them a week to cross Lake Erie on a steamer. They purchased a wagon and a yoke of oxen in Detroit; then the trip progressed at an even slower pace. It took two days to go ten miles, and Burdick's young granddaughter offered her eastern friends this description of Michigan's roads, "There was a great deal of water and no bridges, a great many farms with no fences and one hundred and two mud holes."[13]

No north–south crossroads connected the two branches of the Territorial Road until the late 1840s. Travel north or south between the two roads required that the traveler blaze a path through the woods, an undertaking that rarely succeeded. Woods and marshes were formidable obstacles, and seasonal rains made the swollen St. Joseph River impassable to all but the most skilled Indians. The itinerant preacher Elijah Pilcher vividly described the perils and failures the journey involved:

> There were no cross-roads for a long time. The question then was how to get across to the Chicago road . . . so I hired a man to go with me and work our way. After spending the Sabbath at Marshall, on Monday morning I emptied my saddle-bags of clothes and books and filled them with oats for the horses and raw pork and a bread-loaf for ourselves; then, being armed with a gun and axe, we set forth. . . . We took our course, being diverted sometimes by what appeared to be impassable marshes. With the axe we marked or blazed the trees on the south side, so that we could follow the way back without any trouble. In this way we continued until late in the afternoon . . . when we reached the St. Joseph river. This we found to be full to the banks . . . it was too deep to be forded well. We found a tree near the bank, leaning over. This we felled with the axe, and crawled over on it. . . . Night soon overtook us. . . . We made a camp . . . at the edge of a wide marsh. . . . In the morning we renewed our efforts to find a way through, without success, and returned to Marshall at night.[14]

Given the difficulty of Michigan travel, it is not surprising that settlement came slowly to the lands of southwest Michigan.

FROM 1830 TO 1837 the nation was gripped by land-speculation mania, fueled by the conversion of Indian lands into public domain. The New Republic's citizens, both wealthy and poor, devoted substantial effort to devising ways to get something for nothing. Large land speculators, frequently fur traders turned merchants, often acquired vast tracts of land through Indian indebtedness. They reaped vast profits through the division of these large tracts into smaller, more affordable parcels. Even the poorest farmers profited from this land bonanza. Squatters, without the cash assets to purchase land, sold their improvements and moved on. Squatters intruded on Indian lands and preempted Indian improvements as their own. The Northwest Ordinance commodified the land and transformed it into a saleable asset. Frontier banks magnified the greed for Indian lands through currency inflation. At a time when scarce gold and silver supplies should have restricted purchasing power, these banks dangerously expanded the money supply by issuing paper notes without adequate reserves. By 1836, annual land sales totaled $25 million. The Panic of 1837, coupled with Jackson's Specie Circular, caused land sales to drop to less than a third of that amount by year-end. By 1841, sales had shrunk to $1,500,000, and the fever for public lands east of the Mississippi ended.[15]

Michigan's land office business collapsed dramatically following the Panic of 1837. The previous year the Kalamazoo land office had sold almost 2 million acres of land, but the next year it sold only 313,885 acres. Thousands of people were unemployed, and hundreds of businesses went bankrupt. The failure of Michigan's internal improvement programs undermined the vast network of canals and railroads that had been enthusiastically blazed by engineers and surveyors. Michigan did not solve the problem of incorporating geographically isolated areas of the state until the late nineteenth and early twentieth centuries. The Clinton–Kalamazoo Canal, intended to connect the eastern and western regions of the state, never materialized. Of all the grand improvement schemes planned in 1837, only one small section of the twenty-five railroads that had been chartered became a reality.[16]

Michigan farmers were plagued by high transportation costs prior to the Civil War. Consequently, many farmers fled west to more fertile Iowa lands. When the banks failed in 1837, most people were unable to pay their taxes. The state attempted to stem the bankruptcy tide by extending tax payment deadlines, but, when prices for farm products continued to decline, incoming migration also declined.

The economic disaster was worsened by a rash of epidemics that carried death into almost every Michigan village and city. Cholera swept away entire families and widespread malaria compounded the health problems. Waves of sickness dashed Michigan's hopes to surpass the population levels of its neighbors.[17]

Rampant enthusiasm of an upwardly mobile Euro-American populace was now tempered by the simple desire to survive: "A few years ago, people here were in a rage to get *rich;* now the chief concern of many is, how shall we get *a living.*"[18] From 1838 until the mid 1840s, farm animals, unable to forage in nearby woods, often died of starvation, and people themselves barely survived. People in Vermontville, a western community founded near the proposed east–west canal, survived on "bread, potatoes, and a little salt." One missionary, funded by the American Home Missionary Society, discovered that his horses were doomed to live on "the leaves of the forest, till one died of actual starvation, and the other became so emaciated that I sold him for a mere trifle."[19] More established communities fared no better than their counterparts in the western part of the state. Farmers found that cash crops like wheat could be harvested, but the return was inadequate. Market crops "fetch no cash & not over one or two shillings per bushel in any thing." Children went barefoot, and people's clothing was so frequently patched that there was no cloth left on which to mend.[20] Boxes of clothing were sent by eastern church societies to help hard-pressed farm families.[21] By 1840, ministers were so encumbered by poverty that they even lacked the clothing necessary to preach their sermons. In 1840, three years after the depression struck, Justin Marsh wrote:

> I must tell you one fact. I have of late found the seats of many of our professors [of religion] vacant on the Sabbath. Having inquired the reasons, I find that sickness is one; but another is, they are not . . . [decently] clothed to attend.[22]

Hundreds of letters, written by church missionaries to the Home Missionary Society, describe the severity of the economic depression in Michigan. The missionaries reported widespread poverty, "I have seen dark times before but none like the present." Return to the east ensured the survival of some families, and in letters written to distant families, it is not unusual to read, "I must leave the state. The desolations now are appalling."[23]

When Michigan's boom economy went bust, towns planned for former Indian lands failed to materialize. Joseph Bailly, a French fur trader who had relocated from Michilimackinac to the Calumet River, surveyed and platted Baillytown, but the 1837 panic struck soon after the town was laid out. Few settlers purchased lots, and Bailly's efforts ended almost as soon as they began. Eventually, Baillytown became part of Michigan City, Indiana.[24]

Joseph Bertrand's real estate speculations lasted slightly longer, but fared no better. In 1833, the town of Bertrand was surveyed and platted. It was on the St. Joseph River, not far from present-day Niles. Joseph and Madeleine Bertrand formed the Bertrand Village Association, a real estate company, with five other investors. The company surveyed nearly one square mile of the Michigan lands granted to Madeleine Bertrand.

The land was platted prior to the 1837 panic, a number of houses built and farms established nearby. In 1836, one thousand and two hundred lots were sold, but during the next year the company went bankrupt.[25] By 1840, as unpaid debts mounted, the six men who had platted and sold lots became legal foes. Several hundred Bertrand residents moved to more prosperous communities, and by the turn of the century, fewer than fifty people lived in the village.

Had the 1830s economic boom continued, even the most invisible of Indian villages would have been driven from their secluded marshland locations. Depressed land prices also dampened removal enthusiasm. Fur trade families, like the Bertrands and Baillys, who failed as land speculators, still remained dependent on the Indian trade. After the 1837 depression, even towns located farther west along the St. Joseph River welcomed the Indian trade. In Marshall, Michigan, for instance, furs emerged as one of the few cash crops with a ready market.[26]

Michigan Indian agents rarely discussed the continued Potawatomi presence in their correspondence. There was little incentive for them to discuss their inability to move Native Americans westward. Indian agents, subagents, and even interpreters were political appointees with uncertain job security. Incumbancy changed with each newly elected president.[27] These men lived in a wilderness where there were no supervisors to check on their success or failure, and they lived during an economically tenuous time. Indian agents were among a select few frontier inhabitants who were paid in hard currency.

DURING THE last decade of the nineteenth century when the Census Bureau announced the closing of the "frontier," the first emigrants recorded their memories of their early days in the Old Northwest. These narratives offer further evidence that Indians who were forcibly removed were neither on the brink of poverty nor near collapse. Unintentionally, these descriptions of forced removals provide the evidence for Indian prosperity and reinforce Winter's portrayal of the Potawatomi as better clad and fed than their settler neighbors. Particularly interesting is the description of one eastern Potawatomi village and its leader, Baw Beese, who were forcibly removed from Michigan.

> Mr. Holloway has furnished us a description of the mournful cortege as it passed through Jonesville, the next day after leaving camp. At the head of the column rode the aged chieftain in an open buggy. . . . A single infantry soldier, with musket on shoulder, preceded the buggy, while another marched on each flank. . . . His wife, a woman of sixty, followed

> next, mounted on a pony, a single soldier being considered sufficient for her guard. After her came Baw Bee, a sub-chief, and half-brother of Baw Beese, with a dozen more middle-aged and youngerly Indians and squaws . . . on ponies.[28]

In 1840, there were few carriages in Michigan. Baw Beese traveled west in a coveted luxury item while his people rode ponies.

If we are to understand how cultures change and evolve as different societies confront each other, then we must identify the myths that conditioned past cultural perceptions and reshaped the ideas, ideologies, and discourses of historical narrative. The "Pioneer Narratives" recorded by historical societies in the Old Northwest provide some of the most striking information about Indian persistence.[29] These writers followed the popular storyline about Indian demise and describe the disappearance of the Indians while simultaneously providing evidence for their continued existence.[30] Deconstructed, these narratives reveal the increasingly complicated social dynamics of an antebellum Old Northwest where Indian and mixed-ancestry women acted as cultural mediators, were crucial to Indian persistence, and were fictively depicted in ways that bolstered an image of the Old Northwest that was welcoming of progressive, civilized emigrants. These women became helpmates in the cause of civilization. They were often depicted as self-assertive women with a "knack" for solving Indian problems, with those remaining Indians who proved troublesome. These women were nonthreatening because, like the Indians, they would also disappear.

The central figures of such narratives were the descendents of women such as Marie Rouensa and Marie Madeleine L'archevêque Chevalier. The stories and tales circulated and recorded about them masked and fictionalized their Indian and mixed-ancestry heritage, as does this description of Marie Madeleine L'archêveque Chevalier's daughter:

> [She] possessed a strong mind, with the courage and energies of a heroine. She was also blessed with an extraordinary constitution. She was scarcely ever sick, altho exposed often in traveling and otherwise to the inclemency of the weather and hardships.
>
> The Indians were her neighbors and friends from infancy to nearly her death. By a wise and proper course with these wild men, and by sage councils to promote their interest, she acquired a great deal of influence over the Pottawatomies, Kickapoos, and other nations bordering on the lakes.
>
> She was familiar not only with the language of the Indians, but also with their character.

> On many occasions this lady was awakened in the dead hours of the night by her Indian friends, from the hostile warriors, informing her of the intended attack, that she might leave. . . . No one knew Indian character better than she did. A female on foot approaching several hundred armed warriors would produce a sympathy that she followed up with wise councils to the Indians that were irresistible. She often remained with them for days appeasing their anger.[31]

These cultural mediators were transformed into "frontier exotics" and acquired the aura of community curiosities, similar to the Indian artifacts that many migrants collected for their curiosity cabinets. Only remnants of those memories remained, and in the tales told by emigrants these women were removed from the context of their fur trade world. Thus, Madeleine Bertrand, judged against the more somber homespun cloth and colors associated with American clothing, became an "exotic" so rare that people stared at her in public or peered at her through windows. There was nothing unusual about her dress or her family; they looked much like the Potawatomi in George Winter's paintings. They wore the silks and trade silver that was fashionable among fur traders and Indians. But when Madeleine lived in Bertrand, there was only one church and it was Catholic. Sunday mass offered curious Protestant children an opportunity to scrutinize both the Bertrand family and a Roman Catholic service.[32]

> Old residents relate that on a memorable occasion while they were yet little children they mounted a carpenter's horse and gazed with awe and amazement into the window of the church, where the Bertrand girls and their mother sat, tricked out in gay attire.[33]

Creative memory held full sway where Indians were concerned and reinforced the myth of the primitive Indian. Although Madeleine Bertrand's two-story home remained extant, later writers described her dwelling as a tepee.[34] There was not a tepee in the St. Joseph River valley.

The characteristics that defined these women as cultural intermediaries stemmed from their mixed-ancestry heritage. But this blending of two cultures implied intermarriage, a taboo topic, especially in antebellum borderlands. Consequently, these narratives rarely discussed their subject's backgrounds: their parents, where or how they were raised, how they came to live adjacent to and were so familiar with Indian behaviors. Instead, these women became single-generational phenomenon—unique, unusual, uncommonly helpful to white men—and they often lacked family or kin, thus ensuring their eventual extinction.[35]

Exoticizing these women led readers down a road of comfortable misinterpretation where these women became the handmaidens of white civilization and the foils against which Indians could be depicted as "savages." One of the most illustrative examples was Magdelaine Marcot La Framboise who was described as "A Pocahontas of Michigan."[36] As Rayna Green has pointed out, the only Indian woman who can become a Princess is one who "must save or give aid to white men. The only good Indian—male or female, Squanto, Pocahontas, Sacagawea, Cochise, the Little Mohee or the Indian doctor—rescues and helps white men."[37]

Like all good princesses, Magdelaine married a good pious man, a devout Catholic fur trader who read daily devotional services and publicly prayed on a daily basis. Writers attributed Magdelaine's Christian transformation to her husband and consequently transformed her into an even more devout religious figure, a woman who often publicly dropped down on her knees and prayed on an hourly basis. Bathed in Christian piety, Magdelaine became the true Christian who forgave the heathen Indians who murdered her husband. When presented with the murderer by her loyal Indian friends, Magdelaine refused to exact revenge; she rejected savage ways by forgiving him. These narratives were distinguished by the exaggerated ways in which Indian women sacrificed to promote white behaviors and paved the way for civilization's westward movement.

The reality of Magdelaine's life was far different from this stereotypical narrative. Magdelaine was not Pocahontas: She did not become the wife of a white man and adopt the dress and manners of his society. Instead, her life was shaped by the intersection of disparate worlds, Indian and French, Indian and Anglo, Indian and American. Her primary allegiance resided with her Odawa people, as she helped them remain in Michigan as "Catholic Indians."

The background of Magdelaine's life, prior to her marriage to Joseph La Framboise is rarely mentioned in the "pioneer narratives" written about her. But her life was indicative of cultural mediators. She was raised to be part of a world that mediated complex cultural contacts and exchanges. She was born during the opening years of the American Revolution to a French father, Jean Baptiste Marcot, and an Odawa woman, Thimotée, at Fort St. Joseph.[38] The Marcot family, like the Chevaliers, was forcibly removed from Fort St. Joseph in 1781. But while the Chevaliers were a well-established kin network, with children and family members scattered at posts throughout the Great Lakes, the Marcots were younger and less well established. After being forcibly removed,

Jean Baptiste Marcot headed west into Wisconsin. Thimotée neither spoke the language nor possessed the relationships necessary to ensure her husband's access to Wisconsin peltry. She returned to her Grand River valley village and raised Magdelaine and her siblings among the Odawa.[39] Because Thimotée was the daughter of Chief Kewinaquot, or Returning Cloud, a reportedly powerful Odawa headman, Magdelaine was raised as Odawa, not French.[40] Magdelaine, however, like her sisters, was baptized at Michilimackinac, and her godparents were members of the Catholic kin network of fur trade families. Baptized as Thérèse Magdelaine Marcot she was identified by the priest as Odawa. Despite her French ancestry and her Catholic religion, Magdelaine was part of an Indian world.[41]

The Grand River Odawa community was much like the Potawatomi villages in the St. Joseph River valley. The Odawa had more than three thousand apple trees and almost two thousand five hundred acres of corn and vegetable crops.[42] As elsewhere, the agricultural surplus produced by women was an important part of the exchange process.

The marriage of Thimotée's daughters was grounded in indigenous custom, despite their baptisms in the Catholic Church. Magdelaine and her sisters married young. When she was fourteen, Joseph La Framboise paid the bride's price required by the Odawa. Magdelaine and Joseph remained in the Grand River valley, where her indigenous kin networks ensured access to peltry. Joseph La Framboise's access to trade goods came through Michilimackinac, probably from his brother in Montreal, and this entailed annual trips to the island.[43]

Magdelaine's marriage cannot be defined initially as Christian. She was married "after the custom of the country" two children were born, and ten years elapsed before the couple legitimated their marriage in the eyes of the church. In 1804, at Michilimackinac, the La Framboise marriage was witnessed by members of well-known fur trade families, with their old friends, the Chevaliers, among them.[44]

Several years later, when Joseph La Framboise was killed by an irate Odawa, Magdelaine's life moved in a direction far different from that of previous generations of fur trade widows.[45] Magdelaine did not remarry but, instead, established herself as an independent trader. Magdelaine continued to winter among the Odawa, as she had done for the previous twelve years of her life, and she returned with furs in the spring to Michilimackinac. She was accompanied by her two small children; her two Indian slaves, Angelique and Louison, and twelve voyageurs.[46] Magdelaine lived in a transitional fur trade world that allowed her to remain independent. Her centrality in the Catholic kin networks of fur trade society, her social prominence among the Odawa, and her experience as a trader were distinct advantages. John Jacob Astor readily supplied her with trade goods, and, in return, Astor received access to the best peltry. She remained an independent and successful trader at a time when John Jacob Astor and the American Fur Company eliminated many independent male traders. Magdelaine obtained trading licenses, first from the British and, later, from the Americans. She secured trade goods, hired voyageurs to accompany her, and returned each June to Michilimackinac to sell her furs and to resupply her outfit. The Grand River territory shipped about a hundred packs of furs a year to Michilimackinac. Magdelaine reportedly earned as much as £5,000 to £10,000 per year, while the average fur trader probably earned no more than £1,000 a year. In 1800, furs were valued at £20 per pack, and Magdelaine secured the majority of furs exported from the Grand River valley.[47] The first furs Madame La Framboise had sold to Ramsay Crooks, Astor's representative in the Great Lakes, established her credit with Astor's newly formed company.[48]

Nineteenth-century women, like Magdelaine, continued to expand or reinvent their roles as cultural mediators. Magdelaine consciously chose the appellation *Madame.* She was not referred to by her first name, nor by her Indian name. Her marriage to La Framboise and her subsequent widowhood were compatible with Anglo-American standards of behavior. Joseph's death occurred before the War of 1812, and Magdelaine transformed herself into a French widow just as the British relinquished control of Michilimackinac. The French would, of course, being more fondly remembered by the incoming Americans than the British. The title *Madame* determined how Magdelaine was publicly greeted and enabled her to establish a formality that commanded the respect of first, the British and, then, the incoming Americans. Eventually, her use of *Madame* led to her inclusion in this exotica of fur trade women.

Magdelaine's behavior was interpreted in a variety of ways and suggests that the people in these narratives were actively engaged in public performances that were meant to be interpreted in different ways. For example, when Madame La Framboise retired from the trade, she opened her year-round residence at Michilimackinac to all visitors. She was a celebrated hostess, and this facilitated her continued influence in a changing world, especially when she sponsored specific fur traders or newcomers. Even such a distinguished visitor as de Tocqueville took notice of her.[49] But to visiting Odawa, her behaviors were those associated with indigenous kin: She extended hospitality, clothed the poor, fed the hungry, and housed many of the area's orphans at her own expense.[50] She shared the material resources that she possessed and, in doing so, her actions could be interpreted as those of an Odawa woman or of a conscientious Christian. At the same time, such behaviors further enhanced Magdelaine's power and prestige. Madame La Framboise's move to Michilimackinac expanded her role as a cultural broker when she opened a school and trained Indian and mixed-ancestry women as teachers.[51] Magdelaine possessed the financial resources to hire literate Catholics to come to her Michilimackinac home to teach catechism. Religion served as a premise for acquiring literacy and related skills. In 1823, Magdelaine further extended her educational efforts to include Protestant missionaries and rented out part of her house for their school. Her efforts incorporated both Ojibwa and Odawa children, and then, in 1824, with her help, the school enrolled children who were "only a quarter blood, and a few poor destitute whites."[52] Magdelaine was subsequently involved in the establishment of a Catholic mission school on Michilimackinac Island.[53] Some of Magdelaine's former students, such as Marianne Fisher and Sophia Bailly, Joseph Bailly's daughter, went on to establish their own schools. Religion enabled women to become literate, and their literacy allowed Indians to cope with an increasingly intrusive system of United States governance and the imposition of a new legal system. Schools became integral to the process of cultural adaptation when the United States assumed control over the Great Lakes.

American arrival changed the dynamics of Indian persistence. Indian communities learned to use the language of the invaders both to affirm kin-based relationships and to contextualize those relationships within the parameters established by treaty making. Indians reaffirmed the intermediary role traditionally exercised by women through the gift of land. Thus, in 1823, members of the Grand River Odawa presented Madame La Framboise with land in the river valley. They situated that land transaction within an American legal tradition:

> Know all whom these may concern by these payments that whereas we the undersigned chiefs of the Indian Tribes of Grand River are connected by BLOOD related with Madelon La framboise of Michilimackinac And whereas also we are desirous of doing good unto her and her descendants or offspring to wit Joseph La framboise and her lawful Son Benjamin Langdon Pierce Grand Son & Josett Harriet Pierce Grand Daughter of her the said Madelon La framboise.[54]

This deed demonstrates how kinship obligations were embedded within American legal documents. First, the gift defined the relationship that existed between the Grand River Odawa and Madame La Framboise as one of "Blood" and, thus, relied on the type of racial distinction familiar to antebellum Americans. It also incorporated the legal language that ensured the valid and uncontestable transfer of land from her Odawa village to Madame La Framboise.

Although the land granted to La Framboise's children and grandchildren appeared to be given freely and disinterestedly, it was given to maintain an established social relationship. Within indigenous society, gift-giving entailed reciprocal behaviors.[55] When she retired from the fur trade and took up permanent residence at Michilimackinac, her hospitality, charity, and educational efforts were characterized by Americans as works of charity. But her behaviors reflected the indigenous world in which her charity had been prepaid through the gift of land. The "gift economy," when situated within an Anglo legal framework, was masked by the interpretation of Magdelaine's behavior one way by Americans and another way by the Odawa.

Magdelaine successfully presented herself through a series of multiple identities. To residents of Michilimackinac, she was a devout and public Catholic, one who knelt in public to pray, and was actively engaged in Christian charity. But her behavior toward Indian people was kin based. As kin, she sheltered family members, fed and clothed them, and taught them to read. Behaviors that could be viewed differently but were acceptable to disparate cultures were central to being a nineteenth-century cultural mediator.

Women played a prominent role in Indian persistence, and Madame La Framboise was not a "unique" phenomenon. Her high visibility attracted the attention of incoming emigrants, and stories written about her within an American cultural context masked her role in Indian persistence. There were a variety of ways in which these women approached the issue of persistence, but in great part the direction of those efforts was affected by the Chicago Treaty of 1832/33. In exempting Catholic Indians from removal, Catholicism acquired a presence along the Great Lakes shoreline that it did not possess in the interior of Michigan or in other areas of the Old Northwest.

MADAME LA FRAMBOISE's role as a cultural mediator changed when she moved from the Grand River valley to Michilimackinac. But other Native and mixed-ancestry women who played an important role in Indian persistence lived in a world that had changed little from that of the eighteenth century. Where black raccoon pelts were harvested, women continued to be involved in the fur trade. They were less prominent participants because they and their Indian kin lived in sparsely populated northwest Indiana and southwest Michigan. It was this fur trade world that was routinely excluded from the "pioneer narratives." Ironically, it remains the least remembered and yet it became the most highly romanticized when late-nineteenth-century narratives transformed these fur trade families into French settlers.

The most important fur trade family in northwest Indiana, Joseph and Marie Bailly, were incorrectly described as French homesteaders by later writers. Marie Bailly who was raised in the Odawa community at L'Arbre Croche and had married an Odawa medicine man, was depicted as a striking beauty of irresistible charm, stereotypically nicknamed the "Lily of the Lakes." Joseph Bailly became the heroic French gentleman who, "impressed by her beauty and her fine Christian faith," rescued Marie from her Indian husband and the "uncivilized" Indian life that was reportedly forced on her.[56] Marie became the exotic Scheherazade of the *Arabian Nights.* Her Indian stories captivated strangers, holding them entranced for hours. Few settlers, however, would have remembered those tales, much less understood them, since she spoke Odawa. Marie neither learned nor understood French or English.[57]

There was nothing in the early travel diaries of nineteenth-century visitors to the Bailly fur trade post that suggests either that Marie Bailly was an exceptional beauty or that her husband's demeanor was that of an exiled French gentleman. When Bailly's granddaughter wrote *The Story of a French Homestead in the Old Northwest,* she described her grandfather as "a first class business man . . . one of the most able business men engaged in the fur trade . . . [whose] name could draw a carte blanche almost anywhere."[58] Both published and unpublished travel diaries refute this imaginary version and reveal the indigenous lifestyle of a family thoroughly immersed in the black raccoon trade of the Calumet River valley.[59]

> Arrived at the Old Boys . . . as he is called. His name I believe is Bailey he is a Frenchman and to all appearances he merits the name of "Old Boy"—he is a fat dirty fellow and he sits on a rush mat and smokes his pipe for hours together. He is and has been for years a fur trader and he has a large fat squaw for a bosom companion. . . .
>
> He had a number of little log buildings on a bank by the Big Calumet and it presents the appearance of a small village. It puzzles one at first

> to know which house to go into. There is the dining house . . . the kitchen or cooking house, the sleeping house . . . one for his girls beside outhouses without number for ought I know.[60]

In *The Story of a French Homestead in the Old Northwest,* Frances Howe fictionalized her family portrait in order to mask her own Indian heritage. Her white New England ancestors were a genealogically constructed cocoon that isolated her from an inherently racist world where a "drop of Indian blood" created "mixed bloods." It was a fiction Frances created around an idealized image of her father, who had moved to Chicago from Connecticut. Her parents had lived in Chicago for a short time, when it was a fledgling community and when early business ventures involved the fur trade.[61] When Rose Howe's husband died, the young widow returned to her parents' home to raise her two young daughters. Young Frances Howe spent most of her life in her grandparents' home and on the extensive adjacent lands. The Bailly Homestead, as Frances called it, bore remarkable similarity to an Indian village. It consisted of "6 or more log shanties, for storage purposes together with his house in which his family resided and a stable for his cattle and horses."[62]

Marie Bailly, Rose Howe's mother and Frances's grandmother operated the homestead as a trading post until her death in 1865. Marie's daughter from her first marriage was also involved in the trade. Both Marie Bailly and her daughter remained part of an Odawa world. They dressed in Indian fashion and spoke Odawa. The only other language they understood was French, but only when it was spoken very slowly.[63]

Rose Howe distanced herself from her mother and her Indian sister. She ignored the perpetual stream of Indian visitors. She was determined to mask all evidence of her identity and secluded herself from the outside world. She confined herself to her bedroom, under pretense of failing health, and raised a daughter equally isolated from American society. Her other daughter, sent to a Kentucky boarding school, had died tragically as a young woman. Frances, Rose's surviving daughter and the author of *Story of a French Homestead,* was sent to a Catholic boarding school. Frances never married and she returned to the large house, where she and her mother remained secluded from the surrounding world.

It is difficult to uncover the evidence of persistence because both Rose and her daughter, Frances Howe, deliberately destroyed the evidence of the Indian trading post where they lived. Following Marie Bailly's death, in 1866, Rose Howe took her two daughters on a pilgrimage to France to visit a number of Catholic shrines. On their return, Rose

Howe severed the remaining ties to her neighbors, probably in an attempt to ban curiosity seekers from the area's Indian burying ground. She ordered the bodies of those who were not Bailly relatives removed from the cemetery. After her neighbors relocated their kin to another cemetery, Rose then ordered the removal of all headstones from the graves of nonfamily members.

After her mother's death, Frances erased the physical evidence of her indigenous ancestors further. Frances Howe transformed the trading post into a French homestead, remodeled the house, removed the old Indian cabins, and transformed a larger Indian cabin into a private Catholic chapel. Frances also redesigned the Bailly cemetery and removed all traces of her Indian past. Even the markers that had indicated the burial locations of Marie Bailly's first Indian husband and Marie's Odawa mother were destroyed. Then, Frances designed and constructed a rather elaborate earthwork around the graves with a large masonry wall, surmounted by a large cross. Only four graves remained marked with headstones, those of Marie and Joseph Bailly and of Rose Howe and her husband Francis. Frances thus shielded the burying ground from further public scrutiny by constructing it as a private family plot.

When neighbors openly gossiped about Frances's Indian ancestors, Frances considered hiring lawyers to stop their tongues from wagging. Despite the fact that Frances and her mother had deliberately reconstructed the Indian burying ground adjacent to their home and transformed it into a Catholic cemetery, they were angered by the rumors about the Indians buried in their family cemetery. "I consider the statement that this site is an 'Injun' Cemetery a slander really punishable by law."[64] She combated gossip about her Indian heritage by drawing attention to her father's New England ancestry. Frances sent her librarian friend at the Chicago Historical Society a genealogy of her Howe ancestors. "I want you to see what sort of stuff the forgotten part of my ancestry was. I say forgotten, not by myself, but by those who consider me a part of a vanishing race, when I so clearly belong to the wheat that was thrice sifted for the planting of the nation."[65]

By the end of the nineteenth century, Frances Howe had destroyed the busy fur trade community where the Grand River Odawa had wintered on an annual basis. Isolated and alone, Frances Howe wrote and personally financed the printing and publication of *The Story of a French Homestead in the Old Northwest.* That book was written to confirm Frances's white identity. There is little doubt that Frances appeared Indian and that her neighbors treated her as a curiosity. People peered at her through the windows of her house and stared at her in the private Catholic chapel that she built. People proclaimed publicly that she was an Indian.[66] One Gary, Indiana, librarian, described her as having a "swarthy" complexion and "brownist eyes and "[knowing] her to have Indian blood, you would believe it visible in her features, which were coarse in texture."[67] Frances remained isolated and bitter. Her book, meanwhile, remained unsold, although it was later incorporated into the pantheon of pioneer narratives.

Despite extensive renovations, the Bailly Homestead retained the architectural and material evidence of a fur trade world, where Frances's grandparents, Joseph and Marie Bailly, had lived and traded while the Odawa camped in a "clearing nearby and stayed weeks at a time, visiting, hunting, preparing maple sugar, as they had done for many, many years."[68] What Frances had successfully masked was that world created by intermarriage where the success of the remaining fur trade families was linked directly to Indian persistence. The Baillys had purposefully relocated to the Odawa wintering ground and obtained their land from the Odawa, through treaty concessions.[69]

There is little doubt that Frances was unaware of her Odawa heritage. She arrived as a small child at the Bailly house, in 1850, when her grandmother was actively engaged in the trade. One of her aunts lived and worked in the trade with her grandmother, and they both spoke Odawa and dressed in traditional fashion. Frances was at least fifteen years old when her grandmother died. In addition, Rose Howe's sister, Eleanor, also identified herself as an Odawa woman.

Frances Howe reinvented the past because the world no longer held a place for a Catholic woman of mixed ancestry. Frances was raised with models of assertive Indian women, but as an adult, such roles were no longer open to her. Kinship had linked women like Marie Bailly to the exchange process, but her daughters by Joseph Bailly were not part of that kin network. Joseph Bailly had sent his daughters to be educated at Montreal, Detroit, and the McCoy Mission. They were taught to be accomplished young women. Unfortunately, although they dressed and sounded like Americans, they still looked like Indians.

> They have been schooled at Detroit and they can talk of the beauties of Cologne water, Cooper, and a retired life admirably and eloquently. . . . They dress in the English fashion and look very tidy unlike their mother whose dress is squaw.[70]

Education constructed a facade of acceptable female behavior, but the Bailly family adjustment to the antebellum world beyond the confines of their homestead appeared problematic. The women were also raised to be independent frontier Catholics, and this further complicated their acceptance. Visitors to the homestead noted that the daughters conducted the evening and Sunday devotional services. "One of the girls acted as priestess. She read the service from a book while the others on their knees crossed themselves and responded at intervals something like ou-ooh the language I believe must have been Indian."[71] Missionary priests were nonexistent then, Catholic churches too far distant, and even the closest house was a long fifteen miles away. Social isolation ensured the Bailly women control over their religious lives. When priests began to appear, they were abashed by the independence of these Catholic women.

These young women were educated with the other daughters of fur traders, and their independence and physical distinctiveness problematized their adjustment to American society. When Marie Bailly's daughter, Eleanor, was tentatively accepted as a novitiate at Saint Mary-of-the-Woods, the impressions of the Mother Superior suggest that Eleanor was identifiably different from the other young women who joined the order.

> A new postulant arrived last week. . . . She alone could serve as proof that the Lord had His elect everywhere and that He watches over them. She only seems half civilized, but she has received the direction of the Holy Spirit. . . . I do not know if she will remain, as I wish only those whom God would choose, and . . . we would not receive her if as to virtue she was not suitable.[72]

Eventually Eleanor was accepted and became Sister Cecilia. Unlike her sister Rose, who married an American, she had made no effort to disguise her Indian identity. Her portrait at the convent testifies to her Indian appearance, and, in her correspondence, she describes herself as an Odawa woman. Eleanor signed her letters to her French correspondents, "J'ai femme Odawa."[73] She chose the convent over a cloistered life in an increasingly isolated family setting, where the issue of "mixed blood" transformed women into recluses. Eleanor's educational and religious activity allowed her to maintain an active, independent lifestyle in a cloistered setting. She became principal of Indiana's Catholic academy, Saint Mary-of-the Woods, and she even later attempted to transform the old Bailly homestead into a school for Indian children.[74]

MADAME LA FRAMBOISE, Madeleine Bertrand, and Marie Bailly lived in a fur trade world undergoing dramatic change. They were born when the French controlled the face-to-face exchange of peltry for trade goods, but lived to see the management of the trade and the profits from peltry controlled, first by the British, and then subsequently by John Jacob Astor during the American period. These women had lived in two worlds, that of the Indians and French, but as adults they became negotiators in a third world. These women learned their mediation skills in a world where identity was kin based and where ethnicity had limited meaning. But they lived in cultural borderlands during a time of change. Their children and grandchildren were raised in a dramatically different world. American society determined identity through ethnicity and, increasingly, by race. Being civilized did not save the Indians from removal and people of mixed ancestry from discovering that skin color could also determine their fates. Marie Bailly's children lived in an American world where racial prejudice mitigated against their acceptance. It is not surprising that Madeleine Bertrand's children chose to live among the Pokagon Potawatomi or in St. Mary's Mission, Kansas.

Although Sister Cecilia was open about her Odawa heritage, she lived in a cloistered setting. Outside the convent walls, Sister Cecilia's niece became an anomaly, a curious creature subject to public scrutiny. The rejected Frances Howe sought refuge in an imagined social superiority. As part of an elaborate defense mechanism she transformed her Odawa aunt into a cloistered aristocratic Frenchwoman and her fur trade family into French Catholic settlers.[75] When the Sisters of Providence wrote the history of the founding of their order, the Bailly family underwent a further dramatic transformation. Joseph Bailly became "a Canadian fur magnate of a distinguished French family."[76] Indian persistence is obscured by this kind of pioneer fable and these stories were often created by the descendents of Indians themselves.

FROM THE sixteenth to the early-nineteenth century, the fur trade lands west of the Appalachians and east of the Mississippi River, were a foreign country. People spoke Potawatomi, Miami, Ilini, Delaware, Odawa, and numerous other indigenous languages. Pidgin French, not English, was the lingua franca of the trade. Farmers appropriated the cultivated lands of Indian women, reinvented Native Americans as primitive nomads, and transformed mixed-ancestry women into exotics. While the trans-Mississippi West was gendered as a male domain, the frontier east of the Mississippi became the province of the family. Many writers of fictional "frontier" remembrances expressed nostalgia for imaginary traditions that focused on the family.[77] On this fictive frontier, husbands, wives, and children worked together to transform the empty frontier into farmland. Upward mobility was associated with hard work, always constructed within the context of family and community. No peoples so completely challenged notions about the nature of community, the appropriate roles of women, and the adaptability of Indian society as the diverse groups that lived in the river valleys southwest of Lake Michigan. But actual people who differed from these imagined norms were not accorded a place on the Old Northwest frontier by late-nineteenth-century historians.

For too long, Midwestern history has revolved around the fiction of the farm family. This is history too narrowly remembered, for the frontier had a multiplicity of other success stories. There is much we can learn from the Old Northwest, if we can remember these missed opportunities differently.

The Old Northwest was a region where racial boundaries were crossed, with apparent and obvious frequency. Antebellum black settlements, for instance, appear to have been intentionally located near the Potawatomi lands of southwest Michigan. The stories of slaves of mixed ancestry can be accessed through oral histories. Thus, the example of Ezekiel Anderson, an escaped slave, may not have been unusual one. He was either Kickapoo or Miami and had been kidnapped as a ten-year-old and forced into slavery. He worked on a South Carolina plantation, where he met and married a woman of mixed ancestry. When they returned to his Ilini village, they found it had been destroyed. They continued northward along the river network and found refuge in Michigan, near the Silver Creek Potawatomi.[78] Nearby villages in Cass County were the terminals for the Indiana and Ohio Underground Railroad and they experienced a large influx of black settlers, whose northern route to freedom followed the river pathways of the fur traders of the previous century.[79]

During the 1840s, almost 80 percent of the Old Northwest residents were foreigners, and by the 1850s that percentage had increased to almost 90.[80] Many immigrants came directly from Europe. Irish immigrants streamed into southwest Michigan to work on the Clinton–Kalamazoo Canal.[81] Many Germans, even Russian-born Germans arrived, from Russia's Volhynin region.[82] In 1849, Michigan actively encouraged German immigration by distributing the pamphlet, "Auswanderer Wegweiser nach dem Staat Michigan," in Europe.[83] German Lutherans, originally from the Palatinate, and referred to as "Pennsylvania Dutch," also settled near the village of Bertrand.[84] French Canadians also migrated to Michigan and settled near Bertrand in the small village of Mendon, with additional French families arriving from Ann Arbor and Detroit.[85]

Ethnic diversity here does not correspond to common perceptions, either popular or historical, of the Old Northwest. We presently possess little more than a fleeting glimpse of this borderland. Strategies of persistence were often characterized by invisibility rather than visibility. Anonymity proved more conducive to survival and was often a deliberate and conscious decision. When forced removals ceased, removal contractors appeared and became an ever-present threat. These contractors received bounties for each Native American removed west. Alexis Coquillard, a South Bend trader, proved especially dangerous. When the fur trade dwindled, he profited from this bounty system, and became a recognized "conductor."[86] "Conductors" were like slavecatchers, who were feared in the African American community. They traveled silently and quickly along the same network of rivers. Abduction was a pervasive fear and deliberate strategies evolved that ensured anonymity. Oral traditions among Cassopolis blacks describe deliberate undercounting in both the 1840 and the 1850 census.[87] Michigan Indians also avoided the census takers.

Like their Potawatomi and black neighbors, the Catholic religious orders increasingly were discovering that anonymity brought autonomy. Indians, African Americans, and society's outliers, especially Catholic religious, purposefully faded into society's shadows.

Late-nineteenth-century writers reinvented the Old Northwest and ignored the tensions posed by racial and ethnic diversity. In the years that followed the transformation of the Northwest Territory into states, Americans remembered almost nothing of the persistence of indigenous society. Demise was deemed inevitable. Indians were depicted as minimally agricultural and primarily nomadic. Protestant missionaries left extensive correspondence about failed Indian attempts at farming, but Native people often scorned these missionaries and turned to Catholic priests, whose writings were frequently ignored in histories of the western Great Lakes. The failure to appreciate the nature and extent of change among Native Americans has been further compounded by fur trade histories that have promoted notions of overhunting and, consequently, equated Indian demise with decline in the fur trade.[88] Scant attention has been paid to the ledger sheets of fur trade houses or export records, which demonstrate the continued nineteenth-century market in Indian processed furs.[89] Nor has anyone questioned how a trade that consisted primarily of cloth, rather than guns or liquor, led to dependency.

Nineteenth-century artists with romanticized versions of half-naked

Native Americans dressed in feathers and animal skins further reinforced the belief that Indians had failed to adapt to an agricultural landscape. Few histories, even recent community studies, have adequately assessed the uneven transformation of the Old Northwest into Euro-American farmland. Removal reduced but did not eliminate Michigan's Native American population. Out of a population of 7,600 to 8,300 Indians, only 651 Indians were officially removed.[90] The most persistent focus of removal was the Potawatomi of southern Michigan, where emigrants were very intent on transforming prairies into farms. But river valleys, with their less desirable lands, continued to shelter and sustain many Native communities. The Indians of northern Michigan were less threatened with forcible removal than their southern neighbors were. Again, the northern lands were considered unproductive agriculturally. Indian petitions addressed to the President and the Michigan legislature, coupled with the government's vacillation in removing them, meant that, by the 1840s, western lands were being more rapidly settled than those of Michigan.[91] Indians survived on Michigan's marginal lands and, in many instances, again engaged in subsistence activities that incorporated hunting, agriculture, and trapping. Indians remained in Michigan on lands overlooked by white farmers. Our present-day rush to rely on Indians as symbolic of environmental consciousness should also remind us of how much Indians knew about the land and how they survived successfully in regions most Americans considered marginal.

Notes

Abbreviations

AN	Archives Nationales, Versailles
ANCol	*Archives Nationales, Colonies,* Versailles
CHS	Chicago Historical Society
CIHSL	*Collections of the Illinois State Historical Library*
DCB	*Dictionary of Canadian Biography*
GW DMV	George Winter, "Journal of a Visit to Deaf Man's Village"
GWMSS	George Winter Manuscript Collection, Tippecanoe County Historical Association, Lafayette, Indiana
InHC	*Indiana Historical Collections,* Indianapolis, 1888–1931
ISHS	*Collections of the Illinois State Historical Society,* 1903–1975
ISL	Indiana State Library
JIHS	*Journal of the Illinois State Historical Society*
JR	*Jesuit Relations and Allied Documents, 1896–1901*
MPHC	*Michigan Pioneer and Historical Collections*
MVHR	*Mississippi Valley Historical Review*
NYCD	*Documents Relative to the Colonial History of the State of New York,* 1885–1887
RAPQ	*Rapports de l'Archiviste de la Province de Québec,* 1929
WHC	*Collections of the State Historical Society of Wisconsin*
WMH	*Wisconsin Magazine of History*

Introduction

1. Robert Berkhofer contends that television script writers borrowed the brutal Indian stories of old movies and western literature but also concludes that the Indian image improved slightly later because of Indian involvement in World War II. Nevertheless, the dominant television image became that of the "person of little culture and less language." See Robert F. Berkhofer, *The White Man's Indian* (New York: Vintage, 1979), 103.

2. The historiography of the "vanishing Americans" or of Indians as tangential to the "central narrative" of American history is discussed by Dane Morrison, "In Whose Hand Is the Telling of the Tale?" in *American Indian Studies,* ed. Dane Morrison (New York: Peter Lang, 1979), 5–25. For the ways in which Indians

have been stereotyped, particularly as a vanishing race, see Robert F. Berkhofer, "White Conceptions of Indians," in *History of Indian-White Relations,* vol. 4 of *Handbook of North American Indians,* ed. William C. Sturtevant (Washington, D.C.: Smithsonian Institution Press, 1988), 522–47; also see Berkhofer, *White Man's Indian;* Brian W. Dippie, *The Vanishing American* (Middletown, Conn.: Wesleyan University Press, 1982); and Roy H. Pearce, *Savagism and Civilization: A Study of the Indian and the American Mind* (Berkeley: University of California Press, 1988).

See Anthony F. C. Wallace, *The Death and Rebirth of the Seneca* (New York: Vintage, 1972), for one of the first books that envisioned Indian history as a series of renascences rather than declines. James Axtell, J. Frederick Fausz, Francis Jennings, James Ronda, Neal Salisbury, and Wilcomb Washburn were among the more prominent of these early ethnohistorians whose interest in early American history reshaped how historians depicted the encounter between Indians and Europeans. See James Merrell, "Some Thoughts on Colonial Historians and American Indians," *William and Mary Quarterly,* 3d ser., 46 (1989): 94–119, for a discussion of the reasons many early ethnohistorians were ignored by the larger community of early American scholars; see also David E. Stannard, "The Invisible People of Early American History," *American Quarterly* 34 (1987): 649–55.

3. Kinship as an effective means for urban Indians to reestablish their indigenous identity is explored by Susan Krouse in "Kinship and Identity: Mixed Bloods in Urban Indian Communities," *American Indian Culture and Research Journal* 23, no. 2 (1999): 73–89. How white society structures Indian identity is examined by Ward Churchill in "The Crucible of American Indian Identity: Native Tradition versus Colonial Imposition in Postconquest North America," *American Indian Culture and Research Journal* 23, no. 1 (1999): 39–67.

4. Persistence is defined as community continuity, most frequently achieved through a kinship system that enabled a community to identify its members. Community members shared a spiritual outlook, reconfirmed either through public meetings, rituals, or ceremonies. This emphasis on cultural continuity differs from the federal government's legal definition of Indians by a blood quantum standard that rested on not less than one-half degree blood (1887 General Allotment Act). Ward Churchill discusses Indian identity in "The Crucible of American Indian Identity: Native Traditions versus Colonial Imposition in Postconquest North America," *American Indian Culture and Research Journal* 23 (1999): 39–67.

5. Calvin Martin maintains that the fur trade, coupled with disease and Christian missionaries, destroyed the indigenous ecology and led to overhunting, in *Keepers of the Game* (Berkeley: University of California Press, 1978). The fur trade as destructive of indigenous cultures is also described by Lewis O. Saum, *The Fur Trader and the Indian* (Seattle: University of Washington Press, 1965). Shepard Krech's criticism of Martin can be found in Shepard Krech III, ed., *Indians, Animals, and the Fur Trade: A Critique of Keepers of the Game* (Athens: University of Georgia Press, 1981). Assumptions that the fur trade and the decline of American Indians were causally connected are also critiqued by Donald F. Bibeau, "Fur Trade Literature from a Tribal Point of View: A Critique," in *Rendezvous: Selected Papers of the Fourth North American Fur Trade Conference, 1981,*

ed. Thomas C. Buckley (St. Paul, Minn.: American Fur Trade Conference, 1981), 83–91.

The idea that the fur trade was a "socio-cultural complex" that lasted for almost two hundred years was first suggested by John E. Foster, "Rupert's Land and the Red River Settlement, 1820–1870," in *The Prairie West to 1905,* ed. Lewis G. Thomas (Toronto: Oxford University Press, 1975). The fur trade as social history is further discussed by Sylvia Van Kirk, "Fur Trade Social History: Some Recent Trends," in *Old Trails and New Directions: Papers of the Third North American Fur Trade Conference,* ed. Carol M. Judd and Arthur J. Ray (Toronto: University of Toronto Press, 1978), 161.

6. Academic scholarship focused on the fur trade has been primarily the province of Canadian scholars. The idea that cheaper goods allowed the British ultimately to dominate the fur trade was first advanced by Harold Innis, *The Fur Trade in Canada* (1930; reprint, Toronto: University of Toronto Press, 1970). Innis viewed the North American fur trade as an extension of a European economic system. Innis's view of the trade was first questioned by E. E. Rich, "Trade Habits and Economic Motivation among the Indians of North America," *Canadian Journal of Economics and Political Science* 26 (1960): 36–53; and by Arthur J. Ray and Donald F. Freeman, *"Give Us Good Measure": An Economic Analysis of Relations between Indians and the Hudson's Bay Company before 1763* (Toronto: University of Toronto Press, 1978). Also see Arthur J. Ray, *Indians in the Fur Trade: Their Role as Hunters, Trappers, and Middlemen in the Lands Southwest of Hudson Bay, 1660–1870* (Toronto: University of Toronto Press, 1974); idem, *The Canadian Fur Trade in the Industrial Age* (Toronto: University of Toronto Press, 1990). The idea that the fur trade exemplified how a common ground of understanding was established between two cultures "without sacrificing their unique characteristics and without annihilating one another" is developed by Carolyn Gilman in *Where Two Worlds Meet: The Great Lakes Fur Trade* (St. Paul: Minnesota Historical Society, 1982), 1–4. But Richard White, in *The Middle Ground: Indians, Empires, and Republics in the Great Lakes Region, 1650–1815* (New York: Cambridge University Press, 1991), asserts that trade was a cultural compromise in which Europeans accommodated the customs of Native people. Native people as assertive initiators of the fur trade are described by Bruce J. Bourque and Ruth H. Whitehead, "Trade and Alliance in the Contact Period," in *American Beginnings: Exploration, Culture, and Cartography in the Land of Norumbega,* ed. Emerson W. Baker, Edwin A. Churchill, David S. D'Abate, Kristine L. Jones, Victor A. Konrad, and Harold E. L. Prins (Lincoln: University of Nebraska Press, 1994), 132–47.

Although less extensive than the Canadian literature, U.S. scholarship focused on the fur trade includes White, *The Middle Ground;* David Lavender, *The Fist in the Wilderness* (Garden City, N.Y.: Doubleday, 1964); Paul C. Phillips, *The Fur Trade,* 2 vols. (Norman: University of Oklahoma Press, 1961); Wayne Edson Stevens, *The Northwest Fur Trade, 1763–1800,* Illinois Studies in the Social Sciences, vol. 14, no. 3 (Urbana: University of Illinois, 1928), 3–204. Attempts to incorporate fur trade histories across national boundaries include the series of papers published by the Fur Trade Conferences, with the proceedings from the Halifax, Canada meeting, in 1995 published as *New Faces of the Fur Trade: Selected*

Papers of the Seventh North American Fur Trade Conference, Halifax, Nova Scotia, 1995, ed. Jo-Anne Fiske, Susan Sleeper-Smith, and William Wicken (East Lansing: Michigan State University Press, 1998). The most notable attempt to deal with the fur trade on the American side of the border is White's *Middle Ground;* for a depiction of the southeastern trade, see Kathryn E. Braund, *Deekskins and Duffels: The Creek Indian Trade with Anglo-America, 1668–1815* (Lincoln: University of Nebraska Press, 1993); and Tanis C. Thorne analyzes the Mississippi River valley trade in *The Many Hands of My Relations* (Columbia: University of Missouri Press, 1996).

7. Charles E. Cleland, *Rites of Conquest: The History and Culture of Michigan's Native Americans* (Ann Arbor: University of Michigan Press, 1992); W. Vernon Kinietz, *The Indians of the Western Great Lakes, 1615–1760* (1940; reprint, Ann Arbor: University of Michigan Press, 1965); Helen Hornbeck Tanner, ed., *Atlas of Great Lakes Indian History* (Norman: University of Oklahoma Press, 1986). There are also well-documented histories of many of the individual nations that lived in the western Great Lakes and are discussed in this book, such as the Potawatomi, Miami, and Odawa. These include R. David Edmunds, *The Potawatomis: Keepers of the Fire* (Norman: University of Oklahoma Press, 1978); James A. Clifton, *The Prairie People: Continuity and Change in Potawatomi Indian Culture, 1665–1965* (1977; reprint, Iowa City: University of Iowa Press, 1998); Stewart Rafert, *The Miami Indians of Indiana: A Persistent People, 1654–1994* (Indianapolis: Indiana Historical Society, 1996); James M. McClurken, *Gah-Baeh-Jhagwah-Buk: The Way It Happened* (East Lansing: Michigan State University Museum, 1991).

8. White, *Middle Ground,* 52.

9. Ibid., 53 n. 6.

10. For a discussion of Pierre Bourdieu's work, including his theories and methods, see Richard Harker, Cheleen Mahar, and Chris Wilkes, eds., *An Introduction to the Work of Pierre Bourdieu: The Practice of Theory* (New York: St. Martin's Press, 1990), and Craig Calhoun, Edward LiPuma, and Moishe Postone, eds., *Bourdieu: Critical Perspectives* (Chicago: University of Chicago Press, 1993). Bourdieu's work as applicable to the Great Lakes fur trade is discussed by Peter Cook in "Symbolic and Material Exchange in Intercultural Diplomacy: The French and Haudenosaunee in the Early Eighteenth Century," in *New Faces of the Fur Trade,* 75–100.

11. "Marriage 'after the custom of the country' was an indigenous marriage rite which evolved to meet the needs of fur-trade society. . . . Although denounced by the Jesuit priests as being immoral, the traders had taken their Indian wives according to traditional native marriage rites and distinct family units had developed." See Sylvia Van Kirk, *Many Tender Ties: Women in Fur-Trade Society, 1670–1870* (1980; reprint, Norman: University of Oklahoma Press, 1990), 28.

12. Marriage between French fur traders and Native American women was central to the growth of the fur trade. Combining both Indian and European marriage customs, these unions, although not always permanent, were neither casual nor promiscuous. For a further explanation of how marriage *à la façon du pays* became institutionalized as integral to the fur trade, see Van Kirk, ibid., 3–4; and idem, "The Custom of the Country," in *Essays on Western History,* ed. Lewis H. Thomas (Edmonton: University of Alberta Press, 1976), 49–82. A

second book that deals with intermarriage between traders and Native American women as a function of the fur trade is Jennifer Brown, *Strangers in Blood: Fur Trade Company Families in Indian Country* (1980; reprint, Norman: University of Oklahoma Press, 1996). See also Jacqueline Peterson and Jennifer S. H. Brown, eds., *The New Peoples: Being and Becoming Métis in North America* (Manitoba: University of Manitoba Press, 1985), especially Jacqueline Peterson, "Many Roads to Red River: Métis Genesis in the Great Lakes Region, 1680–1815," 37–73; also see John E. Foster, "The Origin of the Mixed Bloods in the Canadian West," in *Essays on Western History,* ed. Thomas; John Mack Faragher, "Americans, Mexicans, Métis: A Community Approach to Its Imperial Past," in *Under an Open Sky: Rethinking America's Western Past,* ed. William Cronon, George Miles, and Jay Gitlin (New York: W. W. Norton, 1992), 90–110; Gary Clayton Anderson, "Joseph Renville and the Ethos of Biculturalism," in *Being and Becoming Indian: Biographical Studies of North American Frontiers,* ed. James A. Clifton (Prospect Heights, Ill.: Waveland Press, 1989), 59–81. The Métis and multiracial settlement of early Chicago is described by Jacqueline Peterson in "'Wild' Chicago: The Formation of a Multi-Racial Community on the Midwestern Frontier, 1816–1837," in *The Ethnic Frontier,* ed. Melvin G. Holli and Peter d'A. Jones (Grand Rapids, Mich.: Eerdmans Publishing Co., 1977), 25–73. For a historical survey of attitudes toward mixed-blood people, see Robert E. Bieder, "Scientific Attitudes toward Indian Mixed-Bloods in Early Nineteenth-Century America," *Journal of Ethnic Studies* 8 (Summer 1980): 17–30.

13. Sylvia Van Kirk, "Toward a Feminist Perspective in Native History," in *Papers of the Eighteenth Algonquian Conference* (Ottawa: Carleton University, 1987), 386.

14. In regions such as colonial Chesapeake Bay, where chaotic demographic conditions existed, people relied on the fictive kin network of godparenting to counteract demographic instability. My research supports the contention that similar social networks evolved in the Great Lakes region, but that here they formed the socioeconomic framework of the fur trade. On the Chesapeake, see: Darrett B. Rutman and Anita H. Rutman, "Non-Wives and Sons-in-Law: Parental Death in a Seventeenth-Century Virginia County," in *The Chesapeake in the Seventeenth Century,* ed. Thad W. Tate and Daniel L. Ammerman (New York: W. W. Norton, 1969), 153–82; *A Place in Time: Middlesex County, Virginia, 1650–1750* (New York: W. W. Norton, 1984), 59–60; Lorena Walsh, "Community Networks in the Early Chesapeake," in *Colonial Chesapeake Society,* ed. Lois Green Carr, Philip D. Morgan, and Jean B. Russo (Chapel Hill: University of North Carolina Press, 1988), 240–41; James Horn, *Adapting to a New World* (Chapel Hill: University of North Carolina Press, 1994), 203–34.

15. The role of women as cultural mediators has been developed by Clara Sue Kidwell in "Indian Women as Cultural Mediators," *Ethnohistory* 39 (Spring 1992): 97–107. The role of mixed-ancestry women as the wives of fur traders is central to Sylvia Van Kirk's *Many Tender Ties* and to Jennifer Brown's *Strangers in Blood* and is part of the expanding literature on Canadian Métis people, detailed in note 12 above.

16. In a matrifocal household, the woman evolved as the center of economic and decision-making coalitions with their children, despite the presence of a husband–father. The woman is the focus of the relationship but is not the head

of the household. See Raymond Smith, "The Matrifocal Family," in *The Character of Kinship,* ed. Jack Goody (New York: Cambridge University Press, 1973), 124–25. Also see Karen Fog Olwig, "Women, 'Matrifocality,' and Systems of Exchange: An Ethnohistorical Study of the Afro-American Family on St. John, Danish West Indies," *Ethnohistory* 28 (Winter 1981): 59–78.

17. Jacqueline Peterson, "Prelude to Red River: A Social Portrait of the Great Lakes Métis," *Ethnohistory* 25 (Winter 1978): 48.

18. "The term *frontier Catholicism* suggests that lay Catholics were instrumental in the spread of eighteenth-century Catholicism. This was a result of the scarcity of priests." From my "The World of Marie Madeleine Réaume L'archevêque Chevalier," in *New Faces of the Fur Trade,* 64 n. 7.

19. The continued viability of the nineteenth-century fur trade in the southern Great Lakes, particularly the trade in black raccoon, was discussed by James L. Clayton at the 1965 North American Fur Trade Conference and subsequently published in the selected proceedings of that meeting. James L. Clayton, "The Growth and Economic Significance of the American Fur Trade, 1790–1890," in *Aspects of the Fur Trade: Selected Papers of the 1965 North American Fur Trade Conference* (St. Paul: Minnesota Historical Society), 62–72. The black raccoon trade is also discussed at length in Chapter 7 herein.

20. By 1780, when the European population of Canada remained at ten thousand, French minister Jean-Baptiste Colbert urged the Christianization of the Indians and their intermarriage with the French. W. J. Eccles indicates that this policy failed because young Frenchmen preferred Indian lifestyles to those of their homeland, see his *France in America* (1972; reprint, East Lansing: Michigan State University Press, 1990); Jean Delanglez, *Frontenac and the Jesuits* (Chicago: Institute of Jesuit History, 1939), 36; Peterson, "Prelude to Red River," 47.

21. Alfred W. Crosby, *The Columbian Exchange: Biological and Cultural Consequences of 1492* (Westport, Conn.: Greenwood Publishing Company, 1972). Crosby was one of the first to publish in the emerging field of environmental history, but other authors, such as William Cronon, Carolyn Merchant, and Timothy Silver, have written extensively about the impact of the environment on the encounter between Native Americans and Europeans.

22. Numerous nineteeth-century county histories depict the Indians as hunter–gatherer communities that disappeared before the "pioneers" arrived. Even present-day social historians who have completed studies of the community-formation process in the Old Northwest, however, either omit or inaccurately assess the role of Indians. See Don Harrison Doyle, *The Social Order of a Frontier Community: Jacksonsville, Illinois, 1825–1870* (Urbana: University of Illinois Press, 1983); and John Mack Faragher, *Sugar Creek: Life on the Illinois Prairie* (New Haven: Yale University Press, 1986).

23. Francis R. Howe, *The Story of a French Homestead in the Old Northwest* (Columbus, Ohio: Press of Nitschke Brothers, 1907).

24. Patricia Nelson Limerick, *The Legacy of Conquest: The Unbroken Past of the American West* (New York: W. W. Norton, 1987); Patricia Nelson Limerick, Clyde A. Milner II, and Charles E. Rankin, eds., *Trails: Toward a New Western History* (Lawrence: University Press of Kansas, 1991); Richard White, *"It's Your Misfor-*

tune and None of My Own": A New History of the American West (Norman: University of Oklahoma Press, 1991).

25. For discussion of the linguistic complexity of terms in the Canadian fur trade, see Jennifer S. H. Brown, "Linguisitic Solitudes and Changing Social Categories," in *Old Trails and New Directions: Papers of the Third North American Fur Trade Conference,* ed. Carol M. Judd and Arthur J. Ray (Toronto: University of Toronto Press, 1978), 147–72. The discussion of Métis identity is best addressed by the books included in note 12 above.

26. I am indebted to Barry O'Connell, Peter d'Errico, Jacki Rand, Kathryn Abbott, and Jeani O'Brien-Kehoe for the phrase, "to hide in plain view." It arose from a series of discussions that took place before and after our AHA panel presentation. Barry O'Connell et al., "Strangers in Their Own Land: American Indian Diaspora" (panel presented at the annual meeting of the American Historical Association, Washington, D.C., January 1999).

Chapter 1. Fish to Furs

1. Isabel Wilkinson, "The Mississippi Reclaims Its True Domain," *New York Times,* July 18, 1993, Week in Review section; Ted Steinberg, *Acts of God: The Unnatural History of Natural Disaster in America* (New York: Oxford University Press, 2000), xv–xxiii.

2. Information about the earliest encounters is detailed in David B. Quinn, *North America from Earliest Discovery to First Settlement: The Norse Voyages to 1612* (New York: Harper & Row, 1977).

3. Early European exploration was directed by a geographic logic that presumed the presence of a Northwest Passage to the East and consequently led sixteenth-century explorers to focus their activity along the North Atlantic coast. See John L. Allen, "The Indrawing Sea: Imagination and Experience in the Search for the Northwest Passage, 1497–1632," in *American Beginnings: Exploration, Culture, and Cartography in the Land of Norumbega,* ed. Emerson W. Baker, Edwin A. Churchill, Richard S. D'Abate, Kristine L. Jones, Victor A. Konrad, and Harold E. L. Prins (Lincoln: University of Nebraska Press, 1994), 7–35.

4. W. J. Eccles, *The Canadian Frontier, 1534–1760* (New York: Holt, Rinehart, and Winston, 1969; reprint, Albuquerque: University of New Mexico Press, 1974), 5; Marcel Trudel, *The Beginnings of New France, 1524–1663* (Toronto: McClelland and Stewart, 1973), especially chap. 4, 54–81. Also see James Wilson, *The Earth Shall Weep: A History of Native America* (New York: Atlantic Monthly Press, 1998), 37.

5. John A. Dickinson, "Old Routes and New Wares: The Advent of European Goods in the St. Lawrence Valley," in *Le Castor Fait Tout: Selected Papers of the Fifth North American Fur Trade Conference, 1985* ed. Bruce G. Trigger, Toby Morantz, and Louise Dechêne, (Montreal: Lake St. Louis Historical Society, 1987), 37. By 1520, fishing boats arrived each spring and anchored along the coast from Labrador to Cape Sable. Most did not leave till the fall, and because the crews lived on land, they not only fished alongside Native people but also relied on Indian people for their food supply. These fishermen bartered European goods

for corn, beans, squash, fresh meat, and even firewood. Basque crews routinely traded axes and knives for deerskin and marten furs. Europeans often encountered friendly Natives who understood French, English, Gascon, or Basque. H. P. Biggar, ed., *A Collection of Documents Relating to Jacques Cartier and the Sieur de Roberval* (Ottawa: Public Archives of Canada, 1930); Dickinson, "Old Routes and New Wares," 32–34; Thomas R. Weasel, "Agriculture, Indians and American History," *Agricultural History* 50 (1976): 9–20. Both types of fishing, green and dry, involved interaction with Native people. Green fishing took place almost completely at sea. Fifteen to twenty men fished while the remaining crew processed the catch. It took three months to complete a cargo. These fishermen, like their land-based counterparts, varied their bland diet of shipboard fare by bartering with Native people for meat and agricultural produce. See H. P. Biggar, *The Early Trading Companies of New France* (Clifton, N.J.: Augustus M. Kelley Publishers, 1972), 25. The more profitable economic enterprise was dry fishing, a land-based operation that entailed interaction over a period of years. Lodges were constructed along the shoreline, in which the fishermen lived during the spring and summer months rather than aboard ship. Nearby staging areas were built where cod was processed and dried. These men fished in small boats or dories, launched from the shoreline, which were built by the carpenters who were part of these transatlantic fishing expeditions. When the ships returned to France, these extensive land-based operations were often guarded by resident fishermen, for many of whom these initially temporary arrangements became a permanent residence. One of the earliest descriptions of fishing along the Atlantic coasts was completed by Nicolas Denys, *The Description and Natural History of the Coasts of North America* (1672; reprint, Toronto: Champlain Society, 1908), especially 273–74. A brief but accurate discussion of sixteenth-century North American fishing is contained in W. J. Eccles, *France in America* (1972; reprint, East Lansing, Michigan State University Press, 1990), 10–13.

6. Fishermen returned with furs, such as marten, that trimmed the velvet and silk clothing of the upper classes, rather than beaver. For a description of the early trade in furs, see chapter 9, "At the Water's Edge: Trading in the Sixteenth Century," in James Axtell, *After Columbus: Essays in the Ethnohistory of Colonial North America* (New York: Oxford University Press, 1998), 144–81.

7. Beaver has a double coating of fur, an underlayer of soft, curly fur next to the skin covered by an outer layer of stiff, bristly hairs. Hat felt was manufactured by rolling mercury across the pelt to remove the bristles. Mercury poisoning led to the expression "mad as a hatter." The pace of trade quickened as furs acquired market value. The highly transportable nature of furs, being both light in weight and of high value relative to bulk, made them extremely profitable. Of greater import, they did not require the large, relatively skilled labor force of fishing expeditions.

8. Fur trade contracts initially appeared around 1580. See Dean Lloyd Anderson, "Documentary and Archaeological Perspectives on European Trade Goods in the Western Great Lakes Region" (Ph.D. diss., Michigan State University, 1992), 13; also see Laurier Turgeon, "Pour redecouvrir notre 16e siècle: Les peches à Terre-Neuve d'après les Archives Notariales de Bordeaux," *Revue d'histoire de l'Amérique française* 39, no. 4, (1947): 523–49. Fishing expeditions

during the second half of the sixteenth century grossed around 4,000 livres. The early fur trade was not so profitable. In 1583, a fur trade expedition to Maine fetched 2,640 livres. See Dickinson, "Old Routes and New Wares," 27–29.

9. South of the St. Lawrence River, the Indians who lived along the North Atlantic coast, referred to as Etchemins in early French sources, controlled the trade from the Gulf of Maine to Nova Scotia during the sixteenth and early seventeenth century. They sailed European-styled shallops, gathered furs from coastal villages, and transported them to Tadoussac on the St. Lawrence Gulf. See Bruce J. Bourque and Ruth H. Whitehead, "Trades and Alliances in the Contact Period," in Baker et al., *American Beginnings,* 131–47.

10. For discussion of Huron involvement in the early fur trade, see Conrad E. Heidenreich and Arthur J. Ray, *The Early Fur Trades* (Toronto: McClelland and Stewart, 1976). Heidenreich has also written a historical geography, *Huronia: A History and Geography of the Huron Indians, 1600–1650* (Toronto: McClelland and Stewart, 1971).

11. José António Brandao has suggested that the Beaver Wars should not be equated with Iroquois–French relations. He also views the New France settlement process as more like the Anglo-American experience, but with the rather unique experience of Indian interaction. See his *"Your Frye Shall Burn No More": Iroquois Policy toward New France and Its Native Allies to 1701* (Lincoln: University of Nebraska Press, 1997).

12. Trudel, *Beginnings of New France,* 218.

13. James A. Clifton offers a description of the diaspora that occurred in the southern Great Lakes and the resettlement of these refugees, in *The Prairie People* (1977; reprint, Iowa City: University of Iowa Press, 1998), 35–41. For a description of Green Bay and the refugee centers located along the shorelines of Lake Michigan and the Mississippi River valley, see Richard White, *The Middle Ground: Indians, Empires, and Republics in the Great Lakes Region, 1650–1815* (New York: Cambridge University Press, 1991), 1–49.

14. Anderson, "European Trade Goods in the Western Great Lakes," 25.

15. *Iliniwek* derives from *ilini,* meaning man; *iw* can be translated "is"; and the last letters, *ek,* designate the plural termination. They were renamed the Illinois by the French, who changed the ending of their name to their more familiar *ois.* Early in the seventeenth century, when the English arrived in Jamestown and the French established Quebec, the Iliniwek numbered approximately twenty thousand people. Wayne C. Temple, *Indian Villages of the Illinois Country* (Springfield: State of Illinois, 1958), 11; Clarence Walworth Alvord, *The Illinois Country, 1673–1818* (Springfield: Illinois Centennial Commission, 1920; reprint, Urbana: University of Illinois Press, 1987), 31.

16. There were at least twelve different Iliniwek tribes but those which persisted the longest and with the clearest histories are the Kaskaskia, Peoria, Cahokia, Tamaroa, Michigamea, and Loingwea. The Kaskaskia absorbed the Michigamea and Tamaroa, and the Cahokia merged into the Peoria. The Iliniwek were not politically linked nor was there any overall intertribal organization. Rather, these were people who shared a common language and similar origin traditions. See Charles Callender, "Illinois," in *The Northeast,* ed. Bruce G. Trigger, vol. 15 of *The Handbook of North American Indians,* ed. William C. Sturevant,

(Washington, D.C.: Smithsonian Institution, 1978), 673. For descriptions of the Illinois, see Emily J. Blasingham, "The Depopulation of the Illinois Indians," part 1, in *Ethnohistory* (Summer 1956): 193–224, and part 2, in *Ethnohistory* (Fall 1956): 361–412; Ellen M. Whitney, "Indian History and the Indians of Illinois," *Journal of the Illinois State Historical Society* (May 1976): 139–146 (hereafter referred to as *JIHS*). Erminie Wheeler-Voegelin, *Anthropological Report on the Indian Occupancy of Royce Areas 77 and 78,* in *Indians of Western Illinois and Southern Wisconsin,* ed. David Agee Horr (New York: Garland, 1974).

17. *The Jesuit Relations and Allied Documents,* ed. Reuben Gold Thwaites, 73 vols. (Cleveland: Burrows Brothers Company, 1896–1901), 58, 97; 59, 189 (hereafter cited as *JR*); Blasingham, "Depopulation of the Illinois Indians," part 2, 361–64; Callender, "Illinois," 679.

18. Kaskaskia was located on the northern bank of the Illinois River, between the towns of Ottawa and Utica. See Marion A. Habig, "The Site of the Great Illinois Village," *Mid-America* 16 (1933): 12; Joseph Jablow, *Indians of Illinois and Indiana: Illinois, Kickapoo, and Potawatomi Indians* (New York: Garland 1974), 85.

19. Jablow, *Indians of Illinois and Indiana,* 81; *JR,* 59, 123, and 58, 97; Blasingham, "Depopulation of the Illinois Indians, 362–63.

20. Jablow, *Indians of Illinois and Indiana,* 81; *JR,* 60, 159.

21. Carl J. Ekberg contends that, by the end of the French regime (1763), the Illinois Country had shrunk in size to include the "settlement area" on both sides of the Mississippi, from Kaskaskia in the South to St. Louis in the North, in his *French Roots in the Illinois Country: The Mississippi Frontier in Colonial Times* (Urbana: University of Illinois Press, 1998), 33.

22. Present-day Lake Michigan was at first called Lac des Puants and then named after the Illinois. It was subsequently renamed Lac St. Joseph and then Lac Dauphin by the French. See Trudel, *Beginnings of New France,* 183.

23. Daniel H. Usner, Jr., *Indians, Settlers, and Slaves in a Frontier Exchange Economy* (Chapel Hill: University of North Carolina Press, 1992), 14.

24. Archaeological descriptions of the settlement and trade patterns of this region can be found in Thomas E. Emerson and R. Barry Lewis, eds., *Cahokia and the Hinterlands* (Urbana: University of Illinois Press, 1991). The rich legacy of material artifacts is superbly detailed in David S. Brose, James A. Brown, and David W. Penney, *Ancient Art of the American Woodland Indians* (New York: Harry N. Abrams, 1985).

25. Neal Salisbury, "The Indians' Old World: Native Americans and the Coming of Europeans," *William and Mary Quarterly,* 3d ser. 80, no. 3 (July 1996): 435–37.

26. Alvord, *Illinois Country,* 3.

27. La Salle is best known to American historians in this version of his name. His proper French name, however, was Réne-Robert Cavelier de La Salle.

28. Francis Jennings, *The Ambiguous Iroquois Empire* (New York: W. W. Norton, 1984), 175.

29. The *Griffon* reflected La Salle's hostility toward the Jesuits. Louis Hennepin reports that La Salle constructed the ship with Governor-General Louis

de Baude Frontenac's financial support and he named it the *Griffon,* in order that it might "fly above the ravens." The ship alluded to the Comte de Frontenac's coat of arms, which contained two griffins. The mythical ravens were La Salle's sarcastic allusion to the black gowns of the Jesuits. See Louis Hennepin, *A New Discovery of a Vast Country in America,* ed. Reuben Gold Thwaites (Chicago: A. C. McClurg, 1903), 1, 93.

30. Soon after his arrival at the Miami River, in present-day southwest Michigan, La Salle learned that the *Griffon* had been lost. Manned by a helmsman and a five-man crew, the ship had been sent back to Niagara Falls. Hennepin, in *Discovery of a Vast Country,* 120–21, suggests that it went down in an autumn storm. Larry Massie, whose work has focused on Great Lakes history, agrees with Hennepin's conclusion, in "La Bibliothèque," *Michigan History* 76 (November/December 1992): 52–54; Harrison John MacLean, *The Fate of the Griffon* (Toronto: Griffin House, 1974), 65–68.

31. In 1682, La Barre received orders from the king to prevent the outbreak of warfare between the Iroquois and Illinois: "By all means prevent the Iroquois making war on the Illinois and other tribes, neighbors to them . . . whose furs constitute the principal trade of Canada." See Jablow, *Indians of Illinois and Indiana,* 94; E. B. O'Callaghan, ed., *Documents Relative to the Colonial History of the State of New York* (Albany: Weed, Parsons, and Company, 1885–1887), 9, 171. (Hereafter referred to as *NYCD.*)

32. This natural defensive site was protected by steep sides with only one, very difficult means of access. It was known as "Starved Rock," because here a group of Ilini warriors successfully defended themselves against attack but starved to death in the process. La Salle reported that 3,880 Ilini warriors were assembled at Starved Rock. This suggests an overall population perhaps as high as twenty thousand. La Salle's former lieutenant, Henri Tonti, moved the fort from the Starved Rock location to Pimiteoui, or Peoria, in 1692, when the Indians complained about the scarcity of wood and the difficulty of getting water to the fort. See Floyd Mulkey, "Fort St. Louis at Peoria," *JIHS,* 37 (1944): 303.

33. A recently translated record of La Salle's 1682 exploration of the Mississippi describes his effort to unite various refugee Indian communities. See Minet, "Voyage Made from Canada Inland Going Southward during the Year 1682," in *La Salle, the Mississippi, and the Gulf,* ed. Robert S. Weddle (College Station: Texas A&M University Press, 1987), 29–68, especially 63–64. Patricia Galloway provides background on this expedition and on the two participants, Nicolas de La Salle and Gabriel Minime, Sieur Barbier, whose oral recollections are the basis for this narrative, in ibid., 17–27.

34. Richard White maintains that the French were compelled to act as an Algonquian father in order to maintain Indian loyalty and to engage Indian allies in the defense of New France. White contends that only the French possessed the wealth and contacts across this broad geographical expanse to mediate indigenous disputes successfully (*Middle Ground,* 29–38, 142–49).

35. Ouilamette was later adopted by the Potawatomi and became more commonly known as Catfish, head of the Fish clan. *Ouilamette* is the French spelling for the eastern Algonquian name, *Wilamek.* Wilamek's name was first transformed

into Winamek; this represented the more familiar sounds of the Potawatomi language. Today, the name and clan remain prominent among the Kansas and Oklahoma Potawatomi (Clifton, *Prairie People,* 20).

36. Robert L. Hall, "The Archaeology of La Salle's Fort St. Louis on Starved Rock and the Problem of the Newell Fort," in *French Colonial Archaeology,* ed. John A. Walthall (Urbana: University of Illinois Press, 1991), 14–15.

37. Alvord, in *Illinois Country,* 88–89, cites, as the original source of his information, Pierre Margry's *Découvertes et établissements des Français dans l'ouest et dans le sud de l'Amérique septentrionale, 1614–1698, mémoires et documents originaux,* 6 parts (Paris: D. Jouaust: 1876), Part 3: 563, (hereafter cited as Margry, *Découvertes et éstablissements* (1876))

38. For a description of the fur trade rivalry, see W. J. Eccles, *The Canadian Frontier, 1534–1760* (1969; reprint, Albuquerque: University of New Mexico Press, 1974), 109–10. Recently translated French documents suggest that La Salle's geographic knowledge of the Mississippi River was inaccurate and that there was no reason to believe that he knew where the Mississippi flowed into the Gulf of Mexico, and this casts doubt on his plans to link effectively the Great Lakes fur trade to a warm-water port (Galloway, "Minet Relation," 22–27).

39. La Salle, "Memoir of the Sieur de la Salle Reporting to Monseigneur de Seignelay the Discoveries Made by Himself under the Order of His Majesty," *Collections of the Illinois State Historical Library* (Springfield, 1903), vol. 1, 119, 122 (hereafter referred to as *CISHL*).

40. Eccles, *France in America,* 108; Weddle, *La Salle, the Mississippi, and the Gulf,* 7. The Jesuit land grant was not confirmed by the French court until almost three years later, May 24, 1689, a little over two years after La Salle's death. Confirmation of Concessions, Versailles, May 24, 1689, *Archives Nationales, Colonies,* series B, vol. 15, 218, 223 (hereafter cited as *AnCol*).

41. W. J. Eccles, *Canada under Louis XIV, 1663–1701* (Toronto: Mc Clelland and Stewart, 1964), 63–64.

42. Ibid., 106.

43. Eccles, *France in America,* 93–94.

44. La Salle, "Memoir of the Sieur de la Salle Reporting to Monseigneur de Seignelay, *CISHL* 1: 119, 122; Eccles, *France in America,* 91; Minet, "Voyage Made from Canada Inland," 31.

45. Eccles, *Canadian Frontier,* 110, see especially chap. 6, 103–31.

46. Eccles, *France in America,* 103. The Ilini moved from Fort St. Louis at Starved Rock in 1691, because "'their firewood was so remote and because it was difficult to get water upon the rock.'" The Ilini relocated to Lake Pimitoui despite the French preference for Starved Rock (Jablow, *Indians of Illinois and Indiana,* 110).

47. "Marriage 'after the custom of the country'" is discussed in notes (11 and 12) to the Introduction. See especially Van Kirk, *Many Tender Ties,* 28; Brown, *Strangers in Blood,* 62–63.

48. Brown, *Strangers in Blood,* 65.

49. Carolyn Gilman, *Where Two Worlds Meet: The Great Lakes Fur Trade* (St. Paul: Minnesota Historical Society, 1982), 80–81.

50. Unfortunately, many baptismal and marital records also effectively mask

indigenous identity. Often Native women who were either baptized or married by missionary priests were identified by their baptismal names or by the surnames of their husbands. Many of the Native women in this book, however, are identifiable in the Jesuit records by both their Indian and Christian names.

51. For the parallel circumstance of Catholic women among the Iroquois, see Nancy Shoemaker, "Kateri Tekakwitha," in *Negotiators of Change,* ed. Nancy Shoemaker (New York: Routledge, 1995), 49–71; and Natalie Zemon Davis, "Iroquois Women, European Women," in *Women, "Race," and Writing in the Early Modern Period,* ed. Margo Hendricks and Patricia Parker (New York: Routledge, 1994), 243–61.

52. This perspective, espoused in both Carol Devens' *Countering Colonization* and Karen Anderson's *Chain Her by One Foot,* views Christianity as the means through which indigenous female autonomy was subverted. For a discussion of an assimilationist model of missionization among Native American women, see Karen Anderson, *Chain Her by One Foot: The Subjugation of Women in Seventeenth-Century New France* (New York: Routledge, 1991); Carol Devens, *Countering Colonization: Native American Women and Great Lakes Women, 1630–1900* (Berkeley: University of California Press, 1992); Eleanor Burke Leacock, "Montaignais Women and the Jesuit Program for Colonization," in *Myths of Male Dominance: Collected Articles on Women Cross Culturally* (New York: Monthly Review Press, 1981), 43–62.

53. David Thelen, "Memory and American History," Special Issue: Memory and American History, *Journal of American History* 75 (March 1989): 1117–29. See note 17 above for *Jesuit Relations.*

54. The French referred to the western Great Lakes as the *pays d'en haut* and initially included all the "lands bordering the rivers flowing into the northern Great Lakes and the lands south of the lakes to the Ohio." See White, *Middle Ground,* x–xi.

Chapter 2. Marie Rouensa and the Jesuits

1. Nancy Shoemaker, "Kateri Tekakwitha," in *Negotiators of Change,* ed. Nancy Shoemaker (New York, Routledge, 1995), 51.

2. Claude Charles Le Roy, Sieur de Bacqueville de La Potherie, *History of the Savage Peoples Who Are the Allies of New France,* in *The Indian Tribes of the Upper Mississippi Valley and the Region of the Great Lakes,* ed. Emma Helen Blair (1911; reprint, Lincoln: University of Nebraska Press, 1996), 295–300; Joseph Jablow, *Indians of Illinois and Indiana: Illinois, Kickapoo, and Potawatomi Indians* (New York: Garland, 1974), 49–50.

3. *JR,* 60, 161; Eric Hinderaker, *Elusive Empires: Constructing Colonialism in the Ohio Valley, 1673–1800* (New York: Cambridge University Press, 1997), 59; W. Vernon Kinietz, *The Indians of the Western Great Lakes* (1940; reprint, Ann Arbor: University of Michigan Press, 1990), 204. Kinietz relies on the La Salle documents in *Official Account of the Enterprises of La Salle,* in Margry, *Découvertes et établissements* (1876), part 2, 527.

4. During the seventeenth and eighteenth centuries, violence against women by men was also reported among the Miami, Wea, Piankeshaw, and Shaw-

nee, and included mutilation and scalping as well as gang rape. Tanis C. Thorne, "For the Good of Her People: Continuity and Change for Native Women of the Midwest, 1650–1850," in *Midwestern Women: Work, Community, and Leadership at the Crossroads,* ed. Lucy Eldersveld Murphy and Wendy Venet (Bloomington: Indiana University Press, 1997), 101; John Moore, "Evolution and Historical Reductionism," *Plains Anthropologist* 26, no. 94 (1981): 261–69; Lawrence A. Conrad, "An Early Eighteenth-Century Reference to 'Putting a Woman on the Prairies,'" *Plains Anthropologist* 28, no. 100 (May 1983): 141–42.

5. "Memoir of De Gannes concerning the Illinois Country," ed. Theodore Calvin Pease and Raymond C. Werner, *The French Foundations, 1680–1693, CISHL* 23 (1934): 335. This memoir was reportedly written by Pierre Deliette. Margaret Kimball Brown, "The Illinois Country before 1765," in *Guide to the History of Illinois,* ed. John Hoffmann (New York: Greenwood Press, 1991)

6. "Memoir of De Gannes," 334–35.

7. The most comprehensive article about her is that of Carl J. Ekberg, with Anton J. Pregaldin, "Marie Rouensa-8cate8a and the Foundations of French Illinois," *Illinois Historical Journal* 84 (Autumn 1991): 146–60. The figure 8 represents the phoneme *ou.* Ekberg and Pregaldin depict Marie as an Indian who identified with the French. In his later book, *French Roots in the Illinois Country: The Mississippi Frontier in Colonial Times* (Chicago: University of Illinois Press, 1998), Ekberg locates Marie as part of a transitional world that evolved into a French community (33). By 1720, within the first generation of its founding, Kaskaskia was a sedentary agricultural community. Eric Hinderaker, in *Elusive Empires,* also considered Marie as an assimilated Frenchwoman and describes her as one of the "leading matrons of Kaskaskia." Hinderaker also believes that her children chose to become French, rather than Illinois Indians (115). Richard White identifies Marie Rouensa as Indian and refers to her as Aramepinchieue: He focuses on Marie as a young woman and does not discuss her later life *The Middle Ground: Indians, Empires, and Republics in the Great Lakes Region, 1650–1815* (New York: Cambridge University Press, 1991), 70–75.

8. "Marriage 'after the custom of the country' was an indigenous marriage rite which evolved to meet the needs of fur-trade society. . . . Although denounced by the Jesuit priests as being immoral, the traders had taken their Indian wives according to traditional native marriage rites and distinct family units had developed." See Sylvia Van Kirk, *Many Tender Ties: Women in Fur Trade Society, 1679–1870* (Norman: University of Oklahoma Press, 1980), 28. For a further explanation of how marriage *à la façon du pays* become institutionalized as integral to the fur trade, see also notes 11 and 12 to the Introduction.

9. Marie married Michel Accault within the church. Father Gravier described the circumstances of the wedding and baptized their first son, Peter Accault, on March 20, 1695, at Pimiteoui. For the baptism, see "Kaskaskia Church Records," *Transactions of the Illinois State Historical Society,* vol. 2 (Springfield, 1904), 394; Marthe Faribault-Beauregard, *La population des fort français d'Amérique,* vol. 2 (Montreal: Bergeron, 1982), 108.

10. Gravier's Journal, February 15, 1694, *JR,* 64, 193.

11. Richard White uses Marie Rouensa to show how "the prospect of a marriage between a Christian Illinois woman and a Frenchman precipitated a crisis which was ultimately decided on the middle ground" (*Middle Ground,* 70–75).

12. Father Gravier entered the Society of Jesus in 1670 and taught at several Jesuit schools before he arrived in New France in 1687. Then, Gravier traveled west to live among the Iliniwek, where he remained for the next thirteen years. Father Gravier's most successful missionization occurred among the Kaskaskia, because other Ilini people, especially the Peoria, proved openly hostile to his missionary work. He was, in fact, eventually fatally wounded by the Peoria. Some of his writings were preserved in the *Jesuit Relations,* especially vols. 64 and 65.

13. "Memoir of De Gannes," *CISHL,* 23, 361.

14. *JR,* 64, 229.

15. The novelty of these pictures acted as magnets, but not all Jesuits had copperplate Bibles. Many Jesuits relied on pictographs rather than factual depictions to communicate Christianity's message. At St. Francis Mission in Green Bay, Father Claude Allouez used pictographs that incorporated familiar Native symbols to represent the twelve tenets of the Apostles' Creed. See James T. Moore, *Indian and Jesuit* (Chicago: Loyola University Press, 1982), 134; *JR,* 24, 83, 95–97, 135.

16. From Father Gabriel Marest, Missionary of the Society of Jesus, to Father Germon of the Same Society, November 9, 1712, *Lettres Édifiantes* (Toulouse, 1810), 6, 207.

17. For a parallel circumstance among the Iroquois, see Shoemaker, "Kateri Tekakwitha," in *Negotiators of Change,* 49–71; Caroline Walker Bynum, *Holy Feast and Holy Fast: The Religious Significance of Food to Medieval Women* (Berkeley: University of California Press, 1987); Donald Weinstein and Rudolph M. Bell, *Saints and Society: The Two Worlds of Western Christendom, 1000–1700* (Chicago: University of Chicago Press, 1982).

18. Raymond E. Hauser, "Warfare and the Illinois Indian Tribe during the Seventeenth Century: An Exercise in Ethnohistory," *The Old Northwest* 10 (Winter 1984–1985): 381.

19. *JR,* 64, 205.

20. Ibid., 213.

21. Ibid., 195.

22. Ibid., 203.

23. Ibid., 205, 213.

24. Ibid., 217.

25. Jacqueline Peterson, "The People in Between: Indian-White Marriage and the Genesis of a Métis Society and Culture in the Great Lakes Region, 1680–1830" (Ph.D. diss., University of Illinois, Chicago Circle, 1981), 88.

26. *JR,* 64: 207, 211.

27. Ibid., 209.

28. Ibid., 209–10.

29. Ibid., 205–9; 233; Mary Borgios Palm, *The Jesuit Missions of the Illinois Country, 1673–1763* (Cleveland: p. p., 1931), 26.

30. In *Kinsmen of Another Kind,* Gary Anderson shows how the traders among the Sioux relied on presents and the creation of kinship ties to gain access to furs. Among the Sioux many of these traders also established long-term relationships and raised families, and even sent their mixed-blood children east to school. See *Kinsmen of Another Kind: Dakota-White Relations in the Upper Missouri Valley, 1650–1862* (Lincoln: University of Nebraska Press, 1984), 30–31.

31. In a matrifocal household the woman is the focus of the relationship but not the head of the household. Women evolved as the center of economic and decision-making coalitions with their children, despite the presence of a husband–father. See Raymond Smith, "The Matrifocal Family," in *The Character of Kinship,* ed. Jack Goody (New York: Cambridge University Press, 1973), 124–25. The social complexity of Indian communities wherein patrilineal clans intersected with matrilocal residence patterns, is explored by Charles Calendar in "Great Lakes–Riverine Sociopolitical Organization," in *Northeast,* ed. Bruce G. Trigger, vol.15 of *Handbook of North American Indians,* ed. William C. Sturtevant (Washington, D.C., 1978), 610–16.

32. This comment was made by an English trader in the last quarter of the eighteenth century but it is equally relevant to the seventeenth century when canoes were even smaller in size. Alexander Henry, the Elder, *Travels and Adventures in Canada and the Indian Territories* (1809; reprint, Ann Arbor: University Microfilms, 1966), 243–44.

33. Thorne, "For the Good of Her People," 107–8; Jeanne Kay, "The Fur Trade and Native American Population Growth," *Ethnohistory* 31 (1984): 282.

34. For detailed information on gristmills in Illinois Country, see Ekberg, *French Roots,* 265–73.

35. Margry, *Découvertes et établissements des Français* (1879), 5, 375–586; Palm, *Jesuit Missions,* 44; also in Father Watrin's summary of his work among the Kaskaskia, *JR,* 70, 211–301.

36. Brown and Laurie C. Dean, *The Village of Chartres in Colonial Illinois, 1720–1765* (New Orleans: Polyanthos Press, 1977), 871; Ekberg with Pregaldin, "Marie Rouensa," 156; Daniel H. Usner, *Indians, Settlers, and Slaves in a Frontier Exchange Economy: The Lower Mississippi before 1783* (Chapel Hill: University of North Carolina Press, 1992), 229.

37. Ekberg with Pregaldin, "Marie Rouensa," 154; Kaskaskia Manuscripts, Randolph County Courthouse, Chester, Ill., 25: 6: 13: 1. The Kaskaskia documents are classified by the year (two digits), followed by the month, day, and then, the sequence of the transaction for that day. Natalia M. Belting, *Kaskaskia under the French Regime,* Illinois Studies in the Social Sciences, vol. 29 (Urbana: University of Illinois Press, 1948), 14.

38. Ekberg with Pregaldin, "Marie Rouensa," 154.

39. For a description of black slavery in Illinois Country, see Carl J. Ekberg, "Black Slavery in Illinois, 1720–1765," *Western Illinois Regional Studies* 12 (1989): 5–9; Winstanley Briggs, "Slavery in French Colonial Illinois," *Chicago History* 18 (1989–1990): 66–81. For Native American slavery in the Great Lakes, see Russell M. Magnaghi, "Red Slavery in the Great Lakes Country during the French and British Regimes," *The Old Northwest* 12 (Summer 1986): 201–17.

40. An arpent is a French unit equal to about 0.84 acre or when used as a linear measure, to 192 English feet. See Winstanley Briggs, "Le Pays des Illinois," *William and Mary Quarterly* 47 (January 1990): 38 n. 18.

41. Faribault-Beauregard, *La population des forts,* 107–81.

42. The contents of the Kaskaskia records have been methodically analyzed by Margaret Kimball-Brown, "Documents and Archaeology in French Illinois," in *French Colonial Archaeology: The Illinois Country and the Western Great Lakes,* ed. John A. Walthall (Urbana: University of Illinois Press, 1991), 78–84.

43. Susan C. Boyle, "Did She Really Decide? Women in Ste. Genevieve, 1750–1805," *William and Mary Quarterly* 44 (October 1987): 783–84.

44. Lucy Eldersveld Murphy, "Autonomy and the Economic Roles of Indian Women of the Fox–Wisconsin River Region, 1763–1832," in Shoemaker, *Negotiators of Change*, 81–82.

45. Jacqueline Peterson, "Many Roads to Red River: Métis Genesis in the Great Lakes Region, 1680–1815," in *The New Peoples: Being and Becoming Métis in North America*, ed. Jacqueline Peterson and Jennifer S. H. Brown (Manitoba: University of Manitoba Press, 1985), 57.

46. Ekberg, *French Roots in Illinois Country*, 178. For the original documentation, see André Pénicaut, "Relation," in Margry, *Découvertes et établissements* (1876), part 5, 489.

47. Gilbert J. Garraghan, "New Light on Old Cahokia," *Illinois Catholic Historical Review* 11: 99–146.

48. John A. Walthall and Elizabeth D. Benchley, *The River L'Abbe Mission: A French Colonial Church for the Cahokia Illini on Monks Mound*, Studies in Illinois Archaeology no. 2 (Springfield: Illinois Historic Preservation Agency, 1987), 71–73.

49. During the European Counter-Reformation, the Jesuits had learned that accommodation, rather than confrontation with dissenters, won more converts. This doctrine, identified as probabilism, held that there was no one universal moral code that could be applied uniformly to people in different cultures. "The Jesuits thus refined missionary techniques . . . by adapting to specific limitations. Instead of condemning existing cultures outright, they tried to build on common denominators and gradually reshape native ways towards closer approximations of a Christian norm." See Henry Warner Bowden, *American Indians and Christian Missions: Studies in Cultural Conflict* (Chicago: University of Chicago Press, 1981), 84.

50. To be a saint required canonization by the Roman Catholic Church. Saints' names were given to children at baptism and had a prominent place in individual devotional exercises. "They were popular spiritual heroes and were offered to young men and women as models of virtue. Unlike God, saints were human; they walked on earth, and lived and died as other mortals." See Jay Dolan, *The American Catholic Experience* (Garden City, N.Y.: Image Books, 1985), 230.

51. *JR*, 64, 235.

52. Moore, *Indian and Jesuit*, 93; *JR*, 58, 267. Father Allouez described how food offerings included the name of Jesus Christ and was invoked with a litany of Manitous. "They honor our Lord among themselves in their own way, putting his Image, which I have given them, in the most honored place on the occasion of any important feast, while the Master of the banquet addresses it as follows: 'In thy honor, O Man-God, do we hold this feast; to thee we offer these viands.'" Moore, *Indian and Jesuit*, 145; *JR*, 60, 49–51.

53. *JR*, 64, 205.

54. Shoemaker, "Kateri Tekakwitha," 54–57.

55. Ramón A. Gutiérrez discusses the ways in which role reversals of men and women were used as effective Christian techniques by the Franciscans in the Christianization of Mexico, in his *When Jesus Came, the Corn Mothers Went Away* (Palo Alto, Calif.: Stanford University Press, 1991).

56. *JR*, 64, 227.

57. Ekberg with Pregaldin, "Marie Rouensa," 154; Kaskaskia Manuscripts, 25: 6: 13: 1.

58. White, *Middle Ground*, 70–75.

59. Ekberg with Pregaldin, "Marie Rouensa," 149 no. 14.

60. Jean Baptiste Ducoigne was the son of an Indian woman named Elizabeth Michel Rouensa. Jean Baptiste was the Kaskaskia chief when George Rogers Clark captured Illinois from the British in 1778. See "Jean Baptiste Ducoigne," in *Indians of the Chicago Area*, ed. Terry Strauss (Chicago: NAES College Press, 1989), 37.

61. Natalie Zemon Davis has suggested that Christianity provided Native women a public voice that they were otherwise denied, in "Iroquois Women, European Women," in *Women, "Race," and Writing in the Early Modern Period*, ed. Margo Hendricks and Patricia Parker (New York: Routledgc, 1994), 243–58.

62. Kateri Tekakwitha has been nominated for sainthood in the Catholic Church. See Shoemaker, "Kateri Tekakwitha," 49–71; Daniel K. Richter, *The Ordeal of the Longhouse* (Chapel Hill: University of North Carolina Press, 1992), 126–28; K. I. Koppedrayer, "The Making of the First Iroquois Virgin: Early Jesuit Biographies of the Blessed Kateri Tekakwitha," *Ethnohistory* 40 (Spring 1993): 277–306; "Lily of the Mohawks," *Newsweek* 12 (August 1, 1938): 27–28; "The Long Road to Sainthood," *Time* 116 (July 7, 1980): 42–43.

63. Richter, *Ordeal of the Longhouse*, 111–15.

64. Burial sites with numerous Catholic artifacts can be found throughout Michigan, they have been excavated and reported on by Charles Cleland, George Quimby, Arthur Jelinek, Ruth Herrick, research teams from Michigan State University and the University of Michigan, as well as the Upper Grand Valley and the Saginaw Valley Chapters of the Michigan Archaeological Society. For more information regarding the excavation of burial sites, see James E. Fitting's *The Archaeology of Michigan* (Garden City, N.Y.: Natural History Press, 1970), 205–23. Also see Bonnie L. Gums, William R. Isseminger, Molly E. McKenzie, and Dennis D. Nichols, "The French Colonial Villages of Cahokia and Prairie du Pont, Illinois," in *French Colonial Archaeology* ed. John A. Walthall (Urbana: University of Illinois Press, 1991), 105–6; Walthall and Benchley, eds., *River L'Abbe Mission*, 71–73.

65. Shoemaker, "Kateri Tekakwitha," 67.

66. Daniel K. Richter, "Iroquois vs. Iroquois: Jesuit Missions and Christianity in Village Politics, 1542–1686," *Ethnohistory* 32 (1985): 4.

67. Emily J. Blasingham, The Depopulation of the Illinois Indians," part 2, *Ethnohistory* 3 (Fall 1956): 361–72; also see part 1, *Ethnohistory* 3 (Summer 1956): 193–224.

Chapter 3. Marie Madeleine Réaume L'archevêque Chevalier

1. James A. Clifton, *The Prairie People: Continuity and Change in Potawatomi Indian Culture, 1665–1965* (Lawrence: Regents' Press of Kansas, 1977), 85–87.

2. Ibid., 83; W. Vernon Kinietz, *The Indians of the Western Great Lakes, 1615–1760* (Ann Arbor: University of Michigan Press, 1965), 309–10.

3. According to the French scholar Joseph L. Peyser, French officials commonly used the term Saint Joseph River post and not, Fort St. Joseph. Despite this inaccuracy, Fort St. Joseph is used most frequently by historians and it is this name that appears in the historical literature. Joseph L. Peyser, *On the Eve of the Conquest: The Chevalier De Raymond's Critique of New France in 1754* (East Lansing: Michigan State University Press, 1997). This post guarded the river portage from the St. Joseph to the Kankakee River and was an important entry point for reaching the Mississippi River. R. David Edmunds, *The Potawatomis: Keepers of the Fire* (Norman: University of Oklahoma Press, 1978), 32. For a description of the fort as a military post under the French, see Dunning Idle, "The Post of the St. Joseph River during the French Regime, 1679–1761" (Ph.D. diss., University of Illinois, 1946). Information on the fort can also be found in Ralph Ballard, *Old Fort Saint Joseph* (Berrien Springs, Mich.: Hardscrapple Books, 1973); Gérard Malchelosse, "Genealogy and Colonial History: The St. Joseph River Post, Michigan," *French Canadian and Acadian Genealogical Review,* nos. 3–4 (1979): 173–209; Mildred Webster and Fred Krause, *French Fort Saint Joseph: De la Poste de la Rivière St. Joseph, 1690–1780* (p.p., 1990). The genealogical information in these articles is problematic and often requires further verification.

4. Clifton, *Prairie People,* 85.

5. Claude Charles Le Roy, Sieur de Bacqueville de La Potherie, *History of the Savage Peoples Who Are the Allies of New France,* in *The Indian Tribes of the Upper Mississippi Valley and the Region of the Great Lakes,* ed. Emma Helen Blair (1911; reprint, Lincoln: University of Nebraska Press, 1996), 319. (Hereafter cited as La Potherie, *History.*)

6. *The Jesuit Relations and Allied Documents,* ed. Reuben Gold Thwaites, 73 vols. (Cleveland: Burrows Brothers Company, 1896–1901), 65, 199.

7. Ibid., 197.

8. Royal Proclamation, Versailles, May 21, 1696, *Archives Nationales, Colonies,* series B, 19–1: 129–30, and a copy dated May 23, 1696; ibid., 156–69 (hereafter referred to as *ANCol*). The *Archives Nationales, Colonies* is an extensive body of records, housed in the French archives in Paris, that includes a large collection of primary source documents related to Canada and Louisiana. Canadian material is primarily located in series A, B, C^{11}, and F. The series B is used extensively because it contains letters from French officials to colonial administrators. Much of this material is calendared in the *Canadian Archives Reports* (Ottawa, 1884–1905) for 1899, 1904, and 1905. The series C^{11}A includes official correspondence sent from Canada to New France. The *Canadian Archives Reports* for 1885, 1886, and 1887 contains a partial calendar for this series. These transcribed materials are available at the National Archives of Canada, in Ottawa. Some of these materials are also available in microfilm from various university libraries. The Library of Congress in Washington, D.C., also possesses numerous transcribed documents. The sources used in this research often came through interlibrary loan at the University of Michigan and therefore, the footnote listing is complicated by numbers used to identify rolls of microfilm. Researchers who intend to travel to either Paris or Ottawa should ignore these numbers while scholars limited to campus resources may find these numbers helpful for interlibrary loan requests. Unfortunately, there is no bibliographic guide that cata-

logs the location of these materials. For those with access to substantial travel monies, the standard reference procedures for locating the original documents within the *Archives Nationales, Colonies* are contained in the footnote references. The folio page is indicated by a number, which is then followed by r for recto and v for verso, in the margin, e.g., 192v. The National Archives of Canada pagination is designated by the letters NAC and the transcript page number, e.g., NAC 2218. How these references should be understood is rarely explained, and they can appear rather intimidating to the uninitiated scholar. Scholars who wish to pursue their interest in these archives may find it helpful to consult the work of Joseph L. Peyser, who provides an insightful explanation of this complicated research process. Peyser, *On the Eve of Conquest,* 1–46, especially 45–46.

9. Clifton, *Prairie People,* 84.

10. Sylvia Van Kirk, "Toward a Feminist Perspective in Native History," in *Papers of the Eighteenth Algonquian Conference,* ed. William Cowan (Ottawa: Carleton University, 1987), 386.

11. Kenneth M. Morrison, "Baptism and Alliance: The Symbolic Mediations of Religious Syncretism," *Ethnohistory* 37 (Fall 1990): 421.

12. Another child was born to Jean-Baptiste de St. Ours while he lived among the western tribes, and this son later became a commandant at Fort St. Joseph. He was M. Roch de St. Ours De Chaillon and was appointed in 1755.

13. Priests at the reestablished forts served the religious needs of French *habitants,* as well as of the Indians. Indian converts were often ostracized by the French Catholic families of these farmers and tradesmen. For example, four years after Marie Rouensa's death, open hostilities erupted when French settlers from Montreal, Quebec, and New Orleans moved into Kaskaskia and Cahokia. Although the French purchased their cultivated fields from the Ilini, they encountered trouble when they pressured the Ilini to sell them additional land. In 1733, one Frenchman was killed, and the French negotiated with the Catholic Ilini to move twelve leagues from the village of Kaskaskia. A new Native community was established, nine miles away, and a separate chapel was constructed for Indian use. Henceforth, the Indians worshiped in one building and the French settlers in another. See Mary Borgias Palm, *The Jesuit Missions of the Illinois Country, 1673–1763* (Cleveland: p. p., 1931), 42–46; Clarence Walworth Alvord, *The Illinois Country, 1673–1818* (1920; reprint, Urbana: University of Illinois Press, 1987), 222–23.

14. One marital and two baptismal registers are part of this research and include "The Mackinac Register, 1725–1821: Register of Marriages in the Parish of Michilimackinac," *Collections of the State Historical Society of Wisconsin* (Madison: Wisconsin Historical Society, 1854–1931), 18, 469–513 (hereafter cited as *WHC*); "The St. Joseph Baptismal Register," *Mississippi Valley Historical Review* 13: 201–39; "The Mackinac Register, 1695–1821: Register of Baptisms of the Mission of St. Ignace de Michilimakinak," *WHC* 19: 1–162. The original St. Joseph Baptismal Register is in the archives of the Quebec Seminary.

15. Simon Réaume led 400 Wea and Piankashaw warriors and 28 Frenchmen in battle against the Fox. The Fox War began in August of 1727 when Governor-General Charles de Beauharnois of 1727, acting on the advice of his New France advisors, decided to attack the Fox. The campaign opened in the summer of 1727 and quickly evolved into a French initiated war of extermina-

tion against the Fox. Despite the Fox surrender in 1731 the fighting continued intermittently until 1734, when Beauharnois sent the last of the Fox leaders into slavery in the Indies. The Fox remained wary of the French. R. David Edmunds and Joseph L. Peyser, *The Fox Wars* (Norman: University of Oklahoma Press, 1993), 109–201; Joseph L. Peyser, "The Fate of the Fox Survivors: A Dark Chapter in the History of the French in the Upper Country, 1726–1737," *Wisconsin Magazine of History* 73 (Winter 1989–1990): 104 (hereafter referred to as *WMH*).

16. The first official reference to Jean Baptiste Réaume was in 1720, when New France Governor General Philippe de Rigaud de Vaudreuil, sent him to the reestablished Fort St. Joseph post with two canoes loaded with gifts for the Miami. Marie Madeleine Réaume first appears in the St. Joseph Register when she was listed as a godmother in March of 1729 and identified as the daughter of Simphorose Ouaouagoukoue and the post's interpreter, Sieur Jean Baptiste Réaume. See "St. Joseph Register," *MVHR* 13: 212. Réaume is also often spelled Rheaume. Réaume's appointment as interpreter probably took place in 1731, when Villers was ordered to reopen and assume command of Green Bay (Peyser, "Fate of the Fox Survivors," *WMH,* 73, 94).

17. Joseph L. Peyser, "The Fall and Rise of Thérèse Catin: A Portrait from Indiana's French and Canadian History," *Indiana Magazine of History* 91 (December 1995): 364.

18. Thérèse first came to public attention when she had a child out of wedlock at twenty-one. Several years later she married Simon, who was at least twenty years older. During one of her husband's frequent trips west, Thérèse rented rooms to Charles-François-Marie Ruette d'Auteuil de Monceaux, the son of the former attorney general of New France. He continued to live in her apartments when Simon returned and refused to leave her home even when ordered to do so by the New France Governor-General and the Bishop of Quebec. After Simon's death, they couple eventually married, in September of 1834. They had lived together for fourteen years. See Peyser, "The Fall and Rise of Thérèse Catin," 91 361–79; Peyser, "Fate of the Fox Survivors," 109.

19. Louise Dechêne illustrates not only the involvement of French wives in the trade but demonstrates that small merchants depended on their wives' business skills, exercised during their prolonged absences in the west. By the beginning of the eighteenth century, all transactions relating to the fur trade were recorded in notarized contracts. Many of these women can be identified because they were granted legal power of attorney by their husbands. See her *Habitants and Merchants in Seventeenth-Century Montreal* (1974; reprint, Montreal: McGill–Queen's University Press, 1992), 117, and especially "Trade Relations," 90–133.

20. Historian Leslie Choquette maintains that the men in New France were entrepreneurial but that, following the conquest of Canada, British land policies and a declining market transformed the French into peasants, in her *Frenchmen into Peasants* (Cambridge: Harvard University Press, 1997). For a detailed description of the conquest of Canada see Fred Anderson's *Crucible of War: The Seven Years' War and the Fate of Empire in British North America, 1754–1766* (New York: Alfred A. Knopf, 2000), 325–72.

21. Jacqueline Peterson, "Prelude to Red River: A Social Portrait of the Great Lakes Métis," *Ethnohistory* (Winter 1978): 50.

22. "St. Joseph Register," *MVHR* 13: 212, 214, 218, 219, 224, 227, 238.

23. Readers familiar with French spelling and phonetics will often find that the spelling of some names appears non-standard and often varies among holders of the same name. These are not typographical errors but rather, an attempt to reproduce faithfully the spellings as given in the baptismal and marriage registers used in this research. This is done to facilitate further research into these families. Where possible, the *Dictionary of Canadian Biography* (University of Toronto Press) has been used to standardize spelling.

24. The first daughter, Marie Catherine, was born the day after her mother and father were married. She was baptized on January 13, 1731. Her godfather was the post commandant, Nicholas Coulon de Villiers, and her godmother Marie Catherine, of the Illinois nation ("St. Joseph Register," *MVHR* 13: 213). The second daughter Marie Esther (referred to as Marie Joseph Esther) was born sometime in 1733 and baptized one year later at Michilimackinac on January 1, 1734 ("Mackinac Baptisms," *WHC,* 19, 4). The third daughter, Marie Anne, was twenty-one months and eight days old at the time of her baptism at St. Joseph in April of 1740. Her godfather was also Nicholas Coulon de Villiers, the commandant, and her older sister, Marie Joseph Esther, her godmother ("St. Joseph Register," *MVHR* 13: 218). The fourth daughter, Marie Amable, was baptized at St. Joseph on July 27, 1740, by the post commandant de Villiers and, subsequently, by Father Lamorine on June 29, 1741. Her godparents were Claude Caron and Charlotte Robert, the wife of the post interpreter (ibid., 219). The fifth daughter was Angelique (Agathe), baptized in March of 1744. Her godfather was Monsieur de Lespiné de Villiers, a cadet in the marine detachment troops of the colony. Her godmother was her oldest sister, Marie Catherine (ibid., 221). Only after the birth of their last child, a son, would Madeleine deviate from this pattern when she chose a godfather with a Native mother. All five daughters took the first name of their mother Marie, a common baptismal name, and the five were distinguished by their second names. The daughters lived to maturity, but the son probably did not reach adulthood.

25. Variant spellings for L'archevêque include Larchesveque and Larche. Certificate, Montreal, signed de Villiers, July 18, 1745; *ANCol,* C[11]A, 117, 325. In 1741 Augustin L'archevêque contracted to hire canoemen to accompany him to Illinois Country. For engagements or contracts hiring canoemen at St. Joseph from 1722 to 1745, see *RAPQ,* 1929–30, 233–465.

26. "St. Joseph Register," *MVHR* 13: 213.

27. "St. Joseph Register," *MVHR* 13: 214.

28. The names of the priests who served at the St. Joseph mission are enumerated in the baptismal register (ibid., 203–4).

29. Two-year-old Augustin's godparents were Augustin Maras Langlade, Esquire, and Mlle. Bourassa, the elder (Marie Catherine de La Plante). See "Mackinac Register," *WHC,* 19, 24–25. Several signatures of witnesses are illegible, but those that are legible include members of both the Langlade and Bourassa families ("Mackinac Register," ibid., 18, 476).

30. The groom was Jean Baptiste Jutras (Joutras); the wedding took place at St. Ignace on July 7, 1748. Witnesses included Legardeur de St. Pierre Verchere, Bourassa, Langlade, and Charles Langlade (ibid., 18, 475).

31. The wedding of Marie Joseph Esther and Jacques Bariso de La Marche

took place at St. Ignace on August 2, 1748 (ibid., 476). In 1729, Jean Baptiste Réaume owed Charles Nolan La Marque 4,000 livres (in furs). See Idle, "Post of the St. Joseph," 185; *RAPQ*, 1929–1930, 244–408, passim. La Marche and La Marque were probably different spellings for the same surname, see note 23.

32. Eventually, Joseph Esther was widowed and then remarried. Of all the siblings, only she repeatedly reappeared in later written documents. Joseph Esther was twice widowed and, at the age of forty-six on June 8, 1779, she married Thomas M. Brady. He became the Indian agent at Cahokia. She had children and grandchildren living in Cahokia until well into the nineteenth century. Joseph Esther had four children baptized at St. Joseph. When a second son was born in 1752, she was living at Fort Pimiteoui (Peoria). In 1753 they took this child along with his elder brother to be baptized at St. Joseph. Esther's children included Etienne Joseph born in 1750, Louis born in 1752, Marie Joseph born in 1753, and Angelique born in 1756 (Webster and Krause, *French Fort Saint Joseph,* 114–15).

33. The Chevaliers were a large French family: There were at least sixteen children. Jean Baptiste Chevalier and his wife, Marie Françoise Alavoine, probably moved from Montreal to Michilimackinac in 1718. Baptismal registers at Michilimackinac provide information about eleven of the sixteen children born to Jean Baptiste Chevalier and Marie Françoise Alavoine. Five or six children were born at Montreal; eleven children were baptized at St. Ignace. The children born in Montreal included Marie Charlotte (1710), Marie Anne (1712), Catherine (1714, died 1714), Michel Jean Baptiste (1715, died young?), Marie Joseph (1718). The eleven children baptized at the St. Ignace Mission included Constance (1719), Louis Thérèse (1720), Marguerite Josephe (1723), Marie Madeleine (1724), Anne Charlotte Véronique (1726), Charles (1727, died young?), Joseph Maurice (1728), Louis Paschal (1730), Anne Thérèse Esther (1732), Angélique (1733), and Luc (1735).

This source for this information is John M. Gram's unpublished paper, "The Chevalier Family and the Demography of the Upper Great Lakes," completed for the Mackinac Island Park Commission, Lansing, Michigan. It appears to provide the most accurate geneaological information on the Chevalier family. Gram contends that there were two Louis Chevaliers within one family. The father was Jean Baptiste Chevalier, who sired sixteen children and named two of his sons Louis Chevalier. Both sons were born at Michilimackinac: Louis Thérèse in 1720 and Louis Pascal in 1730. According to John Gram's research, it was Louis Thérèse who married Marie Madeleine Réaume L'archêveque. Gram's research is supported by documentation in French geneaological sources: Rene Jetté, *Dictionnaire généalogique des families du Québec* (Montreal: University of Montreal Press, 1983) and Cyprien Tanguay, *Dictionnaire généalogique des families canadiennes depuis la foundation de la colonie jusqu'au nos jours,* 7 vols. (Montreal: Senecal, 1871–90; reprint, New York, 1969). A more widely used but less accurate source on Fort St. Joseph is Mildred Webster and Frederick Krause's *French Fort Saint Joseph* (see note 3). They list a third Louis Chevalier, born to the elder Jean Baptiste Chevalier when he resided in Montreal in 1712. However, the existence of this Louis Chevalier cannot be documented in the original French sources. The privately printed *French Fort Saint Joseph* does not provide documentation through footnotes and identifies only two primary sources as the basis for its information, the "St. Joseph Register" and the *Jesuit Relations and Allied Documents*. This discrepancy is problematic because it creates an obvious age disparity between Marie Madeleine and Louis Chevalier at the time of their marriage; she was forty-one and he was perhaps ten years younger. This problem is then further complicated by a 1780 petition filed by Louis Chevalier when he sought reimbursement from the British for the goods he had forfeited through forced removal. In that 1978 petition, he listed himself as sixty-eight years of age and his wife as seventy. That petition would indicate a birthdate of 1712, but this information is contradicted by the birth of Marie Anne, Louis' sister, in 1712. "Petition of Louis Chevallier," *Michigan Pioneer and Historical Collections,* 40 vols. (Lansing, 1877–1929) 10: 438–40.

34. Louis Chevalier was born in October 1751 and baptized by his uncle, Louis Pascal Chevalier. In April 1752, he was baptized by the priest Father DuJaunay. His godfather was his oldest stepsister's husband, Joutras, and his godmother was another stepsister, Madeleine Chevalier ("St. Joseph Register," *MVHR* 13: 223).

35. Webster and Krause, *French Fort Saint Joseph,* 113. Louis Chevalier's son, Amable, was raised among the Odawa. Like his father he married an Odawa woman and their children were baptized at Michilimackinac ("Mackinac Register," *WHC,* 19, 93, 95).

36. In 1718 Governor Vaudreuil issued six *congés* for the St. Joseph post. Jean Baptiste Chevalier, Louis's father, received a permit for a canoe with two crewmen and himself. *Congés* granted in 1717 and 1718 are linked to the letter from Vaudreuil and Bégon dated November 11, 1718; *ANCol,* C[11]A, 38, 85–88[VO;] *RAPQ,* 1929–30, 278; also see John M. Gram's "The Chevalier Family and the Demography of the Upper Great Lakes," an unpublished paper in the archives of the Mackinac Island State Park Commission, Lansing, Mich.

The reimbursement records from the post commandant to Deshêtres were for his work as a blacksmith. Charlotte Chevalier Deshêtres lived at St. Joseph with her family for over twenty years. Charlotte first appeared as a godmother at the St. Joseph mission in 1730 ("St. Joseph Register," *MVHR* 13: 213). Charlotte and Antoine Deshêtres moved to Detroit sometime in 1750 or 1751 (Webster and Krause, *French Fort Saint Joseph,* 118–19).

37. "St. Joseph Register," *MVHR* 13: 213–14.

38. Marie Magdelaine L'archevêque appears to have been one of Madeleine's daughters, but this cannot be confirmed by the baptismal registers. Louis Pascal was baptized at Michilimackinac on July 22, 1730. He died before January 1, 1779. Louis Paschal and his wife had four children baptized at St. Joseph between 1758 and 1773. See ibid., 223 n. 38; *WHC,* 18, 490; ibid., 19, 3; Webster and Krause, *French Fort Saint Joseph,* 120–21.

39. The Chevaliers were partners, but they were not related. Charles Lhullic dit Chevalier's trading partner now became his stepfather-in-law. Charles and Angelique were married at St. Joseph, and three of their children were baptized there. Chevalier died in 1773, at about sixty-four. His death was the last entry in the "St. Joseph Baptismal Register." See Webster and Krause, *French Fort Saint Joseph,* 115–17; Idle, "Post of the St. Joseph," 253–54 n. 104; "St. Joseph Register," *MVHR* 13: 230.

40. The register does not mention the marriage of Anne L'archevêque and Augustin Gibault; however, when she served as godmother to the daughter of her sister Marie Joseph in 1756, she was identified as Anne L'archevêque, and by 1758, she was identified as the wife of Gibault ("St. Joseph Register," *MVHR* 13: 228, 230).

41. Marie Amable married Jean Baptiste François Lonval. Lonval's ties were to the fur trade community at Trois Rivières. The Longvals settled in Cahokia where they appear on the 1787 Cahokia census. See Webster and Krause, *French Fort Saint Joseph,* 117–18; "St. Joseph Register," *MVHR* 13: 231, 233–34.

42. Gram, "Chevalier Family," 10; Natalie Maree Belting, *Kaskaskia Under the French Regime* (Urbana: University of Illinois Press, 1948), 118; Margaret C. Norton, "Cahokia Marriage Records," *Illinois Libraries* 28 (1936): 260–72, especially 268.

43. Marthe Faribault-Beauregard, *La population des forts français d'Amérique,* vol. 2 (Montreal, 1948); Frederick Billon, *Annals of St. Louis in Its Early Days under the French and Spanish Dominations, 1764–1804* (1886; reprint, New York: Arno Press, 1971), 20.

44. Both Joseph Esther's and Marie Amable's children were baptized at the Fort St. Joseph mission. Four of Esther's children were baptized here. In 1753, her sister Catherine was the godmother to her sixteen-month-old son, Louis, and to her three-year-old son, Etiennne Joseph. Esther's sister Anne was the godmother to Esther's three-year-old daughter, Marie Joseph, and in 1756, Esther's sister Magdaleine was the godmother to her five-month-old daughter, Angelique ("St. Joseph Baptismal Register," *MVHR* 13: 225, 225–26, 228.) In 1761, Amable's two-month-old daughter was baptized at St. Joseph (ibid., 233–34).

45. For a parallel figure, see James H. Merrell's description of Andrew Montour, son of Madame Montour and also an interpreter and go-between in "'The Cast of His Countenance': Reading Andrew Montour," in *Through a Glass Darkly: Reflections on Personal Identity in Early America,* ed. Ronald Hoffman, Mechal Sobel, and Fredrika J. Teute (Chapel Hill: University of North Carolina Press, 1997), 13–39; Nancy Hagedorn, "'Faithful, Knowing, and Prudent': Andrew Montour as Interpreter and Cultural Broker, 1740–1772," in *Between Indian and White Worlds: The Cultural Broker,* ed. Margaret C. Szasz (Norman: University of Oklahoma Press, 1994), 44–60; Jon Parmenter, "Isabel Montour: Cultural Broker on the Frontiers of New York and Pennsylvania," in *The Human Tradition in Colonial America,* ed. Ian K. Steele and Nancy L. Rhoden (Wilmington: Scholarly Resources, 1999), 141–59.

46. For the Detroit settlement plan, see Lionel Grouls, *Roland-Michel Barrin de La Galissoniére, 1696–1756* (Toronto: University of Toronto Press, 1970); Etienne Taillemite, "Roland-Michel Barrin de La Galissonière, *Dictionary of Canadian Biography* (Toronto: University of Toronto Press, 1966) 3, 32–36. (Hereafter cited as *DCB.*)

47. The term "baptized conditionally" appears frequently in baptismal registers and indicates that a child had previously received lay baptism when a priest was unavailable. For an explanation of the term "baptized conditionally," see "The Mackinac Register, 1696–1821: Register of Baptisms of the Mission of St. Ignace de Michilimakinak," *WHC,* 19, 7 n. 25.

48. "St. Joseph Register," *MVHR* 13, 218, 238. Marie Jeanne is identified in

the register as Panis. The Indian slaves who resided in Indian villages were called *Panis* by the French. This term was probably derived from Pawnee and was applied to Indians captured from west of the Mississippi and traded to towns and villages east of the river. Helen Hornbeck Tanner, *Atlas of Great Lakes Indian History* (Norman: University of Oklahoma Press, 1987), 4.

49. The numeral 8 appears throughout the "St. Joseph Baptismal Register" as the phonetic equivalent for the parts of Native American languages that were not spelled in French. Š was a digraph or shorthand for *ou*. Pierre Mekbibkas8nga's godfather was Marin de la Perriere and his godmother was Madeleine de Villiers, de la Perriere's wife. Pierre's wife Marie's godfather was Louis Metivier, a master carpenter, and the godmother, Marie Fafard, his wife. Five years later Marie, Pierre's wife, died (ibid., 221–22).

50. On April 22, 1752, one of Pierre and Marie's daughters, 8abak8ik8e, was baptized. She was about thirty-five years old and took the name Marie as her Christian name. Louis Chevalier signed as the godfather. On May 1, 1752, three more of their daughters were baptized; one was twenty-six or twenty-seven, the second was twenty-five, and the third was fifteen or sixteen. The eldest, a widow and identified as Temagas8kia, took the name of Marguerite. Her godmother was Marguerite of the Saki nation. Both the other daughters elected Marie Madeleine Réaume Chevalier as their godmother. The middle daughter was identified as being married to Pi8assin, who was listed as still unconverted. The youngest daughter took the name Suzanne (ibid., 222–23).

51. The prolonged absence of priests at frontier missions led lay Catholics and even non-Catholics to perform baptisms. Priests were only intermittently assigned to the St. Joseph mission but did serve continuously from 1750 to 1761. At other times, the post was reliant on the missionary priests assigned to Illinois Country—who generally resided at either Cahokia or Kaskaskia. Growth of the frontier Catholic Church was thwarted in 1762 when the French government decreed the secularization of the Jesuits. The Supreme Council of New Orleans put the decree into effect on July 3, 1763. Father Meurin was allowed to remain in Illinois Country at Ste. Genevieve on the Spanish side of the river. Priests from other orders served at the St. Joseph mission in 1761, 1768, and in 1773. A new missionary priest, Father Gibault, was assigned to Illinois Country in 1773. See ibid., 204–5; and George Paré, *The Catholic Church in Detroit, 1701–1888* (Detroit: Wayne State University Press, 1951), 78–103.

52. Idle, "Post of the Saint Joseph River," 182; *RAPQ*, 1929–1930, 233–465.

53. Gram, "The Chevalier Family," 1.

54. Native American women in the St. Joseph River valley were subsequently identified in French archival records by their Christian names. Unless their baptisms were recorded, we are unable to distinguish Native Americans from Frenchwomen. In the St. Joseph Baptismal Register the priests recorded Native American names as well as Christian names only at the time of baptism. It is difficult to discern the origins of baptismal sponsors unless they themselves had been baptized at St. Joseph.

55. William B. Hart, "Black 'Go-Betweens' and the Mutability of Race, Status, and Identity on New York's Pre-Revolutionary Frontier," in *Contact Points: American Frontiers from the Mohawk to the Mississippi, 1750–1830*, ed. Andrew R. L.

Cayton and Fredrika J. Teute, (Chapel Hill: University of North Carolina Press, 1998), 93, 88, 92. Hart's use of the term "situational ethnicity" is defined by Anya Peterson Royce, *Ethnic Identity: Strategies of Diversity* (Bloomington, Ind. 1982), 202–15.

56. Jane T. Merritt explores the use of kinship terms as a way that Indians and whites communicated. She contends that metaphoric kinship terms were used to explain political relationships and conveyed "the role and responsibilities of each party." See her "Metaphor, Meaning, and Misunderstanding: Language and Power on the Pennsylvania Frontier," in *Contact Points,* 73–74.

57. Jacqueline Peterson, "The People in Between: Indian–White Marriage and the Genesis of a Métis Society and Culture in the Great Lakes Region, 1680–1830" (Ph.D. diss., University of Illinois at Chicago Circle, 1981), 139–41; R. David Edmunds, "'Unacquainted with the laws of the civilized world': American Attitudes toward the Métis Communities in the Old Northwest," in *The New Peoples: Being and Becoming Métis in North America,* ed. Jacqueline Peterson and Jennifer S. H. Brown (Manitoba: University of Manitoba Press, 1985), 187–88; Tanis C. Thorne, *The Many Hands of My Relations* (Columbia: University of Missouri Press, 1996), 93–96.

58. Peter Lawrence Scanlan, *Prairie du Chien: French, British, American* (Menasha, Wis.: Collegiate Press / G. Banta Pub. Co., 1937), 237–45. Also see Elizabeth Mason and Adele Rahn, "Web of Power in the Fur Trade of the Old Southwest—A Genealogical Approach," a paper presented at the Fifth North American Fur Trade Conference, Montreal, Canada, 1985.

59. R. W. Brisbois, "Recollections of Prairie du Chien," *WHC,* 9, 291–92. The land claims associated with Jean Marie Cardinal also appear in the following volumes/pages of the *American State Papers: Documents legislative and executive of the congress of the United States from the first session of the first congress to the third session of the thirteenth congress inclusive,* ed. Walter Lowrie and Matthew St. Clair Clark (Washington, D.C.: 1832–1861), 2, 712, 714; 5, 309, 310, 327, 329; 8, 63.

60. The conquest of Canada, when the French surrendered to the British at Montreal and Quebec, marked the end of the Seven Years' War in North America. However, the conflict continued in Europe. The French defeat stemmed from a larger conflict over military policy that focused on how New France was best defended. The governor-general of Canada, marquis de Vaudreuil, believed that the best defense relied on wilderness warfare and that successful opposition to the British rested on France's allies in the *pays d'en haut.* Vaudreuil openly opposed the planned defense of Canada by the marquis de Montcalm. Montcalm's plans were endorsed by the French court and decided the fate of the colony. Historian Fred Anderson indicates that Vaudreuil exhibited "a guerilla conception of defense, for it rested upon his confidence that although the British might conquer territory, they could never hold it so long as Canada's French and Indian peoples remained united and capable of resisting in the interior. The true security of New France therefore lay in keeping open communication with the interior. . . . Montcalm had seen matters in almost exactly the opposite way. As a conventionally minded European professional officer, he thought it suicidal to dissipate the forces available for defense by holding western posts. In

his view the only key to Canada was the city of Québec." Anderson, *Crucible of War*, 346.

Chapter 4. British Governance in the Western Great Lakes

1. Paul Chrisler Phillips, *The Fur Trade* (Norman: University of Oklahoma Press, 1961), 2, 550–66.

2. Fort St. Joseph was located close to present-day Niles, Michigan. Recent attempts to fund renewed excavations at its site have so far been unsuccessful. See "Grant Denied for New St. Joseph Dig," *South Bend Tribune*, October 20, 1999, section D4. Well before the onset of the French and Indian War, there was no longer a military presence at Fort St. Joseph. The last effective commandant, François Marie Picote, Sieur de Bellestre, was appointed to the St. Joseph post in 1747. He was rarely present, for his skill as a negotiator entailed frequent and extended appearances in Detroit and Montreal. In 1757, the stepson of the Governor-General of New France, Marquis de Vaudreuill, became the last commandant. But Louis de Varier, stayed less than two years; he had left by 1759. See Ralph Ballard, *Old Fort Saint Joseph* (Berrien Springs, Mich.: Hardscrabble Books, 1973), 25–26.

3. The active involvement of fort commandants in the fur trade was openly acknowledged by New France officials and relied on legally recognized partnerships with Montreal merchants. See Royal Memoir to Beauharnois and Hocquart, Fontainebleau, April 30, 17421, *ANCol*, series B, 74–2, 392–442; *AnCol*, series C[11]A, 125, 446–49[vo] (see chap. 3, note 8).

4. New France governors authorized permissions that sent three to five canoes a year to each commandant from Montreal. The permissions granted for the St. Joseph River post are listed by year and by grantees. See *RAPQ, 1920 to 1941–1942, 1921–1922*, 1943, 219 passim. The government did not stipulate the size of the canoes, and commandants stood to reap a handsome profit from their appointment. Seventeenth-century permissions were based on three-man canoes, but canoe size increased measurably during the eighteenth century. By 1740, crews consisted of four, or even five or six men. Occasionally nine- or ten-men crews headed westward to trade. The canoes were outfitted with trade merchandise from the warehouses of Montreal merchants.

5. The Peace of Utrecht brought an end to Queen Anne's War (1703–1713). Intent on retaining control over their interior French sea, New France subverted the free trade provision of the Peace of Utrecht, which had declared the Great Lakes an area of free trade.

6. Pierre François Xavier de Charlevoix, *Histoire et description générale de la Nouvelle France, avec le journal historique d'un voyage fait par ordre du roi dans l'Amérique Septentrionale*, vol. 3 (Paris: n. p., 1744), 312.

7. The house was constructed shortly before the British took over Fort St. Joseph. The post interpreter, Pierre Deneau dit Detailly, submitted a claim for 1,000 livres for building a house for a medal chief. Certificate, St. Joseph, April 30, 1760, Archives Nationales, v[7], 345–99. (Hereafter referred to as AN.)

8. A similar multicultural community was located along The Glaize, an old buffalo wallow on the Maumee River about fifty miles southwest of present-day

Toledo, Ohio. These Indian towns and trading communities, more recent than Fort St. Joseph, still attest to the close ties that developed between Indians and Frenchmen. See Helen Hornbeck Tanner, "The Glaize in 1792: A Composite Indian Community," *Ethnohistory* 25 (Winter 1978): 15–39; reprinted in *American Encounters: Natives and Newcomers from European Contact to Indian Removal, 1500–1850,* ed. Peter C. Mancall and James H. Merrell (New York: Routledge, 2000), 404–25.

9. Merchants remained resident in Montreal and incurred the debts for outfitting the canoes with merchandise as well as canoemen. Engagements or contracts hiring canoemen, 1722–1745, are found in *RAPQ,* 1929–1930, 233–65.

10. Bruce M. White, "Montreal Canoes and Their Cargoes," in *Le Castor Fait Tout: Selected Papers of the Fifth North American Fur Trade Conference,* ed. Bruce G. Trigger, Toby Morantz, and Louise Dechêne (Montreal: Lake St. Louis Historical Society, 1987), 184, 164–92.

According to Louise Dechêne, *coureurs de bois* appeared after 1665, voyageurs after 1681, and *engagés* after 1700. A small nucleus of voyageurs, however, continued to exist in the eighteenth century; these were men whose sole occupation was the fur trade. See Louise Dechêne, *Habitants and Merchants in Seventeenth-Century Montreal* (1974; reprint, Montreal: McGill–Queen's University Press, 1992), 93–96. For a description of the *engagés* during the first half of the eighteenth century, see Thomas Buckley's "Fur Trade *Engagés,* 1701–1745," in *Rendezvous: Selected Papers of the Fourth North American Fur Trade Conference, 1981,* ed. Thomas C. Buckley (St. Paul, Minn.: North American Fur Trade Conference, 1984), 15–26; Grace Lee Nute, *The Voyageur* (1931; reprint, St. Paul: Minnesota Historical Society, 1955), 27, 27–28, 50–52.

11. The village of L'Arbe Croche was indicative of the type of indigenous community that prospered near fur trade forts. "They raised large surpluses of corn and vegetables, produced fish and later maple sugar, and manufactured canoes, snowshoes, and clothing essential to the Great Lakes fur trade." See James M. McClurken, "Augustin Hamlin, Jr., Ottawa Identity and the Politics of Persistence," in James A. Clifton, *Being and Becoming Indian* (Prospect Heights, Ill.: Waveland Press, 1989), 85.

12. James A. Clifton, *The Prairie People: Continuity and Change in Potawatomi Indian Culture, 1665–1965* (Lawrence: Regents' Press of Kansas, 1977), 101–2; Emily J. Blasingham, "The Depopulation of the Illinois Indians," part 2, *Ethnohistory* (Fall 1956): 384–85.

13. The exchange of presents was surrounded by ceremony and expressed friendship, goodwill, and sympathy. Abraham Rotstein has argued that Indian trade was a means of reaffirming political alliances, in "Trade and Politics: An Institutional Approach," *Western Canadian Journal of Anthropology* 3 (1972): 1–28. Both Arthur J. Ray and Donald B. Freeman, however, find only limited evidence that gift exchanges with traders transformed them into political or military allies, in "*Give Us Good Measure*": *An Economic Analysis of Relations between the Indians and the Hudson's Bay Company before 1763* (Toronto: University of Toronto Press, 1978). Also see Daniel Francis and Toby Morantz, *Partners in Furs: A History of the Fur Trade in Eastern James Bay 1600–1870* (Montreal: McGill–Queen's University Press, 1983), 46–47.

14. Richard White indicates that the wampum belts that circulated prior to Pontiac's Rebellion came from four different sources and that those that originated from Illinois Country and Montreal were French in origin. Richard White, *The Middle Ground: Indians, Empires, and Republics in the Great Lakes Region, 1650–1815* (New York: Cambridge University Press, 1991), 276.

15. Ibid., 269–314; Charles E. Cleland, *Rites of Conquest: The History and Culture of Michigan's Native Americans* (Ann Arbor: University of Michigan Press, 1992), 128–32; Nelson Vance Russell, *The British Régime in* Michigan and the Old Northwest, 1760–1796 (Northfield, Minn. Carleton College, 1939), 11–30; Michael N. McConnell, *A Country Between: The Upper Ohio Valley and Its Peoples, 1724–1774* (Lincoln: University of Nebraska Press, 1992), 175–206; Howard H. Peckham, *Pontiac and the Indian Uprising* (1947; reprint, Detroit: Wayne State University Press, 1994). Sir Guy Carlton described the French interaction with the Indians as highly personalized: "The System pursued by the French Government in Indian Affairs, was mostly according to the Discretion of Their Officers, who learned the language of the Natives, acted as Magistrates, compelled the traders to deal equitably and distributed the King's presents. . . . Thus managing them by Address, where Force could not avail, they reconciled them . . . without giving offense." National Archives of Canada, Q, V, part 1, 383. The National Archives of Canada, formerly the Public Archives, contains transcripts and microfilm from French archives that pertain to Canada. For a guide to the collections see Alan Delvauz, *Public Archives Library* (Ottawa: Public Archives Canada, 1983). (Hereafter cited as Canadian Archives).

16. Letter, Turnbull to Gage, July 5, 1772, in Papers of Thomas Gage, William Clements Library, University of Michigan, Ann Arbor. (Hereafter referred to as Gage Papers.)

17. Louison Chevalier probably refers to the father, not the son. Henry Bassett to Thomas Gage, December 24, 1772, in *The Papers of Sir William Johnson*, ed. Alexander C. Flick (Albany: The University of the State of New York, 1933), 8, 672–73.

18. "Speech of Four Indian Chiefs," May 22, 1773, ibid., 803–6.

19. For a detailed description of Fort St. Joseph as a military post under the French, see Dunning Idle, "The Post of the St. Joseph River during the French Regime, 1679–1761" (Ph.D. diss., University of Illinois, 1946). Information on the fort can also be found in Ralph Ballard, *Old Fort Saint Joseph;* (Berrien Springs, Mich.: Hard Scrabble Books, 1973); Gérard Malchelosse, "Genealogy and Colonial History: The St. Joseph River Post, Michigan," *French Canadian and Acadian Genealogical Review,* nos. 3–4 (1979): 173–209; Mildred Webster and Fred Krause, *French Fort Saint Joseph: De la Poste de la Rivière St. Joseph, 1690–1780* (pp., 1990).

20. Major Henry Bassett served as commanding officer at Detroit from 1772 until 1774. For a list of Detroit commandants, see Russell, *British Régime in Michigan,* 292. Major Henry Bassett to Gen. Frederick Haldiman, April 29, 1773, Haldimand Papers *Michigan Pioneer and Historical Collections,* 40 vols. (Lansing Mich., 1877–1929) 19: 297. (Hereafter referred to as *MPHC.*)

21. The original of the 1762 census is from the Burton Historical Collection. A 1768 census taken by Philip De Jean was enclosed in a letter dated Febru-

ary 23, 1768, from the Detroit Commandant George Turnbull to General Thomas Gage, and the original is in the Gage Papers at the Clements Library. The census completed by Governor Henry Hamilton listed female slaves at 78 and male slaves at 79. The 1765 census has been published in the *Detroit Society for Genealogical Research Magazine* 43: 19–26; Statistical Series, *Illinois Census Returns 1810–1818,* Statistical Series 2, *CISHL* 24: xxi–xxx; Census Tables for the French Colony of Louisiana from 1969 through 1732, ix–xxix, comp. Charles R. Maduell, Jr. (Baltimore, 1972), 150–63; *MPHC* 10: 446.

22. Traditional societies operate in what Marcel Mauss has described as a gift economy. The obligation to give, to receive, and to reciprocate is explained by him in *The Gift: The Form and Reason for Exchange in Archaic Societies* (New York: W. W. Norton, 1990).

23. For descriptions of Pontiac's Rebellion, see Howard Peckham, *Pontiac and the Indian Uprising* (1947; reprint, Detroit: Wayne State University Press, 1994); Ian K. Steele, *Warpath: Invasions of North America* (New York: Oxford, 1994), 237–42; Cleland, *Rites of Conquest,* 134–43; White, *Middle Ground,* 269–314; Gregory Evans Dowd, "The French King Wakes Up in Detroit: Pontiac's War in Rumor and History," *Ethnohistory* 37 (Summer 1990): 254–78; and idem *A Spirited Resistance: The North American Indian Struggle for Unity, 1735–1815* (Baltimore: Johns Hopkins University Press, 1992).

For a description of these events at St. Joseph, see Joseph L. Peyser, ed., *Letters from New France: The Upper Country, 1686–1783* (Urbana: University of Illinois Press, 1992), 215–16; Ballard, *Fort St. Joseph,* 44–46.

24. Johnson to Gage, May 3, 1764, Gage Papers, AS, 18.

25. Ida Amanda Johnson, *The Michigan Fur Trade* (1919: reprint, Grand Rapids, Mich.: Black Letter Press, 1971), 76.

26. Gladwin to Amherst, July 8, 1763, Gage Papers, W. O. 34/49, 196–99.

27. Instructions for Col. Bradstreet, April 2, 1764, enclosed in Gage to Bradstreet, April 2, 1764, ibid., 16.

28. Jack M. Sosin, *Whitehall and the Wilderness: The Middle West in British Colonial Policy, 1760–1775* (Lincoln: University of Nebraska Press, 1961), 73–78.

29. Carlton to Shelbourne, March 2, 1768, Canadian Archives, Q, V, part. i, 383.

30. From Lt. Campbell Commanding at Detroit to Gage, April 10, 1766, Ayers Manuscript Collections, Newberry Library, Chicago, #308.

31. There are numerous examples of these petitions. Canadian Archives, Q, 8, 133.

32. Beaver pelts exported from Canada in 1764 totaled £17,259, and by 1768 exports had decreased to £13,168. See Clarence Edwin Carter, *Great Britain and the Illinois Country, 1763–1774* (Washington, D.C.: American Historical Association, 1910), 94; Carter calculated the annual value of furs exported from the colonies to Great Britain alone as follows:

1764	£28,067/18
1765	£27,801/11
1766	£24,657/0
1767	£20,262/2
1768	£18,923/18

33. The fur trader George Croghan wrote Gage that the furs worth £80,000 were being shipped to New Orleans. Croghan to Gage, January 16, 1767, Shelburne Papers, William L. Clements Library, University of Michigan, Ann Arbor.

34. Turnbull to Croghan, March 1, 1768, and Jehu Hay to Croghan, February 19, 1768, in Croghan, April 14, 1768, Gage Papers, AS, 76; and Turnbull to Gage, February 23, 1768, Gage Papers, AS, 74. Also see Fr. Hamback Account against Louis Chevalier, 1763, in William Edgar Correspondence and Papers, MS., William Edgar, R2, 1750–1775, Burton Historical Collection, Detroit Public Library.

35. From Lt. Campbell Commanding at Detroit to Gage, April 10, 1766. Ayers Manuscript Collection, #308.

36. Turnbull to Gage, Gage Papers, July 5, 1772.

37. A description of British merchant involvement in the fur trade is given by Harry Duckworth in "British Capital in the Fur Trade: John Strettell and John Fraser," in *The Fur Trade Revisited: Selected Papers of the Sixth North American Fur Trade Conference, Mackinac Island, Michigan, 1991,* ed. Jennifer S. H. Brown, W. J. Eccles, and Donald P. Heldman (East Lansing, Mich.: Michigan State University Press, 1994), 39–56.

38. "An Account of the Number of Canoes gone out Wintering from the Post of Michilimackinac, Including the Names of Traders and those that are Bail for them. Also the Value of their Goods and where they are bound," reprinted by Charles E. Lart, ed., as "Fur-Trade Return, 1767," *Canadian Historical Review* 3 (1922): 351–58.

39. *The John Askin Papers,* ed. Milo M. Quaife (Detroit: Detroit Library Commission, 1902), 1: 12–13.

40. February 26, 1765, Sterling Letter Book, Burton Historical Collections, Detroit Public Library; *Askin Papers,* 1: 47 n. 29.

41. The rich fur trade lands of the Canadian Northwest eventually opened new avenues of interaction for the Interior French and British fur traders. The Great Lakes French and their Indian allies became the *engagés,* voyageurs, and canoemen for English traders, in a region where furs promised to be a valuable resource.

42. David A. Armour and Keith R. Widder, *At the Crossroads: Michilimackinac during the American Revolution* (Mackinac Island, Mich.: Mackinac Island Park Commission, 1978), 35.

43. Gladwin to Gage, June 7, 1764, Gage Papers, 19.

44. Turnbull to Gage, September 25, 1767, ibid., 70.

45. Lernoult to Haldimand, March 26, 1779, Haldiman Papers, *MPHC* 10: 328.

46. Captains Turnbull and Campbell, despite their occasional anti-French rhetoric, also proved more skilled at handling Indian affairs in the Great Lakes (Russell, *British Régime in Michigan,* 79).

47. Chevalier requested reimbursement for the following gifts presented to the Indians, on behalf of "His Britannique Majesty: 7 cotton shirts, a bundle bench lines, 2 dozen large knives, 5 pounds of nails, 2 dozen awls, 5 bags of wheat, 12 bags of wheat, 2 large fat pigs, 2 two year old bulls" (Haldimand Papers, *MPHC* 10: 405).

48. S. De Peyster to Gen. Haldimand, August 15, 1778, ibid., 9: 368.

49. Louis Chevallier to Major Arent S. De Peyster, September 15, 1778, ibid., 19: 352–53.

50. Mr. Chevallier to Major De Peyster, July 20, 1778, ibid., 10: 286–87.

51. To Mr. the Captain Langlade and the Lieut. Gautier from At. S. De Peyster, October 26, 1778, *Miscellanies By An English Officer: Arent Schuyler De Peyster,* ed. J. Watts De Peyster (Dumfries, Scotland: p. p., 1813), Appendix 72, no. 3.

52. Louis Chevallier to Gen. Frederick Haldimand, February 28, 1779, Haldimand Papers, *MPHC* 19: 375–76; Major Arent S. De Peyster to Gen. Frederick Haldimand, May 29, 1779, ibid., 425–26; From Mr. Chevalier Unaddressed, March 13, 1780, ibid., 10: 380–81.

53. A. S. De Peyster to Gen. Haldimand, August 15, 1778, ibid., 9: 368–69.

54. Louis Chevallier to Gen. Frederick Haldimand, February 29, 1779, ibid., 19: 375–76.

55. De Peyster to Sinclair, March 12, 1780, ibid., 9: 581.

56. De Peyster to Haldimand, October 1, 1780, ibid., 615–16.

57. Survey of the Settlement of Detroit Taken 31st March, 1779, ibid.: 10, 326; Russell, *British Régime in Michigan,* 84.

58. Keith R. Widder, "Effects of the American Revolution on Fur Trade Society at Michilimackinac," in Brown, Eccles, and Heldman, *Fur Trade Revisited,* 307.

59. Mr. Ainssé to Lieut. Gov. Sinclair, June 30, 1780; Memorial of Louis Joseph Ainssé, August 5, 1780, *MPHC* 13: 55–62; 10: 434–38.

60. The Hamelin family had children baptized at Fort St. Joseph in 1765, 1766, and 1767, and members of the Chevalier family had served as godparents. See "St. Joseph Register," ed. Rev. George Paré and M. M. Quaife, *MVHR* 13 (June 1925–March 1927): 235–36.

61. John Francis McDermott, ed., *Old Cahokia: A Narrative and Documents Illustrating the First Century of Its History* (St. Louis: St. Louis Historical Documents Foundation, 1949), 31, 128; Webster and Krause, *French Fort Saint Joseph,* 123; Idle, "Post of St. Joseph," 182, 188; Malchelosse, "Genealogy and Colonial History: St. Joseph River Post," 204–6; George Paré, *The Catholic Church in Detroit, 1701–1888* (Detroit: Wayne State University Press, 1951), 47.

62. Indian Council: At a Council Held at Detroit, 11th March, 1781, with the Pottewatimies from St. Joseph, Terre Coupé, and Couer de Cerf, Haldimand Papers, *MPHC* 10: 453–55.

63. The attack was led by Eugène Pouré dit Beausoleil. The number of men who accompanied him varies in different historical accounts. Descriptions of the attack on and the destruction of Fort St. Joseph include A. P. Nasatir, "The Anglo-Spanish Frontier in the Illinois Country during the American Revolution, 1779–1783," *Illinois State Historical Society Journal* 21 (October 1928): 291–358; Clarence W. Alvord, "The Conquest of St. Joseph, Michigan, by the Spaniards in 1781," *Michigan History* (Lansing, Mich.: Michigan Department of State, 1930), 14: 398–414.

64. Indian Council, March 11, 1781, Haldimand Papers, *MPHC* 10: 453–54.

65. Necessary Part of the Councils Held by Mr. Bennet with the Potawatamies at St. Joseph, August 3, 1779, ibid., 9, 349–50.

66. Russell, *British Régime in Michigan,* 85.

67. De Peyster to Haldimand, January 26, 1782, Haldimand Papers, *MPHC,* 10: 548.

68. Letter of Lieut. Col. Bolton to Haldimand, March 24, 1779, ibid., 9: 428; Russell, *British Régime in Michigan,* 120.

69. Russell, *British Régime in Michigan,* 120; Claus Papers, Canadian Archives, 3, 181, Report for 1787, 206.

70. John D. Barnhart, *Henry Hamilton and George Rogers Clark in the American Revolution, with the Unpublished Journal of Lieutenant Governor Henry Hamilton* (Crawfordsville, Ind.: R. E. Banta, 1951), 115–16.

71. Tanis C. Thorne, *The Many Hands of My Relations: French and Indians on the Lower Missouri* (Columbia: University of Missouri Press, 1996), 68–97.

72. Carleton to Johnson, March 27, 1767, *MPHC,* 10, 222–24.

73. E. B. O'Callaghan, ed., *NYCD,* 2, 486.

74. Gage to Shelburne, February 22, 1767, Charles Clarence Carter, ed., *The Correspondence of General Thomas Gage with the Secretaries of State, 1763–1775,* 1 (1931; reprint, Hamden, Conn.: Archon Books, 1969), 121–22; Canadian Archives, Dartmouth Transcripts, 1765–1775, 61–62; *NYCD,* 2, 485.

75. John Preston Moore, "Anglo-Spanish Rivalry on the Louisiana Frontier, 1763–1768," in *The Spanish in the Mississippi Valley, 1762–1804,* ed. John Francis MeDermott (Urbana: University of Illinois Press, 1974), 84.

76. Haldimand to Gage, Pensacola, June 17, 1767, in *The New Régime, 1765–1767,* vol. 11, ed. Clarence Walworth Alvord and Clarence Edwin Carter, CISHL, 575.

77. De Peyster to Haldimand, June 1779, *WHC* 9: 131–32.

Chapter 5. Agriculture, Warfare, and Neutrality

1. Edward Countryman, "Indians, the Colonial Order, and the Social Significance of the American Revolution," *William and Mary Quarterly* 53 (April 1996): 354.

2. Helen Hornbeck Tanner has mapped the epidemic outbreaks among Great Lakes people from 1630 to 1830 in *The Atlas of Great Lakes Indian History* (Norman: University of Oklahoma Press, 1987), 169–74. Smallpox proved the most lethal disease, and many Indians who fought in the Seven Years War carried the disease home to their villages. James Merrell blamed smallpox, acquired by involvement in the Seven Years War, for the the decline of the Catawba, in *The Indians' New World: Catawbas and Their Neighbors from European Contact through the Era of Removal* (Chapel Hill: University of North Carolina Press, 1989), 192–96.

3. The last major smallpox outbreak was during Pontiac's Rebellion, when the English reportedly distributed virus-infected gifts, blankets and clothes—and even a handkerchief from a smallpox ward that carried the deadly virus back to the St. Joseph villages (Tanner, *Atlas of Great Lakes Indian History,* 170–73).

4. John Denis Haeger, *John Jacob Astor: Business and Finance in the Early Republic* (Detroit: Wayne State University Press, 1991), 70 and n. 6; John Inglis to

George Grenville, May 31, 1790, in Gordon Davidson, *The North West Company* (Berkeley: University of California Press, 1918), 272–74; Robert Hamilton, "Observations on the Trade of Upper Canada," September 24, 1798, *MPHC* 25: 202–5; "Memorial of Montreal Merchants—McTavish, Frobisher & Co., and Todd McGill & Co. to John Simcoe," December 9, 1791, ibid. 24: 338–42; Wayne Edson Stevens, *The Northwest Fur Trade, 1763–1800,* University of Illinois Studies in the Social Sciences 14 (Urbana: University of Illinois Press, 1928), 106 n. 48; E. E. Rich, *The History of the Hudson's Bay Company, 1670–1870,* 2 vols. (London: Hudson's Bay Record Society, 1958–1959), 2, 189; and D. G. Creighton, *The Commercial Empire of the St. Lawrence* (Toronto: Ryerson, 1937), 132–33.

5. "1777: Spanish Describe Tribesmen," *WHC* 18: 367.

6. Helen Hornbeck Tanner, "The Glaize in 1792: A Composite Indian Community," in *American Encounters: Natives and Newcomers from European Contact to Indian Removal, 1500–1850,* ed. Peter C. Mancall and James H. Merrell (New York: Routledge, 2000), 404–25.

7. Ronald J. Mason, *Rock Island: Historical Indian Archaeology in the Northern Lake Michigan Basin,* Midcontinental Journal of Archaeology (MCJA) Special Paper, No. 6 (Kent, Ohio: Kent State University Press, 1986); James A. Clifton, *The Prairie People: Continuity and Change in Potawatomi Indian Culture, 1665–1965* (Lawrence: Regents' Press of Kansas, 1977), 38.

8. Canoes had increased dramatically in size by the second quarter of the eighteenth century: "Canoes which held three men, required crews of five by 1725, and six or more after 1740," in Louise Dechêne, *Habitants and Merchants in Seventeenth Century Montreal* (Montreal: McGill–Queen's University Press, 1992), 95.

9. La Salle letter 1681, in Margry, *Découvertes et éstablissements* 1879, 2, 158; Abbé Bernou relation, ibid., 1, 542–43.

10. Frontenac to Pontchartrain, Quebec, October 10, 1698, *ANCol,* series 11A, 16, 50; Cadillac to Frontenac, October 10, 1698; "Cadillac Papers," *MPHC* 33: 94–96.

11. The archaeological record suggests that for Native people in the southern Great Lakes, agriculture was always a source of their food supply, even prior to the European arrival. At the precontact Dumaw Creek site in southwestern Michigan, Native people raised corn, beans, pumpkins, and sunflowers during the summer months. See R. L. Bettarel and H. G. Smith, *The Moccasin Bluff Site and the Woodland Cultures of Southwestern Michigan,* Anthropological Papers No. 49 (Ann Arbor, Mich.: Museum of Anthropology, 1973), 134–36; James E. Fitting and Charles E. Cleland, "Late Prehistoric Settlement in the Upper Great Lakes," *Ethnohistory* 16 (Fall 1969): 289–302; George I. Quimby, *Indian Culture and European Trade Goods: The Archaeology of the Historic Period in the Western Great Lakes Region* (Madison: University of Wisconsin Press, 1966); Clifton, *Prairie People,* 32–33. George I. Quimby, "The Dumaw Creek Site: A Seventeenth-Century Prehistoric Indian Village and Cemetery in Oceana County, Michigan," *Fieldiana: Anthropology,* vol. 56 (Chicago: Field Museum of Natural History, 1966), 83.

12. Odawa involvement as agricultural suppliers of the fur trade has been described by James M. McClurken; see his "Augustin Hamlin, Jr.: Ottawa Identity

and the Politics of Ottawa Persistence," in *Being and Becoming Indian,* ed. James A. Clifton (Prospect Heights, Ill.: Waveland Press, 1989), 82–111; also James M. McClurken, *Gah-Baeh-Jhagwah-Buk: The Way It Happened* (East Lansing: Michigan State University Museum, 1991).

13. In areas of established trade routes, settlers as well as traders depended on the Native Americans for food. This interdependency is explained in Daniel H. Usner, Jr., "The Frontier Exchange Economy of the Lower Mississippi Valley in the Eighteenth Century," *William and Mary Quarterly* 44 (April 1987): 175–92. See also Daniel H. Usner, Jr., *Indians, Settlers, and Slaves in a Frontier Exchange Economy: The Lower Mississippi before 1783* (Chapel Hill: University of North Carolina Press, 1992); Donald P. Heldman, "The French in Michigan and Beyond: An Archaeological View from Fort Michilimackinac toward the West," in *French Colonial Archaeology: The Illinois Country and the Western Great Lakes,* ed., John A. Walthall (Urbana: University of Illinois Press, 1991), 216.

14. "Memoir respecting the Indians between Lake Erie and the Mississippi, with remarks upon their territory, manners, habits, etc., October 30, 1718," in *NYCD,* 9, 890.

15. Father Gabriel Marest, S.J., returned to his Ilini mission from Michilimackinac and was happy to find that "there had been an abundant harvest of wheat and Indian corn." See Marest to Father Germon, S.J., in *Lettres Édifiantes et Curieuses* (Paris: Impr. de Bethune, 1829–1832), 226.

16. Pénicault's Relation, in Margry, *Découvertes et éstablissements,* (1876) part 5, 375–586; Father Gabriel Marest to Father Germon, *JR,* 66, 218–95; also in Father Watrin's summary of his work among the Kaskaskia, ibid., 70, 218–95.

17. "Memoir," *NYCD,* 9, 891.

18. Crooked Tree (L'Arbre Croche), an Odawa community opposite Michilimackinac, was provisioner of the fur trade and engaged in a symbiotic relationship with first, the French, and, later, the British. See McClurken,"Augustin Hamlin, Jr.," in Clifton, *Being and Becoming Indian,* 85.

19. Joseph Peyser, *Fort St. Joseph Manuscripts: Chronological Inventory and Translations* (City of Niles, [Mich.] and Joseph Peyser, 1978), 121, 104.

20. Hamilton to Germain, July 14, 1777, Canadian Archives, Q, 14, 94; Nelson Vance Russell, *The British Régime in Michigan and the Old Northwest, 1760–1796* (Northfield, Minn.: Carleton College, 1939), 120.

21. Burnett to Messrs. Innes and Grant, Sandwich, Canada, May 31, 1801, in *Letter Book of William Burnett,* ed. Wilbur M. Cunningham (n.p.: Fort Miami Heritage Society of Michigan, 1967), 143; *History of Berrien and Van Buren Counties, Michigan* (Philadelphia: D. W. Ensign & Co., 1880), 39.

22. "Petition of Louis Chevallier," Haldimand Papers, *MPHC* 13: 61.

23. Burnett to Tabeau, May 14, 1786; Burnett to Sayer, May 25, 1786, *Letter Book of William Burnett,* 1, 7.

24. Burnett to Sayer, St. Joseph, April 11, 1788, ibid., 29.

25. Burnett to Mr. Charles Patterson, Michilimackinac, St. Joseph, February 2, 1790, ibid., 34.

26. Ibid., 32–33.

27. *History of Berrien and Van Buren Counties, Michigan,* 39; Burnett to Messrs.

Innes and Grant, Sandwich, Canada, May 31, 1801, *Letter Book of William Burnett,* 143.

28. Bela Hubbard, "Ancient Garden Beds of Michigan," *MPHC* 2 (1880): 23.

29. Ibid., 22–23.

30. Ibid., 25; *Schoolcraft's Narrative Journal of Travels,* ed. Mentor L. Williams (East Lansing: Michigan State University Press, 1992), 204, 218.

31. *History of Hillsdale County, Michigan* (Philadelphia: Everts & Abbott, 1879), 36.

32. Hubbard, "Ancient Garden Beds," *MPHC* 2: 25.

33. A. H. Scott to Mr. Henry Bishop, St. Joseph, Michigan, January 9, 188[8?], published as an article entitled "Indians in Kalamazoo County," *MPHC* 10: 164; *History of Calhoun County, Michigan* (Philadelphia: L. H. Everts Co., 1887), 195; "The Indian Johnson and Some of the Potawatomi Bands to Which He Belonged," *MPHC* 10: 156.

34. *History of St. Joseph County, Michigan* (Philadelphia: L. H. Everts Co., 1877), 174.

35. Clark to Nanaquina, April 20, 1779, *Collections of the Illinois State Historical Society* (Springfield: H. W. Rokker Co., 1903–1975), 8, 313–15. (Hereafter referred to as *ISHS.*)

36. "Louis Chevallier to Gen. Frederick Haldimand, 28th Feb. 1779," Haldimand Papers, *MPHC* 19: 375.

37. De Peyster to Haldimand, October 24, 1778, and January 29, 1779, ibid., 9:374–76, 377–78.

38. Anthony F. C. Wallace, *The Death and Rebirth of the Seneca* (New York: Vintage, 1972), 150–54; Eric Hinderaker, *Elusive Empires: Constructing Colonialism in the Ohio Valley, 1673–1800* (New York: Cambridge University Press, 1997), 233–34. The colonial background of the Ohio River valley is explored by Michael N. McConnell in *A Country Between: The Upper Ohio River Valley and Its Peoples, 1724–1774* (Lincoln: University of Nebraska, 1992).

39. Helen Hornbeck Tanner has shown that the Indian villages around the base of Lake Michigan have always been characterized by a mixture of tribal people. See her "Tribal Mixtures in Chicago Area Indian Villages," in *Indians of the Chicago Area,* ed. Terry Strauss (Chicago: NAES [Native American Educational Services] College, 1989), 21–25. Pokagon, who figures prominantly in chap. 6, "Catholic Potawatomi and Resistance to Removal," was emblematic of this diversity; he was probably born into a Chippewa or Ottawa community and then incorporated into a Potawatomi community. See Clifton, *The Pokagons, 1683–1983* (Lanham, Md.: University Press of America, 1984), 57–58.

40. Gregory Evans Dowd, *A Spirited Resistance: The North American Indian Struggle for Unity, 1745–1815* (Baltimore: Johns Hopkins University Press, 1992), 106, 113.

41. Elmore Barce, *The Land of the Miamis* (Fowler, Ind.: Benton Review Shop, 1922), 42.

42. R. David Edmunds, *The Potawatomis: Keepers of the Fire* (Norman: University of Oklahoma Press, 1978), 132.

43. Richard White, *The Middle Ground: Indians, Empires, and Republics in the*

Great Lakes Region, 1650–1815 (New York: Cambridge University Press, 1991), 468.

44. Edmunds, *Potawatomis,* 132–33.

45. Ibid., 125; entries for March 9 to April 7, 1791, in "Journal of What Happened at the Miamis and the Glaize with the Ouias and Piccons," *MPHC* 24: 220–22; Reynolds, *Pioneer History of Illinois,* 175; Hamtramck to Sargent, Winthrop Sargent Papers, Massachusetts Historical Society, Boston (microfilm).

46. "The opposing groups were increasingly polarized, with anti-American tribesmen gravitating towards an affiliation with Tecumseh, but at least as many sitting by, taking no position, waiting for tensions to ease. This was particularly true of most Potawatomi village okamek, who found themselves trapped by the perennial problem of dissension among their young men, appeals for support by American agents, and threats coming from the prophet's camp. Few took a position of such open support of the Americans as did Winamek, who regularly served Harrison as messenger, spy, and advocate. Most adopted a stance of uncomfortable neutrality like that of Gomo in his village near Peoria on the Illinois River" (Clifton, *Prairie People,* 198).

47. Ibid., 213.

48. For a more detailed description of the witch-hunts that ensued under Tenskwatawa's direction, see Dowd, *A Spirited Resistance,* 136–39.

49. Barce, *Land of the Miamis,* 38.

50. Governor Ninian Edwards, Illinois Territory to Isaac Shelby, Kaskaskia, May 18, 1813, Ayers Collections Manuscripts, Newbury Library, Chicago, #401.

51. Tanner, *Atlas of Great Lakes,* 111.

52. Ibid., 112; Edmunds, *Potawatomis,* 201.

53. "Court of Inquiry: Proceedings of a Board of Inquiry held on the 5th of January 1815 and continued by adjournment to the 10th of the same month, at the Garrison of Fort McKay Prairie des Chiens in the conquered Countries pursuant to an order from Captn A. Bulger Royal New foundland Regt. Commanding on the Mississippi," *MPHC* 16: 32–33.

54. Chandonai and Kinzie captured three English traders. Chandonai was Burnett's clerk, and Kinzie was a trader Burnett supplied. Chandonai's name is also spelled Chandonnet and Chardronet; see Edmunds, *Potawatomis,* 201–2, and Wilbur M. Cunningham, *Land of Four Flags* (Grand Rapids, Mich.: Eerdmans Publishing, 1961), 94.

55. "Court of Inquiry: Proceedings of a Court of Inquiry held by order of His Excellency, Major General Sir F. P. Robinson, K.C.B. Commanding in Upper Canada & Administering the Government thereof. Fort Drummond, 10 October 1815," *MPHC* 16: 327–34.

56. Clifton, *Prairie People,* 215.

57. Cunningham, *Land of Four Flags,* 90.

58. Clifton, *Prairie People,* 212.

59. Charles J. Kappler, comp. and ed., *Indian Treaties 1778–1883* (1904; reprint, New York: Interland Publishing Co., 1904), 105.

60. Tanner, *Atlas of Great Lakes,* 119.

61. Ida Amanda Johnson, *The Michigan Fur Trade* (1919; reprint, Grand Rapids, Mich.: Black Letter Press, 1971), 99–100; *Letterbook of William Burnett,* iii.

62. *Letterbook of William Burnett,* vi.

63. Kakima's baptismal name was Angelique, and she and William Burnett were married by the Reverend Father Levadoux in Detroit in 1782. Although it cannot be confirmed, her Potawatomi name was commonly believed to mean "one who steals away." Burton Collection, MS 929.2, Detroit Public Library. See also *Letterbook of William Burnett,* vi.

64. William Burnett to Mr. Charles Patterson, Michilimackinac, St. Joseph, February 2, 1790, *Letter Book of William Burnett,* 32; also see Bert Anson, "The Fur Traders in Northern Indiana" (Ph.D. diss., Indiana University, 1953), 73.

65. Burnett to Andrew Todd, St. Joseph, February 10, 1792, *Letter Book of William Burnett,* 52.

66. Burnett's national origins cannot be confirmed. Some writers state that Burnett came from New Jersey, but Hurlbut refers to him as "William Burnett, the Scotchman." See Cunningham, *Land of Four Flags,* 89, and Henry H. Hurlbut, *Chicago Antiquities* (Chicago: p. p., 1880), 75.

67. Cunningham, *Land of Four Flags,* 93.

68. John Kinzie, the more prominent trader, had lived and traded at St. Joseph, and he was outfitted by William Burnett.

69. Inventory Sale of Property, Sold by Point Sable to Jean Lalime, September 18, 1800, Du Sable Collection, Chicago Historical Society, Chicago.

70. Du Sable retired from the trade and took up residence with his daughters in Ste. Genevieve, where he claimed lands based on his military involvement in the war. He lived out the rest of his life in that community and died peaceably in old age.

71. In 1764, almost two thousand mixed-ancestry French crossed the river and resettled at St. Louis, many believing St. Louis still to be under French control. Most settled into a series of villages on the St. Louis periphery and followed the pattern of intermarriage between Native women and fur traders that was common east of the Mississippi. See *CA,* Dartmouth Transcripts, 1765–1775, 223–24; John Anthony Caruso, *The Mississippi Valley Frontier* (Indianapolis: Bobbs-Merrill, 1966), 331; Auguste Chouteau, "Journal of the Founding of St. Louis," in *Missouri Historical Society Collections,* 3 (1911), 352; and Tanis C. Thorne, *The Many Hands of My Relations* (Columbia: University of Missouri Press, 1996), 71–72.

72. Joseph Bertrand was the son of Joseph Laurent Bertrand, a fur trader at Michilimackinac, and of a mixed-ancestry woman. The "Mackinac Register" records his birth as occurring on October 8, 1779, and his baptism on July 20, 1786. "The Mackinac Register, 1695–1821: Register of Baptism of the Mission of St. Ignace de Michilimakinak," *WHC* 19, 83. See also the Appendix: "Family Tree 1," in Gladys Moeller, *Joseph Bertrand, Sr., His Ancestors, His Descendants* (Kansas: p.p., 1980, a copy is in the Archives of St. Mary's College, South Bend, Ind.) Orville W. Coolidge, *A Twentieth-Century History of Berrien County, Michigan* (Chicago: Lewis Publishing Co., 1906), 207.

73. Cunningham, *Land of Four Flags,* 104.

74. Madeleine Bertrand also has been described by genealogists as a woman born into the Chevalier-kin network of the St. Joseph River valley, whose parents relocated to Detroit before the 1780 French removal. See also the Appendix,

"Family Tree 1," in Moeller, *Joseph Bertrand, Sr.* And see George A. Baker to Mrs. Edward G. Mason, April 20, 1892, Historical Society Correspondence, Chicago Historical Society.

75. "History of the Extinct Village of Bertrand," *MPHC* 28:129; A. B. Copley, "Early Settlement of Southwestern Michigan, ibid. 5: 145; Damon A. Winslow, "Early History of Berrien County," ibid. 1: 121.

76. Cunningham, *Land of Four Flags,* 97; Juliette M. Kinzie, *Wau-Bun: The "Early Day" in the Old North-West* (1856; reprint, Urbana: University of Illinois Press, 1992), 126.

77. In Tanner, *Atlas of Great Lakes,* see "The War of 1812: Indian Involvement 1811–1816," 105–21.

78. "Disposition of Abraham Burnett, March 1870, Shawnee County, Kansas." Microfilm of the George Winter Papers held by the Tippecanoe Historical Society in West Lafayette, Indiana. Indiana Historical Society, Indianapolis.

79. Ibid., microfilm, Indiana Historical Society.

80. The eldest son of Kakima and William Burnett was James Burnett, probably born around 1782. He married Menache, daughter of She-cau-go-se-qua, and they had a son named Wimego, or William Burnett. This relationship lasted two years; she later moved to Sugar Creek and remarried. Official copy of depositions taken in Shawnee Township, Topeka, Kansas, November 1, 1878, for the St. Joseph (Ind.) County Court in the case of Menachee vs. L. M. Taylor, Adm. of James Burnett's estate, Case 76, passim.

John Burnett was the second son. He married No-ta-no-quay and eventually was imprisoned for debt in 1821, when the American Fur Company purchased his debts from another trader. The AFC drove the Burnetts out of the river valley. See Bert Anson, "The Fur Traders in Northern Indiana, 1796–1850" (Ph.D. diss., Indiana University, June 1953).

81. Richard White, "What Chigabe Knew: Indians, Household Government, and the State," *William and Mary Quarterly* 52 (January 1995): 154.

Chapter 6. Being Indian and Becoming Catholic

1. Daniel Richter, "'Believing That Many of the Red People Suffer Much for the Want of Food': Hunting, Agriculture, and a Quaker Construction of Indianness in the Early Republic," *Journal of the Early Republic* (Winter 1999) 19: 602–3.

2. Helen Hornbeck Tanner, *Atlas of Great Lakes Indian History* (Norman: University of Oklahoma Press, 1987), 133–37.

3. Reed to Cass, July 25, 1828, in *Letter Book of William Burnett* ed. William M. Cunningham (N.p.: Fort Miami Heritage Society of Michigan, 1967), 220.

4. When Joseph Bertrand first arrived in southwest Michigan he worked for the American Fur Company. He aligned his interests with the Potawatomi villages settled near the former St. Joseph fort and mission, in 1804/5. See Ida Amanda Johnson, *The Michigan Fur Trade* (1919; reprint, Grand Rapids, Mich.: Black Letter Press, 1971), 109; "Early History of Berrien County," *MPHC* 1: 121.

5. Reed to Cass, July 25, 1828, *Letter Book of William Burnett,* 224, 221.

6. Ibid., July 31, 1828, 224–25.

7. Reed to Cass, July 25, 1828, Michigan Record Group: M1, Roll 23, 141–

43, National Archives; Reed to Cass, July 31, 1828, *Letter Book of William Burnett,* 223–25; "L. Cass to Col. L. McKenney, [Library of Congress—Schoolcraft Papers—1828], Sep. 22d, 1828," *MPHC* 36: 565–66.

8. "Articles of a Treaty between the United States and the Potawatomi Indians, September 20, 1828," in *Indian Treaties, 1778–1883,* ed. Charles J. Kappler (1904, vol. 2; reprint, New York: Interland Publishing Company, 1972), 283–84; James A. Clifton, *The Prairie People: Continuity and Change in Potawatomi Indian Culture, 1665–1965* (Lawrence: Regents' Press of Kansas, 1977), 229–30; R. David Edmunds, *Potawatomis Keepers of the Fire* (Norman: University of Oklahoma Press, 1978), 229–30; James A. Clifton, *The Pokagons: 1683–1983* (Lanham, Md.: University Press of America, 1984), 62–63.

9. By mid-nineteenth century, the St. Joseph River had so completely changed its course that Bertrand's former trading post was submerged beneath the old river channel. See "Extinct Village of Bertrand," *MPHC* 28 (1900): 131.

10. Ella Champion, *Berrien's Beginnings* (Berrien County, Mich.: Historical Committee of the County Federation of Women's Clubs in Berrien County 1926), 32; *Letter Book of William Burnett,* 174, n. 2.

11. "Indian Council," *White Pigeon [Michigan] Republican,* August 28, 1839; *MPHC* 10 (1888): 170–72.

12. George A. Schultz, *Indian Canaan: Isaac McCoy and the Vision of an Indian State* (Norman: University of Oklahoma Press, 1972), 64–77.

13. In 1820, Isaac McCoy and his wife had established Carey Mission, one mile east of Niles. By 1826, the mission declined, and McCoy moved west with the Potawatomi to establish a new mission. See Edmunds, *The Potawatomis,* 222–24; Isaac McCoy, *History of Baptist Indian Mission* (Washington D.C.: W. M. Morrison, 1840).

14. Father Gabriel Richard, the Detroit priest, was originally an Illinois Country missionary priest, when he visited among the Potawatomi Indians in 1821 and in 1828. See George Paré, *The Catholic Church in Detroit* (1951; reprint, Detroit: Wayne State University Press, 1983), 332–34; Clifton, *Pokagons,* 65.

15. Arthur J. Hope, *Notre Dame: One Hundred Years* (Notre Dame, Ind.: University of Notre Dame Press, 1928), 38.

16. Ibid., Gilbert J. Garraghan, *The Jesuits of the Middle United States* (New York: America Press, 1938), 177.

17. In addition to Pokagon's close association with Madeleine Bertrand, Pokagon's daughter was married to the Canadian Métis Alexander Mousse. See Clifton, *The Pokagons,* 65; Cecilia Bain Buechner, "The Pokagons," *Indiana Historical Society Publications,* vol. 10 (Indianapolis: Bobbs-Merrill Company, 1933), 288.

18. Although Madeleine Bertrand, baptized Madeon, and also spelled Madeline, Madelene, or Magdelene, was regarded by most historians as related to Topenabe, one Bertrand family historian claims that she was the daughter of a Potawatomi woman and a French trader. She was born in 1781, in the vicinity of Detroit, baptized at St. Anne's Church, and married Joseph Bertrand in 1804. Their children included: Joseph Junior (1808), Benjamin (1810), Laurence (1811), Theresa, Alexander, and Julia. Madeleine died in 1846. See Gladys Moeller, *Joseph Bertrand, Sr., His Ancestors, His Descendants* (Kansas, p. p., 1980); Veronique Decq Odekirk, "Bertrand, Michigan: Its Origins, Development, and

Decline, 1833–1855" (Master's thesis, University of Notre Dame, 1983); see Appendix, "Family Tree 2," in Moeller, *Joseph Bertrand, Sr.;* Clifton, *Pokagons,* 60; See also Christian Dennisein, ed., *Genealogy of the French Families of the Detroit River, 1701–1911* (Detroit: Detroit Society for Genealogical Research, 1976), 34.

Carol Devens, on the other hand, contends that the Jesuits made a calculated effort to appeal to men rather than women, that women resisted conversion, clinging to more traditional belief systems that emphasized communal values. During the early nineteenth century, Protestant missionaries made no gender distinctions in their conversion efforts, but were rejected by Native Americans because they were perceived as agents of "change and destruction." See her *Countering Colonization: Native American Women and Great Lakes Missions, 1630–1900* (Berkeley: University of California Press, 1992), 7–30; 69–89.

19. The term "niece" is English in context, but it is not appropriate in terms of Potawatomi kinship. The relationship between Pokagon's wife and Topenabe is unclear. Pokagon is reported by Clifton to have married a niece of Topenabe's, who, according to their kinship terms, would have been considered a daughter. Kakima was the sister of Topenabe, and it is unclear which Topenabe sibling was the father of Pokagon's wife (Clifton, *Pokagons,* 60).

20. George Paré and Milo M. Quaife, eds., "The St. Joseph Baptismal Register," *Mississippi Valley Historical Review* 13 (September 1926): 205–39. At Mackinac, the Justice of the Peace often baptized children during the priest's absence. "The Mackinac Register: Register of Baptisms of the Mission of St. Ignace de Michilimackinak" *WHC,* 19 (1910): 1–162.

21. "July 22, 1830," Father Badin's Baptismal Register, University of Notre Dame Archives, Notre Dame, Ind.

22. Jacqueline Peterson with Laura Peers, *Sacred Encounters: Father De Smet and the Indians of the Rocky Mountain West* (Norman: University of Oklahoma Press, 1993), 23–24.

23. Clifton, *Pokagons,* 43.

24. Ibid., 61.

25. Joseph Bailly was also referred to as Joseph Bailly de Meissen. See Frances R. Howe, *The Story of a French Homestead in the Old Northwest* (Columbus, Ohio: Press of Nitschke Bros., 1907), 24. Joseph Aubert de Gaspe Bailly Americanized his name by changing it to Joseph Bailly. See "Calumet Region," *Indiana Historical Collection,* 39 (Indianapolis: Indiana Historical Bureau, 1959), 47. (Hereafter referred to as *InHC.*)

26. "Calumet Region," *InHC,* 39 (1959), 47; Sister Mary Borromeo Brown, *The History of the Sisters of Providence of Saint Mary-of-the-Woods* (New York: Benzinger, 1949), 129–30; John C. Bowers, *The Old Bailly Homestead* (Gary, Ind.: p.p., 1922), 7.

27. Howe, *French Homestead,* 64–65.

28. Richard White, *The Middle Ground: Indians, Empires, and Republics in the Great Lakes Region, 1650–1850* (New York: Cambridge University Press, 1991), 26.

29. Catherine L. Albanese, *Nature Religion in America: From the Algonkian Indians to the New Age* (Chicago: University of Chicago Press, 1990), 24.

30. Jacqueline Peterson, with Laura Peers, *Sacred Encounters,* 23–24;

Kenneth M. Morrison, "Baptism and Alliance: The Symbolic Mediation of Religious Syncretism," *Ethnohistory* 37 (1990): 417.

31. Howe, *French Homestead,* 35–36.

32. James Burnett, "Day Book," 1800, unnumbered pages, Northern Indiana Historical Society, South Bend.

33. "American Fur Trade Invoices, 1821–1822," *WHC* 11: 378.

34. Wolcott to Cass, January 1, 1821, Michigan Record Group: M1, Roll 8, 5–6, and March 31, 1821, 244–46, Record Group 75, Records of the Michigan Superintendency, 1814–1850, Bureau of Indian Affairs.

35. Anselm J. Gerwing, "The Chicago Indian Treaty of 1833," *JIHS* 57 (Summer 1964): 117–42.

36. Hope, *Notre Dame,* 39–40. For information on the Odawa, see Blackbird, *History of the Ottawa and Chippewa Indians of Michigan: A Grammar of Their Language, and Personal and Family History of the Author* (Petoskey, Mich.: Little Traverse Regional Historical Society, 1887), 46, 49; also see James M. McClurken's *Gah-Baeh-Jhagwah-Buk: The Way It Happened* (East Lansing: Michigan State University Press, 1991).

37. Clifton, *Pokagons,* 69.

38. Ibid., 71; Rev. Louis Baroux, *An Early Indian Mission: Correspondence to the Reverend M. J. De Neve,* ed. and trans. Rev. E. D. Kelley (Berrien Springs, Mich.: Hardscrabble Books, 1976), 63, 81; Buechner, "Pokagons," vol. 10, 312; Howard S. Rogers, *History of Cass County from 1825 to 1875* (Cassopolis, Mich.: Vigilant Printers, 1875), 169–70; Lowell H. Glover, ed., *A Twentieth Century History of Cass County, Michigan,* (Chicago, 1906) 20, 285.

39. Brady to Commissioner of Indian Affairs, August 24, 1840, Bureau of Indian Affairs Microfilm 234, Reel 361, *National Archives.*

40. Mother Mary of the Compassion's Diary, Sisters of the Holy Cross, St. Mary's College Archives, South Bend, Ind.

41. The first nineteenth-century priest assigned to the St. Joseph River valley was Father Badin, a Belgian. His successors were French: Fathers De Seille, Petit, Baroux, and Sorin.

42. Pepper to Cass, October 16, 1830; Pepper to CGS George Gibson, November 8, 1830; Pepper to De Seille, August 7, 1835; De Seille to Pepper, October 10, 1835; Pepper to De Seille, October 20, 1835, Record Group 75, Bureau of Indian Affairs.

43. Brady to Commissioner of Indian Affairs, August 24, 1840, Bureau of Indian Affairs Microcopy 234, Reel 361, National Archives.

44. Those communities clustered near Pokagon's village and were known as the Silver Creek Potawatomi. They were identified with Wesaw, Shavehead, Wakimanido, Mkago, Pepiya, and Chief Flatbelly (Clifton, *Pokagons,* 71).

45. Edward Sorin, *Chronicles of Notre Dame Du Lac* (Notre Dame, Ind.: Notre Dame University Press, 1992), 28. Still other Michigan Potawatomi villages moved south of the Indiana state line to the headwaters of the numerous rivers. One Catholic village, led by Signowa, moved to the Kankakee, was forcibly removed to Kansas but then returned to Michigan by 1843. The villagers purchased individual homesteads around Rush Lake, north of Hartford, Michigan

(Clifton, *Pokagons,* 717); Rev. Baroux, *Early Indian Mission: Correspondence to Rev. De Neve,* 63; Buechner, "The Pokagons," vol. 10, 281–340, especially 312; Rogers, *History of Cass County* 169–70; Glover, *A Twentieth Century History of Cass County,* 20, 285.

46. Sorin, *Chronicles of Notre Dame,* 46.

47. Madeleine Bertrand was granted lands in both the Chicago Treaty of 1821 and in the Carey Mission Treaty of 1828. She held title to 1,191 acres. Her children were also granted land under these same treaties. In the later treaties of 1832 and 1833, she and her children also received monetary compensation. Since Madeleine had seven children, the family held title to considerable lands in the river valley. From a legal perspective, Madeleine, not Joseph, held the lands granted by the federal government. Permission to sell these lands had to come not only from the government but also from Madeleine (Odekirk, "Bertrand, Michigan," 2, 32).

48. Hope, *Notre Dame,* 55.

49. The school was staffed by Sister Mary of the Crucifixion Augot and Sister Mary of the Holy Cross Sweeney. See Notes from Sister Euphrosine, Sisters of the Holy Cross, St. Mary's College Archives, South Bend, Indiana.

50. Ibid.

51. Father Moreau, "Report on Holy Cross Missions," trans. A. Gagnier, Correspondence, Sorin Period, 1846 Indiana Provincial Archives Center, Notre Dame.

52. Baroux, *An Early Indian Mission: Correspondence,* 53.

53. Notes from Sister Euphrosine, St. Mary's Archives.

54. Letter of Sister Mary of the Five Wounds to Father Sorin, 1845, New York, File: Sorin Period, 1845-B, Edward Sorin Papers, Indiana Province Archives Center, Notre Dame. Sister Mary was the convent superior at Bertrand. She was sent to France by Father Sorin to raise money. See Etienne Catta and Tony Catta, *Mother Mary of the Seven Dolors* (Milwaukee: Bruce, 1959), 75–76.

55. Sister M. Eleanore, *On the King's Highway: A History of the Sisters of the Holy Cross of St. Mary of the Immaculate Conception, Notre Dame, Indiana* (New York: D. Appleton & Co., 1931), 145–46.

56. Ibid., 151.

57. Hope, *Notre Dame,* 82–85.

58. "Contributed Services, Congregation of the Sisters of the Holy Cross, 1843–1855," St. Mary's College Archives; Hope, *Notre Dame,* 83.

59. Hope, *Notre Dame,* 83–84.

60. Odekirk, "Bertrand, Michigan," 91.

61. Wilbur M. Cunningham, *Land of Four Flags* (Grand Rapids, Mich.: William B. Eerdmans, 1961), 112.

62. Richard Hulin, George Heath, Wm. W. Elliott, Trustees of the Presbyterian Society of Bertrand, Berrien Co[unty], to Milton Badger, Musser, "Home Missionaries" 2, Calendar Entry 594. Necia Musser, "Home Missionaries on the Michigan Frontier, a calendar of the Michigan Letters of the American Home Missionary Society, 1825–1846" (Ph.D. diss., University of Michigan, 1967).

63. The Bertrand events were similar to those that took place at the Ursuline Academy in Charleston, Massachusetts. There, the construction of an imposing

brick structure became the focus of mob hysteria when vandals broke into the convent and set it aflame, along with an adjacent building also owned by the sisters. In Boston, as elsewhere, anti-Catholic hysteria was fueled by the anti-Catholic sermons of such well-known ministers as Lyman Beecher, father of Henry Ward Beecher and Harriet Beecher Stowe. The 1855 publication of *The Escaped Nun* had spread inflammatory stories about the barbarity and immorality of Catholic schools and convents. See Ray Allen Billington, *The Protestant Crusade, 1800–1860* (Chicago: Quadrangle Books, 1938), 70–75.

64. Many historians have noted the importance of church building as central to Irish communities. See Jay P. Dolan, *The American Catholic Experience* (Garden City, N.Y.: Image Books, 1958), 164–65. Ethnicity as a divisive force in religion is discussed in Leslie Woodcock Tentler, *Seasons of Grace: A History of the Catholic Archdiocese of Detroit* (Detroit: Wayne State University Press, 1990), 109–12; see also Harold J. Abramson, *Ethnic Diversity in Catholic America* (New York: Wiley, 1973); Harold J. Abramson, "The Relgio-Ethnic Factor and the American Experience," *Ethnicity* 2 (1975): 163–77.

65. Howe, *French Homestead,* 149.

66. "Calumet Region," *InHC,* 39, 48. Brown, *Sisters of Providence,* 127–30; Bowers, *Bailly Homestead;* Howe, *French Homestead,* 63.

67. Simon Pokegon, *O-g i-m aw-ke e mit-i-gw a-k i (Queen of the Woods)* (Hartford, Mich.: C. H. Engle, 1899), 50–52.

Chapter 7. Hiding in Plain View

1. At the beginning of the nineteenth century, the United States engaged in a national debate about the role of the Indian in the New Republic. Thomas Jefferson and his followers identified the yeoman farmer, living in a pastoral setting, as the best of men. They believed Indians possessed the virtues necessary to cohabit that agrarian Garden of Eden. Jeffersonians never doubted that "progress included the Indian and that his pastoral ways gave him unique qualification to take his part in it." Bernard W. Sheehan, *Seeds of Extinction: Jeffersonian Philanthropy and the American Indian* (Chapel Hill: University of North Carolina Press, 1973), 100–101.

2. Roy Harvey Pierce, *Savagism and Civilization: A Study of the Indian and the American Mind* (Berkeley: University of California Press, 1988), 232–36; Eric W. Said, *Orientalism* (New York: Vintage, 1978), 233; Reginald Horsman, *Race and Manifest Destiny* (Cambridge: Harvard University Press, 1981), 43–44.

3. Exceptions to this rule were made in specific cases, such as the law that the United States Congress passed to protect Frances Slocum against forced removal. See John Meginness, *Biography of Frances Slocum, The Lost Sister of Wyoming* (New York: Arno Press, 1974), 131.

4. Brigitte Georgi-Findlay, *The Frontiers of Women's Writing: Women's Narratives and the Rhetoric of Westward Expansion* (Tucson: University of Arizona Press, 1996), especially "Traveling and Settling on the Prairies," 21–66.

5. Indians are omitted from most Michigan histories. Alec Gilpin's territorial history typifies this common perspective when he states that "Michigan's Indian problems were for the most part solved before it became a state." Historians

who include Indians generally depict them as minor participants in the shaping of the midwestern landscape. Susan Gray's recent monograph, *The Yankee West,* includes a chapter on white–Indian interactions, but following this initial encounter, Indians virtually disappear from the book. John Mack Faragher's *Sugar Creek: Life on the Illinois Prairie* (New Haven: Yale University Press, 1986), describes the Kickapoo Indians as part of the initial stage in "successive Indian and American communities" in Illinois (10–43, 113). Don Harrison Doyle's *The Social Order of a Frontier Community: Jacksonville, Illinois, 1825–1870* (Urbana: University of Illinois Press, 1978) and Kenneth Winkle's *The Politics of Community: Migration and Politics in Antebellum Ohio* (New York: Cambridge University Press, 1988) focus on the formation of community ties among white settlers and both exclude Indians from that process. See also Alec R. Gilpin, *The Territory of Michigan, 1805–1837* (East Lansing, 1970), 170; Susan E. Gray, *The Yankee West: Community Life on the Michigan Frontier* (Chapel Hill: University of North Carolina Press, 1996);

6. Richard White, *The Middle Ground: Indians, Empires, and Republics in the Great Lakes Region, 1650–1815* (New York: Cambridge University Press, 1991), 517.

7. The first removal in 1833 effectively relocated only seventy-six Potawatomi to Kansas. See R. David Edmunds, *The Potawatomis: Keepers of the Fire* (Norman: University of Oklahoma Press, 1987), 240–72; James A. Clifton, *The Prairie People: Continuity and Change in Potawatomi Indian Culture* (Lawrence: The Regents' Press of Kansas, 1977), 279–88. Richard White indicates that decline of the middle ground, coupled with settler pressures, depletion of game reserves, and the liquor trade around Vincennes, ultimately brought Native American demise (*Middle Ground,* 482–517).

8. Edmunds, *Potawatomis,* 271.

9. Helen Hornbeck Tanner, ed., *Atlas of Great Lakes Indian History* (Norman: University of Oklahoma Press, 1986), 133. Revised population estimates for 1830 are the result of recent research by Tanner and the staff for the *Atlas of Great Lakes Indian History.* These revisions now include the numerous small villages that existed along Michigan's southern tier. See also James A. Clifton, *The Pokagons, 1683–1983: Catholic Potawatomi Indians of the St. Joseph River Valley* (Lanham, N.Y.: University Press of America, 1984), 141. Former population estimates were significantly lower; most historians formerly believed that only six to seven thousand Potawatomi lived in the entire Great Lakes region at the beginning of the nineteenth century. See Clifton, *Prairie People,* 180–81, and John Tipton to John H. Eaton, April 5, 1831, *Tipton Papers,* part 2, *InHC,* 24, 399–400. Cass and William Clark, the St. Louis Superintendent, estimated the total number in Indiana as 5,500. See U.S. House of Representatives, 25th Congress, 2d sess., Executive Documents, no. 51, vol. 2 (serial no. 322), 17. The *Tipton Papers* were published separately as three volumes (1–3) and simultaneously incorporated as volumes 24–26 of the *InHC.* The volumes in this research were published as vol. 24, sec. 1; vol. 25, sec. 2, and vol. 26, sec. 3.

10. The report sent to Congress stated that Michigan's Indian population was somewhat smaller, but that there were fewer Potawatomi, only 6,500, although the estimated Odawa population was 4,000, and the Chippewa num-

bered 15,000 inhabitants, (U.S. Senate, 20th Congress, 2d sess., Senate Documents, 1828–1829, no. 72, vol. 1, 96).

11. One of the earliest changes in housing style can be traced to the Delawares. Early in their history, they lived in multifamily bark houses that were gable roofed. Among the Iroquois, the Handsome Lake revival produced the first rectangular houses with gabled roofs at the beginning of the nineteenth century. See Peter Nabokov and Robert East, *Native American Architecture* (New York: Oxford University Press, 1989), 86–90.

12. *Indians and a Changing Frontier: The Art of George Winter,* catalogue compiled by Sarah E. Cooke and Rachel B. Ramadhynai (Indianapolis: University of Indiana Press for the Indiana Historical Society in cooperation with Tippecanoe County Historical Association, 1993), 60.

13. Charlotte Copley Diary, 1833, Frank W. Copley Papers, Box 244-A, Bentley Historical Collections, Ann Arbor, Michigan.

14. Original field notes of surveys of several Indian reservations in Indiana by Robert Clark, Jr., and Sylvester Sibley, 1833 and 1834, Indiana Historical Society, Indianapolis.

15. Stewart Rafert, *The Miami Indians of Indiana: A Persistent People, 1654–1994* (Indianapolis: Indiana Historical Society, 1996), 127.

16. Godfroy's father, James or Jacques, married and lived among the Miami and traded at Eeltown. For a description of Jacques Godfroy's trading activities, see Charles B. Lasell, "The Old Indian Traders," *The Indiana Magazine of History* (March 1905) 2: 5; *Combination Atlas Map of Miami County, Indiana* (Indianapolis, 1877), 13; Bert Anson, "The Fur Traders in Northern Indiana, 1796–1850" (Ph.D. diss., Indiana University, 1953), 22.

17. George Winter, "Journal of a Visit to Deaf Man's Village," in *The Journals and Indian Paintings of George Winter, 1837–1839* (Indianapolis: Indiana Historical Society, 1948), 162–63. George Winter's original journal is in the archives of the Tippecanoe County Historical Museum, Lafayette, Indiana. (Hereafter referred to as TCHA). This publication contains no location designation for the George Winter manuscript collections held by the Tippecanoe Historical Museum. For a further description of Godfroy see John Todd, *The Lost Sister of Wyoming* (Northampton, Pa.: J. H. Butler, 1842), 120–21.

18. Tipton to Eaton, April 5, 1831, *Tipton Papers,* part 2 *InHC,* 25, 400; Robert A. Trennert, Jr., *Indian Traders on the Middle Border: The House of Ewing, 1827–54* (Lincoln: University of Nebraska Press, 1981), 40.

19. Meginness, *Frances Slocum,* 85–91.

20. Winter, "Visit to Deaf Man's Village," in *Journals and Indian Paintings of George Winter,* 166–67.

21. Meginness, *Frances Slocum,* 110–11.

22. Ibid.

23. Daniel K. Richter, "'Believing That Many of the Red People Suffer Much for the Want of Food': Hunting, Agriculture, and a Quaker Construction of Indianness in the Early Republic," *Journal of the Early Republic* (Winter 1999) 19: 601–28.

24. Bernard W. Sheehan, "The Problem of the Indian in the Revolution,"

in *The American Indian Experience,* ed. Philip Weeks (Arlington Heights, Ill.: Forum Press, 1988), 67.

25. Robert F. Berkhofer, Jr., *The White Man's Indian* (New York: Vintage Books, 1979), 86–96.

26. Guns constituted a small fraction of trade goods, even at wilderness posts. At Rainy Lake, for example, guns constituted 0.44 percent of the trade goods while, at Nipigon, they were less than 0.03 percent of the trade. See Dean L. Anderson, "European Trade Goods in the Western Great Lakes Region, 1715–1760," in *The Fur Trade Revisited: Selected Papers of the Sixth North American Fur Trade Conference, Mackinac Island, Michigan, 1991,* ed. Jennifer S. H. Brown, W. J. Eccles, Donald P. Heldman (East Lansing: Michigan State University Press, 1994), 107; also see Bruce M. White, "Montreal Cargoes and their Canoes," in *Le Castor Fait Tout: Fifth North American Fur Trade Conference, 1985* eds. Bruce G. Trigger, Toby Morantz, and Louise Dechêne (Montreal: St. Louis Historical Society, 1987), 164–92.

27. This quotation is from a resolution passed by the Commissioners of the Indian Trade In South Carolina. Gail DeBuse Potter, "The Matchcoat," *Museum of the Fur Trade Quarterly* (Winter 1997): 2; William L. McDowell, Jr. ed., *Journals of the Commissioners of the Indian Trade,* September 20, 1710–August 29, 1718 (Columbia: South Carolina Department of Archives and History, 1955), 82.

28. Animal skins were difficult to sew, and iron needles were some of the most frequently found trade goods during early-contact-period archaeological excavations. Father Hennepin listed needles among the trade goods that Robert La Salle carried aboard the *Griffon.* Needles were among the surface items collected in the Fort St. Joseph vicinity; see Charles Hulse, "An Archaeological Evaluation of Fort St. Joseph: An Eighteenth Century Military Post and Settlement in Berrien County, Michigan" (Master's thesis, Michigan State University, 1977), 336–39. A list of trade goods taken into Illinois Country by a fur trader in 1688 included not only a vast quantity of cloth, but also "8 livres of sewing thread (a livre as a unit of weight equals 1 pound)." See George Irving Quimby, *Indian Culture and European Trade Goods: The Archaeology of the Historic Period in the Western Great Lakes Region* (Madison: University of Wisconsin Press, 1966), 65.

29. *Indians and a Changing Frontier,* 50; see also George Winter Manuscript Collection, TCHA, Lafayette, Indiana, 2–5 [10]. (Hereafter referred to as GWMSS). The editors of this volume attempted to directly reference the George Winter manuscript collections and where applicable my footnotes follow their guidelines. The location of sources at the Tippecanoe County Historical Association is indicated by GWMSS (#) and the last line of each entry is followed by a number that indicates the collection catalogue number.

30. *Indians and a Changing Frontier,* 28.

31. Ibid., 76, see also *GWMSS,* 2–10 [3].

32. Disposition of Abraham Burnett, March 1870, Shawnee County Kansas. Microfilm of the Winter Papers held by the Tippecanoe Historical Association in West Lafayette Indiana. Microfilm is located in the archives of the Indiana Historical Society, Indianapolis, Indiana. The Burnett disposition appears to be missing from the manuscript collections at TCHA.

33. Fur traders in the Pacific Northwest also found Indians were particular

about the goods they wished to trade. Alexandra Harmon, in describing the Indians of Puget Sound, demonstrates that British traders had to be not only well intentioned but also had to supply particular types of merchandise. Traders reported that Indians were less interested in guns than in "blankets, textiles, molasses, and rum." When one trader failed to supply the desired items, one Indian "took his skins back and said he would wait." *See her Indians in the Making: Ethnic Relations and Indian Identities around Puget Sound* (Berkeley: University of California Press, 1998), 26.

34. "William Burnett Day Book," 1800, Archives of the Northern Indiana Historical Society, South Bend.

35. There is considerable debate among fur trade historians about the extent to which silk hats reduced the demand for beaver. There is, however, little controversy over the fact that, by 1830, the beaver trade had moved permanently into the American and Canadian Northwest, where large numbers of low-cost pelts were harvested. See James A. Hanson, "The Myth of the Silk Hat and the End of the Rendezvous," *Museum of the Fur Trade Quarterly* (Spring 2000). For a discussion of how the demand for silk hats affected the beaver trade, see Hiram Martin Chittenden, *The American Fur Trade of the Far West,* 2 vols. (New York: Press of the Pioneers, 1935), 1, 364; Leroy R. Hafen, *The Mountain Men and the Fur Trade of the Far West,* 2 vols. (Glendale, Calif.: Arthur H. Clark Co., 1965–72), 1, 174; John E. Sunder, *The Fur Trade on the Upper Missouri, 1840–1865* (Norman: University of Oklahoma Press, 1965), 11.

36. James L. Clayton, "The Growth and Economic Significance of the American Fur Trade, 1790–1890," in *Aspects of the Fur Trade: Selected Papers of the 1965 North American Fur Trade Conference,* ed. Dale L. Morgan, W. L. Morton, K. G. Davies, David Lavender, J. D. Herbert, Merrill J. Mattes, Wilcom E. Washburn, John Witthoft, and James L. Clayton (St. Paul: Minnesota Historical Society, 1965), 64–65, 68.

37. Clayton, "Growth of the Fur Trade," 65–67. The Ewing Brothers focused greater attention on the western fur trade, along the Lower Missouri, in the area vacated by the American Fur Company. Thus, the Ewings left Michigan, Ohio, and even Indiana furs to their competitors. See Robert A. Trennert, *Indian Traders on the Middle Border: The House of Ewing, 1824–1854* (Lincoln: University of Nebraska Press, 1981), 87–89.

38. *Indians and a Changing Frontier,* 64; GWMSS, TCHA, Lafayette, Indiana 1–4 [1], 1–3, 2–30 [1], 1–4 [8].

39. *Indians and a Changing Frontier,* 50; see also GWMSS, TCHA 2–5 [10].

40. Letter 1–15 [13] from George Winter, January 8, 1858, to Judge Petit, member of Congress, GWMSS.

41. Cass to Pepper, January 25, 1836, Bureau of Indian Affairs, M21, Roll 17, 458–61, National Archives; Cass to Potawatomi chiefs, February 9, 1836, Roll 17, 384–85, National Archives; Irving McKee, ed., "The Trail of Death: Letters of Benjamin Marie Petit," *Indiana Historical Society Publications* (Indianapolis: Bobbs-Merrill, 1941), 14, 21–22.

42. Tipton to David Wallace, September 18, 1838 in *Tipton Papers,* part 3, *InHC,* 26, 713–18.

43. Ibid., August 31, 1838, 26, 682; "Journal of an Emigrating Party of Potta-

watomie Indians, 1838," *Indiana Magazine of History* 21 (December 1925): 316–17; Daniel McDonald, *Removal of the Pottawattomie Indians from Northern Indiana* (Plymouth, Ind.: D. McDonald and Company, 1989), 42–45.

44. Dwight L. Smith, ed., "A Continuation of the Journal of an Emigrating Party of Potawatomi Indians, 1838, and Ten William Polk Manuscripts," *Indiana Magazine of History* 44 (December 1948): 403–4; Petit to his family, September 14, 1838, in Irving McKee, ed., "The Trail of Death: Letters of Benjamin Petit," *Indiana Historical Society Publications* 14 (Indianapolis: Bobbs-Merrill, 1941), 90–93; "Journal of an Emigrating Party," *Indiana Magazine of History* 21:317–84; Dwight Smith, "Jacob Hull's Detachment of the Potawatomi Emigration of 1838," ibid. 45 (September 1949): 285–88, describes the subsequent removal of those left behind because of the typhoid outbreak.

45. Trennert, *Indian Traders,* 67–68; Pepper to Harris, September 18, 1838, Tipton to Harris, September 25, 1838, Letters Received, OIA (Office of Indian Affairs, Record Group 75, National Archives), Indiana Agency; Harris to G. W. Ewing, September 17, 1838, Ewing Papers, Indiana State Library (hereafter referred to as ISL); Ewing, Walker & Co. and Allen Hamilton & Co. to Tipton, September 18, 1838, and Tipton to Harris, September 27, 1838, *Tipton Papers,* part 3, InHC, 26, 721, 731–32.

46. Trennert, *Indian Traders,* 77–78; W. G. Ewing to G. W. Ewing, November 14, 1839, G. W. Ewing to W. G. Ewing, November 14, 1839, Ewing Papers, ISL; undated note on the 1839 fur sales, Ewing memo book, 1835–40, ISL.

47. Todd, *Lost Sister,* 156–57.

48. Ibid., 149.

49. Cash settlements of $800 for every man, woman, and child were offered as a reward for land cessions, but these monetary bonuses were only to be paid out west of the Mississippi. It was an extravagant incentive, but necessary for a government intent on moving stubborn Indians west.

50. Meginness, *Frances Slocum,* 131.

51. Ibid., 125–28.

52. *Indians and a Changing Frontier,* 117; GWMSS, TCHA, 2–23 [13].

53. Rafert, *Miami Indians,* 134.

54. Ronald Takaki, *Iron Cages: Race and Culture in Nineteenth-Century America* (New York: Oxford University Press, 1990), 114–15.

55. *Indians and a Changing Frontier,* 114; GWMSS, TCHA, 1–23 [13].

56. Rafert, *Miami Indians,* 175.

Chapter 8. Emigrants and Indians

1. The term *emigrant* was used extensively during most of the nineteenth century; it was popular from the 1830s to the 1890s and was used to denote people who intended to settle in the West. This term was routinely used in guidebooks published during this period to promote settlement in both Canada and the United States. Examples of such usage include: Francis Head, *The Emigrant* (London: Murray, 1847); James M. Horner, *The Modern Emigrant* (New York: Mitchell, 1832); John Murray, *The Emigrant and Traveller's Guide to and through Canada, by Way of the River St. Lawrence . . .* (London: Smith Elder, 1835). *Emigrant*

was also used in newspaper titles: *The Western Emigrant* (Boonville, Missouri), 1833–1838; *Emigrant* (Ann Arbor), 1830–1832; *The Illinois Emigrant* (Shawneetown), founded in 1818. The other main source was literature, especially in poetry relating to settling in America or conveying the emigrant's longing for the home country. Examples include: Frederick W. Thomas, *The Emigrant, Or Reflections while Descending the Ohio* (Cincinnati: Drake, 1872), William R. Dempster, *The Lament of the Irish Emigrant, A Ballad* (Boston: Henry Tolman, 1863). Some government publications also used the term; for example, *Texas: The Home for the Emigrant from Everywhere* (Austin: Cardwell and Texas Bureau of Immigration, 1873).

2. Robert A. Trennert, *Indian Traders on the Middle Border: The House of Ewing, 1824–54* (Lincoln: University of Nebraska Press, 1981), 77–78.

3. Peirce Lewis, "The Landscapes of Mobility," in *The National Road,* ed. Karl Raitz (Baltimore: Johns Hopkins University Press, 1996), 3–7.

4. Community studies constitute the social historian's framework for understanding mobility in the nineteenth-century Midwest. Merle Curti, *The Making of an American Community: A Case Study of Democracy in a Frontier County* (Stanford, Calif.: Stanford University Press, 1959), pioneered the systematic use of demographic data that pointed to the importance of internal migration in the nineteenth-century United States. Curti's model was adopted by social historians who stressed the problems of social discord these new communities experienced. See Allan G. Bogue, "Social Theory and the Pioneer," *Agricultural History* 34 (1960): 21–34; William L. Bowers, "Crawford Township, 1850–1870: A Population Study of a Pioneer Community," *Iowa Journal of History* 58 (January 1960): 1–30; Don Doyle, *The Social Order of a Frontier Community: Jacksonville, Illinois, 1825–1870* (Urbana: University of Illinois Press, 1978); Milford Throne, "A Population Study of an Iowa County in 1850," *Iowa Journal of History* 57 (October 1959): 305–30: Peter J. Colman, "Restless Grant County: Americans on the Move," *WMH* 46 (Autumn 1962): 16–20.

5. *History of Berrien and Van Buren Counties* (Philadelphia: D. W. Ensign & Co., 1860), 127; James A. Clifton, *The Pokagons, 1683–1983: Catholic Potawatomi of the St. Joseph River Valley* (Lanham, Pa.: University Pres of America, 1984), 71.

6. Helen Hornbeck Tanner, ed., *Atlas of Great Lakes Indian History* (Norman: University of Oklahoma Press, 1987), 6.

7. *History of Berrien and Van Buren Counties* (Philadelphia: L. H. Everts Co., 1887), 128.

8. Ibid., 127.

9. Tanner, *Atlas of Great Lakes History,* 135.

10. Charlotte Copley Diary, 1833, Copley Family Papers, Bentley Historical Collections, Ann Arbor, Michigan.

11. The western end survey was done by Daniel G. Garnsey, one of the proprietors who laid out Bertrand. See Judge Orville Coolidge, *A Twentieth Century History of Berrien County* (Chicago: Lewis Publishing Company, 1906), 37.

12. Rev. O. C. Thompson, "Observations and Experiences in Michigan Forty Years Ago," *MPHC* 1: 397.

13. "Lakeford Burdick, One More of the Old Settler's Gone," ibid. 10: 189.

14. Elijah Pilcher, "Forty Years Ago," ibid. 5:83–84.

15. Malcolm J. Rohrbough, *The Land Office Business: The Settlement and Administration of American Public Lands, 1789–1837* (Belmont, Calif.: Wadsworth Publishing, 1968), 211, 238.

16. Willis F. Dunbar, as revised by George S. May, *Michigan: A History of the Wolverine State* (Grand Rapids: William B. Eerdmans, 1970), 270–71.

17. Ibid., 261–85.

18. Hiram Smith to Milton Badger, July 1, 1840, Bristol, Michigan, quoted in Necia Musser, "Home Missionaries on the Michigan Frontier, A Calendar of the Michigan Letters of the American Home Missionary Society, 1825–1846" (Ph.D. diss., University of Michigan, 1967), vol. 2, calendar entry 766. The records of the American Home Missionary Society are housed in the Bentley Historical Collections at the University of Michigan, Ann Arbor.

19. Sylvester Cochrane to Milton Badger, October 5, 1838, Vermontville, Michigan, vol. 2, calendar entry 595, ibid.

20. Justin Marsh to Milton Badger, December 3, 1840, vol. 2, calendar entry 746, ibid.

21. J. P. Cleaveland to C. Hall, July 22, 1842, Ann Arbor, Michigan, vol. 2, calendar entry 806, ibid.

22. Justin Marsh to M. Badger, June 1, 1840, Leoni, Michigan, vol. 2, calendar entry 743, ibid.

23. Elijah Buck to Milton Badger, November 22, 1841, Homer, Michigan, vol. 2, calendar entry 798; August 25, 1841, letter 796b, ibid.

24. Bailly's wife, Tou-se-qua, was an L'Arbe Croche Odawa. See Rollo B. Oglesbee and Albert Hale, *History of Michigan City, Indiana* (La Porte, Ind.: Edward J. Widdell, 1908), 55.

25. Coolidge, *Twentieth Century Berrien County,* 206–7. Veronique Decq Odekirk, "Bertrand, Michigan: Its Origins, Development, and Decline, 1833–1855" (Master's thesis, University of Notre Dame, 1983), 97; Coolidge, *Twentieth Century Berrien County,* 207.

26. Jacob Schellenberger, a German immigrant who arrived in Marshall in 1839, built a tavern near the Kalmazoo portage to Detroit. Here the Potawatomi often exchanged furs for whiskey. See Mabel Cooper Skjelver, *Nineteenth-Century Homes of Marshall, Michigan* (Marshall: Marshall Historical Society, 1971), 50–51.

27. Letters of inquiry for appointment as Indian agents conveyed political loyalty, rather than Indian expertise. "I am a loyal party man," wrote one of the applicants for an interpreter's position. Records of the Michigan Superintendency of Indian Affairs, State of Michigan Archives, Lansing.

28. *History of Hillsdale County* (Philadelphia: Everts & Abbott, 1879), 44.

29. In the Great Lakes region, numerous state historical societies were formed, and their annual publications routinely included interviews with first-generation emigrants, or "reminscences or recollections written by them or their descendents."Most were begun late in the nineteenth or early in the twentieth century. Those with particularly rich resources include: *Reports and Collections of the Michigan Pioneer and Historical Society* (*MPHC*) (Lansing, 1877–1908); *Collections of the State Historical Society of Wisconsin* (*WHC*), ed. Lyman C. Draper and Reuben G. Thwaites (Madison: Wisconsin Historical Society, 1888–1931: *Collections of the Illinois State Historical Society* (*ISHS*) (Springfield: H. W. Rokker Co.,

1903–1975); *Indiana Historical Collections* (*InHC*) (Indianapolis: Indiana Historical Bureau, 1916–1994).

30. Jean O'Brien's work on the Natick Indians reveals how many of the contradictions in early community histories can be used to dispute claims about Indian "extinction and undermine the simplistic narrative of decline." As O'Brien insightfully indicates, the contradictory evidence of these early histories is important in revealing "a complicated story of conquest and Indian resistance." See her *Dispossession by Degrees: Indian Land and Identity in Natick, Massachusetts, 1650–1790* (New York: Cambridge University Press, 1997).

31. John Reynolds, *The Pioneer History of Illinois* (Chicago: Fergus, 1887), 168–69.

32. Wilbur M. Cunningham, *Land of Four Flags: An Early History of the St. Joseph River Valley* (Grand Rapids, Mich.: William Eerdmans Publishing Company, 1961), 112.

33. "Extinct Village of Bertrand," *MPHC* 28 (1900): 130.

34. Cunningham, *Four Flags,* 105.

35. Rayna Green, "The Pocahontas Perplex: The Image of Indian Women in America Culture," *Massachusetts Review* 16 (Autumn 1975): 698–714.

36. Leo C. Little, *Historic Grand Haven and Ottawa County* (Grand Haven, Mich.: p. p., 1931), 91. The author, in describing Madame La Framboise, borrows the title from Vivian Lyon Moore's article, "A Pocahontas of Michigan."

37. Green, "Pocahontas Perplex," 703.

38. Thimotée was also called Marie Neskesh by the Jesuits. Therésè was ten and Magdelaine was six years old when the sisters were baptized on August 1, 1786, "Mackinac Register," *WHC* 19: 86.

39. "Census of the Post of St. Joseph," *MPHC* 10: 406–7.

40. Jean Baptiste Marcot relocated to what is present-day Wisconsin and, in 1783, he was killed by Indians at the portage between the Fox and Wisconsin Rivers, when Magdelaine was a young child. See John E. McDowell, "Thérèse Schindler of Mackinac: Upward Mobility in the Great Lakes Fur Trade," *WMH* 61: 126–27.

41. "Mackinac Register," *WHC* 19: 86.

42. Tanner, *Atlas of Great Lakes History,* 133.

43. "Marguerite-Magdelaine Marcot (La Framboise)," *DCB,* 7, 582; Milo Quaife, *Lake Michigan* (New York: Bobbs-Merrlll, 1944), 201–6.

44. "Mackinac Register," *WHC* 18: 507–8.

45. Claude La Framboise to John Kinzie, June 11, 1807, Solomon Sibley Papers, Burton Historical Collection, Detroit Public Library.

46. Elizabeth Thérèse Baird, "Reminiscences of Early Days on Mackinac Island," *WHC* 14: 38–39.

47. Gordon Charles Davidson, *The North West Company* (Berkeley: University of California Press, 1918), 72; McDowell, "Madame La Framboise," 278.

48. John Denis Haeger, *John Jacob Astor: Business and Finance in the Early Republic* (Detroit: Wayne State University Press, 1991), 149–52.

49. George Wilson Pierson, *Tocqueville and Beaumont in America* (New York: Oxford University Press, 1938), 302.

50. Magdelaine La Framboise to Marianne Fisher, Montreal, August 18,

1841, and May 10, 1842, Baird Papers, State Historical Society of Wisconsin, Madison.

51. James M. McClurken, "Augustin Hamlin, Jr.: Ottawa Identity and the Politics of Persistence," in James A. Clifton, *Being and Becoming Indian* (Prospect Heights, Ill.: Waveland Press, 1989), 82–111.

52. William F. Ferry, "Extracts from William Ferry's Journal," *American Missionary Register* 5, no. 3 (March 1824): 89–90.

53. Mary E. Evans, "The Mission Footnote or the Curé Who Wasn't There," in *Records of the American Catholic Historical Society of Philadelphia* (1973), 84, 199.

54. "Donation of Indian Chiefs to Madelon Laframboise" (1823), Henry S. Baird Papers, State Historical Society of Wisconsin, Madison.

55. Marcel Mauss, *The Gift: Forms and Functions of Exchange in Archaic Societies* (New York: W. W. Norton, 1990), 65.

56. Marie Le Febvre left her Odawa husband, a reportedly powerful shaman, and Joseph parted from his Grand River Odawa wife, whom he had married in the eyes of the church. They married in the "manner of the country," and Marie's two children remained with her, while Joseph's remained with his former wife. Joseph Bailly was born on April 7, 1774, and became the father of five sons and five daughters. His first wife was Angelique McGulpin, daughter of a French trader and an Indian woman who was reputed to have been the niece of Pontiac. Their children included Alexis Bailly, Joseph Philippe Bailly, Michel Bailly, Philippe Bailly, Sophie (Hortense) Bailly. His second wife, Marie Le Fevbre, was born about 1783 and died September 15, 1866. Their children were: Esther, Rose, Ellen or Eleanor, Robert, and Hortense. See "The French-Canadian Background of a Minnesota Pioneer—Alexis Bailly," *Bulletin des recherches historiques* 55, (nos. 7, 8, 9): 137–55; Edward C. Bailly, "Genealogy of the Bailly de Messien Family in the United States," 180–95.

57. Elizabeth Baird, "Reminiscences of Mackinac Island," *WHC* 14: 43.

58. Frances R. Howe, *The Story of a French Homestead in the Old Northwest* (Columbus, Ohio: Press of Nitschke Brothers, 1907), 24–25.

59. For an explanation of the black raccoon trade, see Chapter 7 herein, and James L. Clayton, "The Growth and Economic Significance of the American Fur Trade, 1790–1890," in *Aspects of the Fur Trade: Selected Papers of the 1965 North American Fur Trade Conference,* eds. Dale L. Morgan, W. L. Morton, K. G. Davies, David Lavender, J. D. Herbert, Merrill J. Mattes, Wilcomb E. Washburn, John Witthoft, and James L. Clayton (St. Paul: Minnesota Historical Society, 1965), 62–72.

60. Lemuel Bryant Travel Journal, 1832, Chicago Historical Society, Chicago. (Hereafter referred to as CHS.)

61. Jacqueline Peterson describes early Chicago as ethnically diverse and with an economy completely dependent on trade, especially the fur trade, in "'Wild' Chicago: The Formation and Destruction of a Multiracial Community on the Midwestern Frontier, 1816–1837," in *The Ethnic Frontier: Essays in the History of Group Survival in Chicago and the Midwest,* ed. Melvin G. Holli and Peter d'A. Jones (Grand Rapids, Mich.: William B. Eerdmans Publishing, 1977), 26–71. Also see Ernest E. East, "The Inhabitants of Chicago, 1825–1831," 37 (June 1944) *JIHS,* 131–63.

62. Allen L. Boyer, Reading, Pennsylvania, Diary describing emigration from Danville, Columbia County, Pa., to Chicago in 1833, CHS.

63. Howe, *Story of a French Homestead*, 37.

64. Footnotes written by Frances R. Howe and appended to *The Story of a French Homestead in the Old Northwest*, Bailly Family Collections, CHS.

65. Frances R. Howe to Miss McElvaine, September 27, 1915, ibid.

66. Olga Mae Schiemann, *From a Bailly Point of View* (Chicago: Duneland Historical Society Publication, 1955), 4.

67. Ibid., 3.

68. Rose V. Howe to Mr. Clark, March 27, 1878, Bailly Family Collections, CHS.

69. Marie and Joseph Bailly relocated to northwest Indiana, not far from the St. Joseph River valley, on lands that they thought would become part of Michigan. They returned to a place where Joseph Bailly had traded early in the nineteenth century. This was familiar terrain, a previous generation of Baillys had served in the eighteenth-century military at Fort St. Joseph. This location, proved ideal for the fur trade. These were the campgrounds where the Odawa and the Potawatomi stopped on their way to the wintering grounds of the Kankakee River valley. On January 11, 1801, Joseph Bailly received an American license from Governor Harrison to trade with the Odawa on the Grand River valley. See Charles B. Lasalle, "The Old Indian Traders of Indiana," *The Indiana Magazine of History* (March 1906) 2: 7. In the winter of 1813, Bailly, licensed as a British trader, was captured by the Americans and jailed at Detroit (*MPHC* 16: 332).

70. Bryant Travel Journal, 1832, CHS.

71. Ibid.

72. "A Mère Marie," December 3, 1841. Saint Mary-of-the-Woods Archives, Terre Haute, Indiana.

73. For more information about Sister Cecilia, see Sister Mary Borromeo Brown, *The History of the Sisters of Providence of Saint Mary-of-the-Woods*, vol. 1 (New York: Benzinger, 1949); Sister M. Eleanore, *On the King's Highway: A History of the Sisters of the Holy Cross of St. Mary of the Immaculate Conception, Notre Dame, Indiana* (N.Y.: D. Appletown & Co., 1931).

74. Sister Anita Cotler, *In God's Acre: Biographical Sketches, Mother Cecilia Bailly, Sisters of Providence, Saint-Mary-of-the-Woods* (Terre Haute, Ind.,: 1940), 1–36; Brown, *History of the Sisters of Providence*, 124–31.

75. Howe, *Story of a French Homestead*, 24–25.

76. Brown, *History of the Sisters of Providence*, 125.

77. William Cronon, George Miles, and Jay Gitlin, *Under an Open Sky: Rethinking America's Western Past* (New York: W. W. Norton, 1992), 19.

78. Marcia Renee Sawyer, "Surviving Freedom: African American Farm Households in Cass County, Michigan, 1832–1880" (Ph.D. diss., Michigan State University, 1990), 48–49.

79. George K. Hesslink, *Black Neighbors: Negroes in a Northern Rural Community* (New York: Bobbs-Merrill, 1974), 35–37; William H. Pease and Jane H. Pease, *Black Utopia: Negro Communal Experiments in America* (Madison: State Historical Society of Wisconsin, 1963), 4.

80. Robert P. Swierenga, "The Settlement of the Old Northwest: Ethnic Pluralism in a Featureless Plain," *Journal of the Early Republic* 9 (Spring 1989): 73; Richard K. Vedder and Lowell E. Gallaway, "Migration and the Old Northwest," in *Essays in Nineteenth Century Economic History: The Old Northwest* ed. David C. Klingaman and Richard K. Vedder (Athens: Ohio University Press, 1975), 161.

81. Swierenga, "Settlement of Old Northwest," 83.

82. By the twentieth century, Berrien County had the largest concentration in North America of Germans from Volhynia, a Russian province near the Polish border. They took over the nursery and fruit farms of southwestern Michigan. See George P. Graff, *The People of Michigan* (Lansing: Michigan Department of Education, 1974), 43–44.

83. The pamphlet was written by Epaphroditus Ransom. He also wrote the legal opinion for the Pokagon Potawatomi that their forced removal was illegal. He was a Michigan Supreme Court judge and, at the time of the pamphlet's publication, was Michigan's governor. John A. Russell, *The Germanic Influence in the Making of Michigan* (Detroit: University of Detroit Press, 1927), 56–57.

84. Coolidge, *Twentieth Century Berrien County,* 210–11. Ronald P. Formisano, *The Birth of Mass Political Parties, 1827–1861* (Princeton: Princeton University Press, 1971), 168–69; Fuller, *Economic and Social Beginnings,* 303; *History of Berrien and Van Buren Counties, Michigan* (Philadelphia: D. W. Ensign & Co., 1880), 278–79, 288–90.

85. *History of St. Joseph County* (Philadelphia, L. H. Everts, 1879), 220–21.

86. Clifton, *The Pokagons,* 71; Rev. E. D. Kelley, *Correspondence to the Reverend M. J. DeNeve,* ed. and trans. Rev. Louis Baroux (Berrien Springs, Mich.: Hardscrabble Books, 1976), 45–49; Stewart Rafert, *The Miami Indians of Indiana: A Persistent People, 1654–1994* (Indianapolis, Indiana Historical Society, 1996), 108; Bert Anson, *The Miami Indians* (Norman: University of Oklahoma Press, 1970), 220–21.

87. Sawyer, "Surviving Freedom," 59–60.

88. Calvin Martin, "The European Impact on the Culture of a Northeastern Algonquin Tribe: An Ecological Interpretation," *William and Mary Quarterly* 31 (January 1974): 7–26. Discussions about the rationales for Indian overhunting have been the focus of Calvin Martin, *Keepers of the Game: Indian-Animal Relationships and the Fur Trade* (Berkeley: University of California Press, 1978), and Shephard Krech III, ed., *Indians, Animals, and the Fur Trade: A Critique of "Keepers of the Game"* (Athens: University of Georgia Press, 1981). An argument for overhunting having caused the decline in the deer population in America's southeastern region has been advanced by Charles Hudson in his article, "Why the Southeastern Indians Slaughtered Deer," in Shephard Krech's edited collection, ibid., 162–63.

89. Based on the archaeological data, Gregory Waselkov also contends that the overhunting of animals for furs hypothesis is suspect, in "The Eighteenth-Century Anglo-Indian Trade in Southeastern North America," in *New Faces of the Fur Trade: Selected Papers of the Seventh North American Fur Trade Conference, Halifax, Nova Scotia, 1995,* ed. Jo-Anne Fiske, Susan Sleeper-Smith, and William Wicken Wicken (East Lansing: Michigan State University Press, 1998), 189–91.

90. Elizabeth Neumeyer, "Michigan Indians Battle against Removal," *Michigan History* 55, no. 4 (1971): 278; for more detailed statistics, see Elizabeth Neumeyer, "Indian Removal in Michigan, 1833–1855" (Master's thesis, Central Michigan University, Mt. Pleasant, 1968), 30, 33, 40, 46, 54, and 92.

91. Neumeyer, "Michigan Indians," 283, 287–88.

Index

Page references to illustrations and tables are in italics.

Abenaki people, 16, 60
Accault, Michel, 26, 28–29, 30, 35, 178n. 9
Accault, Peter, 178n. 9
adoption, 39, 55, 59,101
African Americans, 92, 161, 162. *See also* slaves
agriculture: appropriated Indian field, 83–84; community, 69; defined wealth, 32; discouraged war, 74, 84; Indian desire to continue, 97–98; Indian fields, 78–79, *79–81*, 82–84, 199n. 11; Indiana, 124; and lifestyle vulnerability, 86; market-based, 74–75, 77; Michigan, 78–85; and nomads, 117; and portage area villages, 76; and production, 55; shortage in, 69–70; surplus in, 69–70, 76, 151; tools of, 77, 82; and trade, 70; women's controlling role in, 16, 30, 32–33, 75, 77, 82, 91–92. *See also* food crops
Ainssé, Louis, 67
Alavoine, Marie Françoise, 187n. 33
Albany, Fort, 61
Albivi people, 37
alcohol, 40, 60, 117, 162
Allegheny River, 12, *13*
Allouez, Claude Jean, 14, 23, 181n. 52
Amable, Marie, 48
American Fur Company, 94, 105, 130, 134, 152, 160, 204nn. 80, 4
American Home Mission Society, 146
Amherst, Jeffrey, 56, 60
Amouoka people, 37
"Ancient Garden Beds of Michigan" (Hubbard), 78, *79–81*, 83
Anderson, Ezekiel, 161
Anderson, Fred, 191n. 60
Anderson, Gary, 179n. 30
annuity payments, 116, 117, 122, 133, 136–37, 141
arpent, 32, 180n. 40
Askin, John, 63–64
Astor. *See* American Fur Company
Au Glaize River, 85–86
Au Sable River, 19, *20*

Badin, Stephen, 102, 207n. 41
Bailly, Eleanor (Sister Cecelia), 158, 159, 160, 218n. 56
Bailly, Joseph (de Meissen) (Joseph Aubert de Gaspe Bailly), 104–5, 153, 206n. 25; children of, 218n. 56; described, 155, 156, 160; as an emigrant, 146, 216n. 24; in Indiana, 219n. 69; marriages of, 155, 156, 157, 158, 218n. 56
Bailly, Marie (Le Febvre): children of, 218n. 56; described, 155; as an "exotic," 155; family of, 155–59, 160, 218n. 56; in Indiana, 219n. 69; marriages of, 155, 156, 218n. 56; religious life of, 158–59; as a trader, 156
Bailly, Rose (Howe), 156–57, 159, 218n. 56
Bailly, Sophia, 153
Bailly family names, 218n. 56
Bailly homestead, 156–58, 159, 219n. 69
Baillytown, 146
Baird family names, *51*
baptism: Christian versus Native, 104–5; conditional, 189n. 47; and intermarriage, 46, 48, 151, 189n. 44; Kaskaskia, 29, 30, 32; L'archevêque, 186nn. 24, 29,

baptism (*continued*)
187nn. 32–33; lay, 190n. 51, 206n. 20; name recording, 52, 190n. 54; Potawatomi, 106; and social structures, 43. *See also* Chevalier; L'archevêque; Michilimackinac
Baroux, 103, 207n. 41
bartering, 171–72n. 5
Barthe, Marie Archange, 64
Bassett, Henry, 58–59, 64, 194n. 20
bateaux, 63
Baw Bee, 148
Baw Beese, *107,* 147, 148
battles. *See by specific name*
Beauharnois, Charles de, 184n. 15
Beausoleil. *See* Pouré
beaver: exports, 129–30, 195n. 32; for hats, 11, 172nn. 6–7, 213n. 35; trade history, 6, 118
Beaver Wars, 173n. 11
Begon, 188n. 36
Berrien County, Michigan, 220n. 82
Bertrand, Benjamin, 111
Bertrand, Daniel, 102
Bertrand, Joseph, 93–95; appearance of, 114; depression losses of, 146; and the fur trade, 102, 204n. 4; kin network influence of, 98–99, 100, 101–2, 205n. 9; land of, 100; sons, 111–12
Bertrand, Joseph, Jr., 112
Bertrand, Joseph Laurent, 203n. 72
Bertrand, Laurent, 102
Bertrand, Madeleine (Mouto), 93–95, 98, 101, 146, 203n. 74, 205nn. 17–18; as a catechizer, 102, 108; children of, 111–12, 205n. 18; as an exotic, 149; land granted to, 208n. 47; names of, 205n. 18
Bertrand, Marguerite, 102
Bertrand, Michigan (town), *107,* 108, 109, 110–11, 112, 113
Bertrand, Théotés, 102
Bertrand, Thérèse, 102
Bertrand family names, *51,* 102, 205n. 18
Bertrand Real Estate Company, 109
Bertrand Village, *107,* 146–47, 149, 161
Bertrand Village Association, 146–47
bison, 14
Black Partridge, 87
"black robes." *See* Jesuits
Boullenger, Jean-Antoine Le, 31
Bourassa, Daniel, 102
Bourassa family, 47, *51,* 186nn. 29–30
Bourdieu, Pierre, 3
Bouriette, Jean Baptiste, 128
Brady, Hugh, 107
Brady, Thomas M. (Tom), 67, 187n. 32, 197n. 60
British fur trade, 53, 54–72, 74, 191n. 60
Brown, Jennifer, 19
Bryant, Lemuel, 155–56
buffalo, 100
Burdick, Robert, 143–44
Burnett, Abram, 94, 95, 128
Burnett, Abram (Potawatomi), 94, 128
Burnett, James, 95, 204n. 80
Burnett, John, 204n. 80
Burnett, Kakima. *See* Kakima
Burnett, William, 77–78, 82, 90–95, 129, 202n. 54, 203nn. 63, 66, 68; death of, 94, 98; ledgers, 105; removal of, 91; sons of, 94, 95, 204n. 80; and wife, Kakima, 77, 90–91, 93–94, 128, 203n. 63. *See also* Kakima
Burnett, William (Wimego), 204n. 80

Cadillac. *See* La Mothe
Cadot, Joseph, 88–89
Cahokia, 15, 48, 65, 184n. 13, 187n. 32; census, 189n. 41
Cahokia people, 33, *51, 173n. 16;* at Kaskaskia, 35; violence by, 67, 68
Campbell, John, 62, 196n. 46
Campbell, William, 86
Canadian Northwest, 64, 196n. 41
canals, 145, 146, 161
canoes, 30, 55, 63, 180n. 32, 193n. 9; evolution of, 75, 192n. 4, 196n. 41, 199n. 8. *See also* voyageurs
Cardinal, Jean Marie, 52–53, 191n. 59
Carey Mission, 99, 100–101, *107,* 158, 205n. 13
Carlton, Guy, 62, 194n. 15
Caron, Claude, 186n. 24
Cass, Lewis, 96–98, 100, 105–6, 117, 132
Cass County, Michigan, 161
Cassopolis, Michigan, 162
Catawba people, 198n. 2
catechists, 26; female, 29, 49; male, 102
Catin, Thèrése, 45, 185n. 18
Catlin, George, 125
Catholic Church: emigrant versus pioneer, 113; and "frontier Catholicism," 170n. 18; and fur trade, 29–20; and Indians, 112–

15; Irish reshaping of the, 113–14; and kin networks, 43–53, 90, 91, 93–95, 98–99; laymen in the, 44, 102, 184n. 13, 190n. 51; and mixed ancestry, 155–59; Order of the Holy Cross of the, 109–10, 112, 208nn. 49, 54; and the Potawatomi, 100–115; as a removal refuge, 102; and sacrifice, 33–34; and social change, 101–5, 109–15; and social power, 21; violence against the, 10–12, 208n. 63; women, 21, 36. *See also* baptism; Bailly; Bertrand; Burnett; Chevalier; fur trade; godparenting; Jesuits; kin networks; Potawatomi; religion; women
Catholic converts, 5, 21, 22, 50; Indian, 33–34; male focus of, 206n. 18; Natives as, 23, 24, 34, 44; ostracized, 184n. 13; women's' power as, 24, 25, 26, 27–29, 33–37. *See also* Rouensa
"Catholic Indians," 150
Catholic kin networks, 5, 21, 43–53, 90, 91, 93–95, 98–99; Bertrand's reestablishment of, 94; family names, *51*; started, 43
"Catholic party," 108
Cecelia (nun). *See* Bailly, Eleanor
cemeteries: and funerary objects, 15, 33, 182n. 64; hidden, 156; Kaskaskia, 30; Native Catholic women in, 36, 157, 182n. 64; vandalism of Catholic, 112, 157
census and Cahokia, 189n. 41
census of 1768 (Detroit), 60, 194–95n. 21
census of 1840, 162
census of 1850, 162
Chandonai, 202n. 54
Charlevoix, Pierre François Xavier de, 54
Chebanse, 87, 88, 89, 90, 128
Chepoussa people, 37
Chevalier. *See* Lhullic
Chevalier, Amable (Aimable), 65–66, 188n. 35
Chevalier, Anne, 48
Chevalier, Charlotte, 48, 49, 188n. 36
Chevalier, Jean Baptiste, 47–48, 187n. 33, 188n. 36
Chevalier, Louis, 187n. 33
Chevalier, Louison, 58–59, 67, 89, 194n. 15
Chevalier, Louis Paschal (Pascal), 48, 187n. 33, 188nn. 34, 38
Chevalier, Louis Thérèse: and De Peyster, 65–66, 69, 194n. 67; described, 60, 63; as godfather, 50, 190n. 50; and kinship, 57, 67, 187n. 33, 188n. 34; married Marie Madeleine, 47–48
Chevalier, Marie Josephe (Josette) (Locat), 48
Chevalier, Marie Madeleine Réaume L'archevêque: as agriculturist, 76–77; as a Catholic lay practitioner, 49–50; characterized, 44, 50, 148; children of, 46, 47, 48, 148–49, 186n. 24, 188n. 35; as godmother, 46–47, 48, 49–50, 185n. 16, 190n. 50, 197n. 60; kin network expansion by, 44, 47–50; kin network links of, 36, 57, 98; ledgers of, 77; marriages of, 46, 47, 48, 50, 188nn. 33–34; parents of, 45, 185n. 16; removal of, 76–77
Chevalier family names, 48, *51*, 187n. 33, 188nn. 34, 38–39
Chicago, 92, 105–6, 144, 156, 218n. 61
Chicago, Fort, *13*, *39*
Chicago Treaty (1821), 208n. 47
Chicago Treaty (1832), 95, 208n. 47
Chinko people, 37
Choquette, Leslie, 185n. 20
Clark, Fort, 87
Clinton-Kalamazoo Canal, 145, 146, 161
clothing: beadwork, 125, 127, 128; luxury, 127, 128, 129–30, 137–38; from trade goods, 125, 127
Coiracoenatanon people, 37
Colbert, Jean-Baptiste, 17, 170n. 20
"conductor," 162
congé (congés). *See* license
Conti, Prince de, 17
Copley, Charlotte, 119, 143
Coquillard, Alexis, 162
coureurs de bois (illegal traders), 18, 42, 193n. 10
Crooked Tree. *See* L'Arbre Croche
Crooks, Ramsay, 152
Cuillerier, Angélique, 64
Curti, Merle, 215n. 4

Deaf Man, 123, 124, 135, 137
Deaf Man's Village, 123–24, 135–36, 139
Dearborn, Fort, 92, 93; attacked, 94. *See also* Chicago
Dechêne, Louise, 185n. 19
De Jean, Peter, 106
De Jean, Philip, 194n. 21

de La Marche, Jacques Bariso, 47, 186n. 31
de La Perrierre family, 190nn. 49–50
Delaware people, 60, 85, 89, 211n. 11
Deliette, Pierre, 23
"demise," 1, 2, 3, 148, 162
Deneau, dit De Tailly, Pierre, 192n. 7
De Peyster, Arent Schuyler, 65–66, 68–69, 71
depression. *See* Panic of 1837
de Quindre (Lt.), 67, 68
De Seille (priest), 103, 108, 132, 207n. 41
Deshêtres, Antoine, 48, 49, 188n. 36
De Tailly. *See* Deneau
Detroit, *39*, 49, *51*, 69, 101; census, 60, 194–95n. 21; trade goods, *126*
Detroit, Fort, 54, 58; attacks on, 61; British control of, 66, 74; census, 60, 194n. 21; commandants, 62, 64, 65, 66, 194n. 20; De Peyster at, 66; food sources of, 76; slaves, 60; trade at, 66
Devens, Carol, 206n. 18
de Villiers, Madeleine, 190n. 49
de Villiers, Monsieur de Lespiné, 186n. 24
de Villiers, Nicholas Coulon, 185n. 16, 186n. 24
diaries. *See* pioneer narratives
diaspora, 3, 12, 14, 15, 175n. 34
diet, 55–56, 193n. 11
disease: cholera, 111, 145; epidemics, 55–56, 73, 145, 198n. 2; in gifts, 198n. 3; malaria, 145; smallpox, 55–56, 73, 198nn. 2–3; typhoid, 133
D-mouche-kee-kee-awh, 128
Ducoigne, Jean Baptiste, 182n. 60
Du Sable, Jean Baptiste Pointe, 92–93, 203n. 70

Eaton, John, 121
Edwards, Ninian, 88
Eeltown, 211n. 16
Ekberg, Carl, 35, 178n. 7
Elkhart River, 87, 143
emigrants: as 17th-century Iroquois aggression, 3; as 18th-century French traders, 3, 18; as 19th-century British arrivals, 3; defined, 214n. 1; and Indian image, 142, 157–58; narratives by, 144, 146–48, 150, 155–57; as Native refugees, 18; as nomads, 142; and racism, 142; and removal, 142–63; Wisconsin, 151. *See also* Great Lakes
engagés, 193n. 10, 196n. 41
En Nash Go Gwah, 105
environment: affected expansion, 6–7, 170n. 21; affected trade, 70; fur trade destroyed the, 166n. 5; poisons, 172n. 7; waterway, 11
Erie people, 12, 36
Espemikia people, 37
Etchimens, 173n. 9
Euphrosine (nun), 110
Ewing Brothers, 133–34, 141, 213n. 37

facon du pays, à la, 168n. 12
Fafard, Marie, 190n. 49
Fallen Timbers, battle of, 85–86
Fisher, Marianne, 153
fishing: dry, 172n. 5; green, 172n. 5; N. Atlantic, 11, 171–2n. 5
Flatbelly (Papakeecchi), 119, 207n. 44
Folle Avoine, 52
food crops: as a central exchange process, 75, 91–92; Chevalier's, 76–77; at forts, 55, 69; increased demand for, 74–75; inflated prices, 69; Native sources of, 199n. 11; post-war destruction of, 85–86, 88; in pre-contact fields, 78–79, *79–81*, 82–84, 199n. 11; Rouensa, 31–32; shipping, 77–78; shortage, 69–70, 85–86, 92, 133, 145–46; surplus, 30, 32–33, 56, 69–70, 75, 76, 77, 151; types, 75–78, *79–81*, 82–86, 88, 91–92. *See also* agriculture
forts: British, 71; construction of, *13*, 16, 18–19; French, 71; functions of, 54–55, 192n. 4. *See also* Albany; Chicago; Clark; Dearborn; Detroit; La Boeuf; Miami; Michilimackinac; Oswego; Pimiteoui (Peoria); Pontchartrain; Sandusky; St. Joseph (Duluth); St. Joseph (Michigan); St. Louis; Venango; Wayne
Fox people, 12, 38, 184n. 15
Fox River, *13*, *39*, 70
Fox Wars, 45, 184n. 15
Francophobia, 58–66, 71–72
Frontenac, Louis de Buade, (governor), 42, 75, 174–75n. 29
"frontier Catholicism," 170n. 18
"frontier exotics," 149, 150, 152, 155, 160
funeral. *See* cemeteries
furs. *See* peltry
fur trade: in art, 129; Atlantic coast, 172–3nn. 8–9; ban, 42, 43; British, 53,

54–72, 74, 191n. 60; British dominance of the, 167n. 6; British restrictions and the, 61–63; Canadian Northwest, 64, 196n. 41; Catholic kin networks in the, 44, 98–115; as a common ground, 167n. 6; credit system, 133–34; earnings, 152, 195n. 32; environmental impact of the, 166n. 5; exports, 50, 74, 78, 152, 195n. 32, 213n. 35; and food demands, 74–75; function of the, 18; Jesuit opposition to the, 16–17, 40–42; Johnson Plan and, 61–63; La Salle and growth of the, 17; ledgers, 77–78, 105, 162; links to marriage, 28, 29–30, 45; marriage changed the, 4, 42, 168n. 12; long range impact of the, 129; outposts, *13*, 18–19; and overhunting, 162, 220nn. 88–89; poachers, 62; price inflation, 133–34; restrictions, 42; and river travel, 142–43; success factors, 19, 20–22, 45–46, 129; women as independents in, 151. *See also* Catholic Church; *coureurs de bois;* St. Joseph; license; women

fur traders: function of, 41; perspective of, 41; were not farmers, 32–33. *See also coureurs de bois*

Fur Trade Wars, 12, 13, 14, 18–19, 21, 23; and the Beaver Wars, 173n. 11

Gage, Thomas, 58, 60, 61, 62, 64, 66, 71

Galesburg, Michigan, *81*

Gandeateua, Catherine, 36

Garnsey, Daniel, defined, 214n. 11

General Hunter (ship), 78

Gibault, Augustin, 48, 188n. 40, 190n. 51

Giddens, Anthony, 3

"gift economy," 154

gift giving: as diplomacy, 41–42, 56, 60, 185n. 16, 193n. 13, 195n. 22; and disease, 198n. 3; function of, 42, 179n. 30; and land, 153, 154; made allies, 16; to neutral peoples, 88; reciprocal, 154; reimbursement claims for, 133–34; Spanish, 68, 74; via traders, 41

Gladwin, Henry, 61, 64

Glaize, The, 192n. 8

Godfroy, Elizabeth, 110, 111

Godfroy, Francis, 111, 138–39; children of, 136; as Miami chief Pa-Lonz-Wa, 119, 120, 138, 211n. 16

Godfroy, Gabriel, 140

Godfroy, James (Jacques), 211n. 16

Godfroy Reserve, 138

godparenting: Bertrand family, 102; created relationships, 43–44, 46–47, 186n. 24; reinforced kin links, 46, 48–50, 169n. 14, 188n. 36, 189n. 44. *See also* Chevalier

Gomo, 87

Gram, John M., 187n. 33

Grand River valley, 93, 151–54, 157

Gravier, Jacques, 22, 24–29, 33, 34–35, 178n. 9, 179n. 12

Great Lakes, 12, *13*, 18; British governance of the, 54–72; Indians, 168n. 7; Native emigration in the, 141–63, 214n. 1. *See also states and territories by name;* kin networks

Green, Rayna, 150

Green Bay, 8, *13*, 16, 38, *39*, 68*;* diaspora in, 12–13, 14, 40; family names, *51;* interpreters, 45; missions, 179n. 15; refugee area, 75; trade goods, *126*

Greenville Treaty, 90

Griffon (ship), 15–16, 174n. 29, 174–75nn. 29–30, 212n. 28

Gros Loup people, 70

Gull Prairie, 97, 107

guns as trade goods, 125–26, 162, 212n. 26

habitants, 8, 18, 49; and godparenting, 46, 47

Haldimand, Frederick, 65, 69, 71

Hambach, Frederick, 63

Hamelin, Jean Baptiste, 67

Hamilton, Henry, 69–70, 84

Hamlin, Louis, 52–53

Harmer, Josiah, 85

Harmon, Alexandra, 213n. 33

Harrison, William Henry, 219n. 69

Hart, William, 52, 191n. 55

"hide in plain view." *See* "hiding in plain sight"

"hiding in plain sight": strategy, 9, 111, 157–58, 171n. 26; to thwart removal, 7, 8–9, 142, 154

Hinderaker, Eric, 178n. 7

Holloway (narrative), 147

Hopkins, Gerald L., 96

housing (Native), 119, 120–123, *121–22*, 139, 149, 211n. 11; Bailly, 156

Howe, Frances R., 104, 155–58, 160

Howe, Rose (Bailly), 156–57, 159, 218n. 56
Hubbard, Bela, 78, *79–81*, 83
Huron people, 12, 19, 38, 60

identity: and ethnicity, 7–8, 21, 52, 59; and invisibility, 21, 154, 157, 176n. 50; and kinship, 43, 59, 60, 154, 160; and language, 136; and racism, 114–15, 157; and removal refugees, 85. *See also* "hiding in plain sight"; image; kin networks; stereotypes
Iliniwek Confederacy, 14, 15–16, 173nn. 15–16, 175n. 32
Iliniwek people: Gravier among the, 24, 179n. 12
Ilini people, 38, 45
Illinois (state), 15, 141
Illinois Country, *13*, 16, 174n. 21; Native population, 119; violence, 67
Illinois River, *13*, 14, *39*
Illinois Territory: governors, 88; statehood, 141
image, of Indians, 95, 96, 112, 116–17, 124–30, 134–35, 209nn. 1, 5; artistic portrayals and the, 125; and emigrants, 142, 157–58; modern media's, 1–2, 165n. 1; myths, 149
Indiana, 85, 106, 109, 119–40; emigrants, 146; geography of, 142; governors, 132, 219n.69; identity in, 115; Miami people in, 111, 116, 119, 121–23, 130, 134–40; militia, 132, 137; peltry, 130; Potawatomi, 97, 106, 115, 207nn. 44–45; statehood, 141; women traders, 155. *See also* Bailly; Godfroy; "hiding in plain sight"; Slocum
Indian agents, 146, 187n. 32, 216n. 27
Indians: artistic portrayals of, 125; massacres of, 86; as nomads, 85–86, 95, 160; and Pan-Indianism, 86–87; as removal refugees, 85, 201n. 39. *See also* emigrants; housing; identity; image of; land cessions; Native peoples; removal; stereotypes
integration, 59, 96, 156–59; ethnic, 89; at Fort St. Joseph, 55, 193n. 8; of traders, 62–64
Interior French, 56, 63, 64–65, 68
intermarriage: of British and Natives, 64; of French traders, 64, 170n. 20; fur trader and Native, 16, 19, 35, 39–40, 102, 135–36, 149; high rates of, 46; and racism, 156–59, 160; scorned, 63; with slaves, 53. *See also* adoption; marriage; Métis; Chevalier
interpreters. *See* language
invisibility. *See* "hiding in plain sight"
Iowa, 145
I-O-Wah, 130
Iroquois people, 12, 15–16, 18–19, 35

Jackson, Andrew, 117, 141, 145
Jackson, Elizabeth Ann, 112
Jackson, Michigan, 143
Jay's Treaty (1794), 86
Jefferson, Thomas, 209n. 1
Jesuit Relations, The, 21
Jesuits (Society of Jesus): as "black robes," 101, 131; changes in the, 44; disbanded, 36, 44; hated intermarriage, 16–17, 40; and Kaskaskia people, 24–28, 178n. 12; male focused, 206n. 18; and Native conversions, 33–34, 36; opposed the fur trade, 16–17; probabilism doctrine of the, 33, 180n. 49; and power and Native behavior, 34; records of the, 21, 33–34; and rivalry with traders, 16–17, 40–42; shortage of, 47. *See also* Catholic Church; Gravier; marriage; St. Joseph
Johnson, William, 60, 62
Johnston, John, 19
Johnson Plan, 61–63
Jonesville, Michigan, 147
Jutras (Joutras), Jean Baptiste, 47, 186n. 30, 187n. 34

Kakima (Burnett), 77, 90–91, 93–94, 98, 203n. 63; kin network of, 77–78, 91–92, 93, 101, 128, 206n. 19; sons, 94, 204n. 80
Kalamazoo, Michigan, 78, 84, 106, 145, 146, 161
Kalamazoo River, 97
Kankakee River, 77, 78, 85; animals, 118; militants, 87; portage, 38, *39*, 97, 183n. 3, 104
Kansas, 133, 139, 175n. 35, 207n. 45, 210n. 7
Kaskaskia community, 14, 84, 184n. 13; baptisms, 29, 30, 32; church, 30; described, 31–32, 178n. 7; Jesuits and the, 24–28, 178n. 12; slaves at, 60. *See also* Rouensa

Kaskaskia people, 22, 28, 14, 173n. 16; at Cahokia, 35; chiefs, 182n. 60
Kaskaskia River, *13, 39*
Kewinquot (Returning Cloud), 151
Kickapoo people, 16, 148
Kilatica people, 16
kin-based society, 3–4, 19, 42–43, 158, 160; British power and the importance of, 54–72; defined, 166n. 4
King, Charles Bird, 125
kin networks: Chevalier, 93; controlled the fur exchange process, 4–5, 19, 61, 63, 66–67; defined, 166n. 4; Du Sable's, 93; Fort St. Joseph's, 49–50, 93–94, 150; and identity, 43, 59, 60, 154, 160; indigenous, 5; La Framboise, 152; L'archevêque, 93; and marriage "in the custom of the country," 50, 63–64, 218n. 56; matrifocal, 5; replaced French authority, 43; St. Joseph, 49–50, 89, 93–94, 150; St. Louis, 89; symbiotic, 57. *See also* Bertrand; Burnett; Catholic kin networks; Chevalier; integration; Kakima; L'archevêque; marriage; Potawatomi; women
Kinzie, John, 105, 202n. 54, 203n. 68
Kokomo, Indiana, 135
Kouerakouilenoux people, 37

La Barre, Joseph-Antoine Le Febvre de, 16, 17, 175n. 31
La Boeuf, Fort, 60
La Framboise, Joseph, 150, 151, 152, 153
La Framboise, (Thérèse) Magdelaine Marcot, 150, 151–54, 217n. 38
La Framboise family, *51,* 151
La Marque, Charles Nolan, 187n. 31
Lamorine, (priest), 186n. 24
La Mothe, dit Cadillac, Antoine Laumet de, 39
land cessions, 96, 97, 100, 105–6, 118; and growth, 120; and land titles, 116, 120–21, 153; prices for, 99; and profit, 133–34. *See also* reservations
Langlade family, 47, *51,* 186nn. 29–30
language: digraphs, 190n. 49; in the fur trade, 160; Ilini, 31; interpreters, 20, 31, 45, 59, 64, 110; Miami, 136; missionary lack of, 103; Native use of, 114, 155; Odawa, 155, 156; phonemes in Native, 178n. 7, 190n. 49
L'Arbre Croche (Crooked Tree, Wagansgisi), 64, 75, 92, 106, 155, 193n. 11, 200 n. 18, 216n. 24
L'archevêque (Marie Madeleine). *See* Chevalier
L'archevêque, Angelique (Agatha), 48, 188n. 39
L'archevêque, Augustin, 46, 186nn. 25, 29
L'archevêque, Marie Amable, 186n. 24, 188nn. 41, 44
L'archevêque, Marie Anne, 48, 186n. 24, 189nn. 40, 44
L'archevêque, Marie Catherine, 47, 186n. 24, 189n. 44
L'archevêque, Marie Joseph Esther, 47, 186n. 24, 186n. 31, 187nn. 32–33, 189n. 44
L'archevêque, Marie Magdelaine, 48, 188n. 38, 189n. 44
L'archevêque family names, *51;* and spellings, 186n. 25
Lasaliere, Pierre, 93
Lasaliere, Thérèse, 93
La Salle, Nicholas de, 175n. 33
La Salle, Réne-Robert Cavelier de, 15–18, 174nn. 27, 29, 175nn. 30, 32, 176n. 38, 212n. 28; and Accault, 26; crops of, 75; on marriage, 23. *See also Griffon*
law: French, 31; and removal, 107, 220n. 83; wills, 31–32. *See also* license; marriage
Le Febvre, Marie. *See* Bailly
Le Gesse, 86
Lernoult, Richard Beringer, 65
Lhullic, dit Chevalier, Charles, 48, 188n. 39
license, fur trade *(congé),* 18, 30, 43, 188n. 36, 219n.69; given to women, 52–53, 152; revoked, 42
Little, Henry, 84
Locat, Pierre Renaud, 48
Loingwea people, 173n. 16
Lonval, Jean Baptiste François, 188n. 41

Mad Sturgeon, 88
Mahican (Mohican) people, 38
Main Poc, 87, 88, 89
Maine, 173n. 8
Maintenon, Madame de, 42
Manistee River, 19, *20*
Manitou symbology, 33, 181n. 52
Marcot, Jean Baptiste, 150–51, 217n. 40
Marcot family, 150

Marest (Father), 30
Marie Jeanne (Panis), 49
Maronas people, 37
Marquette, Jacques, 14, 23
marriage, sanctioned, 42, 50. *See also* intermarriage; marriage in the "manner (custom) of the country"; polygamy
marriage in the "manner (custom) of the country" (*facon du pays, à la*), 4, 17, 19, 28, 151, 178n. 8; defined, 28, 168nn. 11–12; extended kin networks, 50, 63–64, 218n. 56; Jesuit hatred of, 16–17, 40; rejected by converts, 24; transformed the fur trade, 4, 42, 168n. 12. *See also* adoption; intermarriage; polygamy
"marry out," 5, 42
Marsh, Justin, 146
Marshall, Michigan, 78, 144, 147, 216n. 26
marten, 172n. 6
Mascoutin people, 16
matriarchy. *See* matrifocal
matrifocal: defined, 169n. 16; households, 30, 32–33, 55, 169n. 16, 180n. 31. *See also* kin networks; women
Maumee River, *13*, 19, *20*, *39*, 85–86
McCoy, Isaac, 100, 101, 158, 205n. 13
McGulpin, Angelique, 218n. 56
Mekbibkas8nga, Pierre, 49; family of, 190nn. 49–50
Menache, 204n. 80
Mendon, Michigan, 161
Menominee, 131–32, 134
Merrell, James, 198n. 2
Mesquakie people, 32
Métis (*métis*), 8, 52, 114, 205n. 17
Metivier, Louis, 190n. 49
Miami, Fort, 60, 62, 85, 86
Miami National Reserve, 135
Miami people: attacked, 177n. 4; as British supporters, 87, 88; dress styles of the, 5, 6, 127–29; in the diaspora, 12, 16; Indiana, 111, 116, 119, 121–23, 130, 134–40; lands of the, 38, 85, 123, 185n. 16; Michigan, 97
Miami River, 16, 70, 175n. 30
Michigamea people, 173n. 16
Michigan (state): agriculture, 78, 83–84; canal, 145, 146, 161;emigrants, 161; governors, 107, 220n. 83; land cessions, 106; land speculation, 141–47; Panic of 1837 and, 141–42, 145–47; population, 97–98, 119, 210n. 10; removal, 85, 147–48, 163; statehood, 141. *See also* Cass
Michigan, Lake, 13, 174n. 22
Michigan City, Indiana, 146
Michigan Territory: agriculture, 78–85; cemeteries, 182n. 64; emigrants, 161, 220n. 82; governors, 100; land sales, 145; Miami people, 97; missions, *107;* narratives, 79–84; natural resources, 141–43; population, 97–98, 119, 210n. 10; portages, 142, 216n. 26; Potawatomi, 97, 99–100, 102, 106–9, 119, 207n. 45; removal, 85, 147–48, 163; removal refugees in, 85; rivers, *13*, 19, *20*, 100, 142–43, 205n. 9*;* roads, 143–44, 215n. 11; statehood, 141; village locations, *107;* women traders, 155. *See also forts by specific name;* La Framboise
Michilimackinac, Fort, *13*, *39*, 54*;* attacked, 90; baptisms, 47, 151, 187n. 33; commandants, 39, 66, 71, 92; family names, *51;* Métis, 8; trade at, 63, 66, 92, 153
Middle Ground, The (White), 2–3, 35, 168n. 6
middle ground, 89–90
military: Indiana militia, 132, 137; scorch-and-burn policy, 85–86, 88. *See also* battles; forts; warfare
Milroy (general), 137
Minime, Gabriel, Sieur Barbier, 175n. 33
mining, 32
Mississinewa River, 119, 123, 124, 137
Mississippi River, 12, *39*, 50, 70–71, 100, 105, 134
Mkogo, 102, 207n. 44
Mo-con-no-qua, 123, 124, 128, 135–36, 137
Mohawk people, 36
Mohegan people, 16
Monceaux, Charles-François-Marie-Ruette d'Auteuil de, 185n. 18
Montcalm, Louis-Joseph de (marquis), 191n. 60
Montour family, *51*, 52
Moran, 88
Mousse, Alexander, 205n. 17
Muskingum River, *13*

Nan-Matches-Sin-A-Wa, 119
narratives. *See* pioneer narratives

Nas-waw-kay, 130–31
Natick people, 217n. 30
Native peoples. *See by specific group or family name;* Catholic Church; emigrants; housing; identity; kin networks; marriage; women
natural resources. *See* agriculture; environment; fishing; peltry; rivers
Neskesh. *See* Thimotée
Neutral people, 12, 60
New Arbre Croche, 106
New Orleans, 70–71, 74
Niles, Michigan, 99, 100, 143, 146, 192n. 2, 205n. 13
Nipissing, Lake, *13, 39*
North Dakota agriculture, 83
Northwest Ordinance, 145
Northwest Territory, 15
No-ta-no-quay, 204n. 80
Notawaseppe Prairie, 97; reservation, 99, 100

O'Brien, Jean, 217n. 30
Odawa people, 19, 33, 93, 150–51; baptisms, 106; population, 210n. 10. *See also* L'Arbre Croche
Ohio (state), 141
Ohio River valley, 12, *13,* 85
Ojibway people, 19
Oklahoma, 175n. 35
Onangizes, 42
Onoxa, 90
Osage people, 87
O-Shaw-gus-co-day-way-quah, 19
Oswego, Fort, 61
Ouabona people, 16
Ouaouagoukoue, Simphorose, 45, 185n. 16
Ouilamette (Wilamek, Winamek), 16, 175n. 35, 202n. 46
Ouiatenon (Indiana), 8, *13, 39;* attacked, 60; commandants, 45; family names, *51;* fur trade at, 62; trade goods, *126*
Ouiatenon people, 16, 45, 177n. 4, 184n. 15

Pa-Lonz-Wa. *See* Godfroy, Francis
Panic of 1837 and Michigan, 141–42, 145–47
Pan-Indianism, 86–87
Panis. *See* slaves
parc auz vaches, 100
Patterson, Charles, 91
Pawnee people, 60, 190n. 48. *See also* Panis
Paw Paw, Michigan, *107,* 109
pays d'en haut, 8, *13,* 14, 16–17, 18, 45; British control of, 54, 60, 61, 117; French and the, 177n. 54
peltry: access to, 4; as commerce, 11–13, 41, 128–30; 172nn. 3, 7–9; grades of, 130. *See also animals by specific name;* fur trade
Peoria, 175n. 32, 187n. 32
Peoria, Lake, 16, 87, 92
Peoria people, 31, 35, 173n. 16, 179n. 12
Pepikokia people, 16
Pepiya, 102, 207n. 44
Pepper, Abel C., 108, 132
Pequot people, 2
persistence. *See* land cessions; Potawatomi; removal
Peru, Indiana, 128
Peterson, Jacqueline, 28, 32, 46
Petit, Benjamin (priest), 103, 132, 133, 207n. 41
Petit, Charlotte, 52
Peyser, Joseph, 183n. 3, 184n. 8
Philippe, Michel, 30, 32
Piankeshaw people, 16, 177n. 4, 184n. 15
Picote, François Marie, Sieur de Bellestre, 192n. 2
Pierce, Benjamin Langdon, 153
Pierce, Josett Harriet, 153
Pilcher, Elijah, 144
Pimiteoui, Fort, (Peoria), 48
Pimiteoui people, 175n. 32, 176n. 46
pioneer narratives: collected, 53; Copley, 119, 143; emigrant, 144, 146–48, 150, 155–57; Holloway, 147; Howe, 104; inaccurate, 162; Indiana, 155; Jesuit, 21, 110, 162; La Framboise, 150, 155; Marsh, 146; Michigan, 79–84, 119, 143–44, 147, 155; Pilcher, 144; Slocum, 137–38; Winter, 127–28, 130, 131, 137, 139
Pitchbaon, 59
plows (*en bardeau*), 77, 82
"Pocahontas of Michigan," 150
Pointe. *See* Du Sable
Pokagon, 90; family, 101, 102, 131, 206n. 19; removal of, 106
Pokagon, Elizabeth, 102
Pokagon, Leopold, 102–4, 106–9, 201n. 39

Pokagon, Simon, 102
polygamy, 23, 24, 26
Pontchartrain, Fort, *13*
Pontiac (chief), 56, 60–61, 63, 198n. 3, 218n. 56
population: Cahokia, 15; Ilini, 175n. 32; decreased Native, 37; and disease, 56; emigrant, 161; errors, 210n. 9; French settler, 66; Illinois Native, 119; increased Native, 14; Kaskaskia, 35; male reductions in, 23; Michigan Native, 97–98, 119, 210n. 10; Potawatomi, 39, 73, 97–98, 163; removal and, 163; sex ratios, 23; and treaty negotiations, 97–98; Wisconsin Native, 119. *See also* slaves
portages: Michigan, 142, 216n. 26; principal, *20,* 70*;* St. Joseph, 38, *39,* 70, 97, 183n. 3; taverns near, 216n. 26; villages built near, 18, 76
Potawatomi people: anti-British, 68–69, 86; attacked the British, 58–59; baptism, 106; Catholicism of the, 100–115; in the diaspora, 12; dress styles of the, 5, 6, 127–29; as fickle allies, 68–69; and the fur trade, 42; Green Bay, 38; Indiana, 97, 106, 115, 207nn. 44–45; Kansas, 133, 139, 175n. 35, 207n. 45, 210n. 7; lands of the, 38, *39;* Michigan, 97, 99–100, 102, 106–9, 119, 207n. 45; neutral, 70, 73–74, 84, 87–89, 93; Oklahoma, 175n. 35; Pokagon, 112, 131; population removed, 163, 210n. 7; prosperity of, 128–29, 147; as refugee hosts, 75, 85; and smallpox, 73; Spanish gifts to the, 68, 74; St. Joseph River, *38,* 42, 68–69, 89, 106, *107;* violence by the, 40, 62, 63, 68. *See also* agriculture; Catholic Church; disease; food crops; kin networks; land cessions; marriage; removal; women
Potawatomi Trail, 143
Pouré, dit Beausoleil, Eugene, 197n. 63
Prairie Ronde, *81, 107,* 119
Presque Isle, 60
Proclamation Line of 1763, 56
Prophet, the (the Shawnee Prophet, Tenskwatawa), 87, 88, 90
Prophetstown, 90
prostitution, 40–41
Prout, A. T., 84

raccoon (black), 6, 118, 129–30, 155
racism, 99–100, 101, 114, 116, 118, 134–35; and emigrants, 142; and identity, 114–15, 157; and intermarriage, 156–59, 160; and removal, 134–35. *See also* "hiding in plain sight"
Radisson, Pierre-Esprit, 13–14
railroads, 145
Raisin River, 19, *20*
Ransom, Epaphroditus, 107, 220n. 83
Raparouras people, 37
rape, 23, 178n. 4
Réaume (Marie). *See* Chevalier
Réaume, Jean Baptiste, 45, 185n. 16, 187n. 31
Réaume, Simon, 45, 184n. 15, 185n. 18
Réaume family names, *51*
Red Bird, 100
Reed (observer), 97, 98–99
religion, Native form versus Catholic form of, 103–5, 113–14, 179n. 15. *See also* Catholic Church; cemeteries; Manitou symbology
removal, of Indians from their lands: in art works, 130; British policy of, 67; and cash settlements, 214n. 49; and emigrants, 142–63; exemptions from, 95, 98, 107, 108, 137, 154, 209n. 3; in the Great Lakes, 3, 85, 91, 150; Indiana, 116–40; law and, 107, 220n. 83; Michigan, 85, 147–48, 163; and population changes, 163, 210n. 7; and Potawatomi refugee hosts, 75, 85; and racism, 134–35; resistance to, 7, 8–9, 100, 105–6, 108–9, 118, 162; thwarted, 7, 8–9; violent, 132–33, 162. *See also* "hiding in plain sight"; Indians; land cessions
Removal Act of 1830, 117, 210n. 7
Rese (priest), 102
reservations, 99, 100, 117, 121; Indiana private, 135. *See also* annuity payments
Richard, Gabriel, 101, 102, 109, 205n. 14
Richter, Daniel, 36, 96
Rigaud de Vaudreil, Philipe de, 185n. 16, 188n. 36, 191n. 60
rivers: Michigan, *13,* 19, *20,* 100, 142–43, 205n. 9; Indiana, 143; navigable, 15; and waterways, 11. *See also rivers by specific names;* canoes; portages; voyageurs
roads, 143–44, 215n. 11
Robert, Charlotte, 186n. 24
Rogers (at Detroit), 65
Rogers (trader), 63
Rouensa, Elizabeth Michel, 182n. 60

Rouensa, Marie, 22–37, 148; called Arамepinchieue, 35, 178n. 7; Catholicism of, 24, 25–29, 31, 35, 36; characterized, 27, 35, 178n. 7; children of, 30, 31, 35–36, 178nn. 7, 9; death of, 30; father of, 27–28; husbands of, 4, 26, 28–29, 30–32, 35, 178nn. 9, 11; mother of, 33; as proselytizer, 25–26; as translator, 25; will of, 31–32. *See also* Gravier
Rush family, 111
Rush Lake, Michigan, 207n. 45

Saginaw River, 19, *20*
Sahlins, Marshall, 3
Sandusky, *13*, *39*
Sandusky, Fort, 60
Sauk people, 12, 32, 38, 60; violence and the, 40
Sauk Trail, 100
Sault Ste. Marie, *13*, *39*
Schellenbarger, Jacob, 216n. 26
Schlosser, Joseph, 60
Schoolcraft, Henry, 19, 83
scorch-and-burn policy, 85–86, 88
Seek's Reserve, 121
Seignelay (Marquis de), 17, 18
Senajiwan, 87
Seneca people, 89
Seven Years' War, 55, 71, 191n. 60
Shavehead, 102, 207n. 44
Shawnee people, 16, 60, 85, 87, 89, 137. *See also* Prophet; Tecumseh
Shoemaker, Nancy, 34
Siggenauk, 86
Signowa, 207n. 45
Silver Creek, Michigan, 106, *107*, 119, 161, 207n. 44
Sinclair, Patrick, 66–67, 68, 71–72
Sioux people, 12, 179n. 30
"situational ethnicity" (Hart), 52, 191n. 55
slaves, 31–32, 151; black, 60, 161; Fox, 185n. 15; gender ratio of, 60, 195n. 21; at Kaskaskia, 60; of mixed ancestry, 161, 187n. 31; Panis (Indian), 49, 53, 55, 60, 190n. 48
Slocum, Frances, as Mo-con-no-qua, 123, 124, 128, 136–38, 209n. 3
Slocum family, 124, 138
Society of Jesus. *See* Jesuits
Sorin (priest), 109, 110, 111, 113, 207n. 41, 208n. 54
South Bend, Indiana, 111
Spain, 68, 71, 74, 84
Spring Wells, 89
squatters, 132, 144–45
starvation, 133, 145–46
"Starved Rock," 175n. 32, 176n. 46
St. Clair, Arthur, 85
stereotypes, Indian, 1–2, 84–85, 95, 124
Sterling, James, 64
St. Joseph, Fort (Duluth), *13*
St. Joseph, Fort (Michigan), 8, *13*, *39*; attacked, 58–59, 68, 86, 197n. 63; baptisms, 46–48; Catholic kin network, 49–50, 89, 93–94, 150; commandants, 44, 60, 75, 184n. 12, 186n. 24, 192nn. 2, 4; De Peyster at, 65–66; family names, *51*; fur trade at, 62; garrison, 54–55, 65; housing, 55, 192n. 7; integration at, 55, 193n. 8; interpreters, 45, 192n. 7; location, 55, 192n. 2; mission, 47, 186n. 28; purpose of, 54–55, 192n. 4
St. Joseph mission, 98, 204n. 4
St. Joseph River, *13*, 16, 19, *20*, 144; Potawatomi, *38*, 42
St. Joseph River valley, 38, *39*, 48, 53, 74, 76; fur trade, 91; garden beds, 78, *79–81*, 82–83; Jesuits, 101; portage, 97. *See also* agriculture; Catholic kin networks; Potawatomi people
St. Lawrence River, 11–12, 19, 70
St. Louis, *13*; founding, 70; kin networks at, 89, 93, 203n. 71; Spanish at, 84; trade at, 74, 93
St. Louis, Fort, *13*, 16, 17, *39*, 175n. 32, 176n. 46
St. Mary of the Woods, 159
St. Mary's Academy, 109–11
Story of a French Homestead in the Old Northwest, The (Howe), 155–56, 157. *See also* Bailly
St. Ours, Jean-Baptiste de, 44, 184n. 12
St. Ours de Chaillon, M. Roch de, 184n. 12
St. Pierre, Verchere Legarduer de, 186n. 30
Swift Current, 87
symbolic capital, 4

Tamaroa people, 173n. 16
Tapoura people, 37
Tecumseh, 87, 88, 90, 202n. 46
Tekakwitha, Kateri, 34, 36, 182n. 62
Tenskwatawa. *See* Prophet
Territorial Road, 143, 144
Therese (Potawatomi), 49

Thimotée (Marie Neskesh), 150–51, 217n. 38
Thompson, O. C., 143
Thorntown, *122*
Tippecanoe, battle of, 88, 131, 132
Tipton, John, 120, 121, *121,* 122, 133
Todd, John, 135
Tonti, Henri, 175n. 32
tools, 32, 33, 49, 88. *See also* agriculture
Topenabe, 90, 93, 100, 101, 205n. 18, 206n. 19
To-quoc-yaw, 128
Tou-se-qua, 216n. 24
trade goods: alcohol as, 40, 60, 117, 162; allies built with, 16; Catholicism reflected by, 105; changed Indian images, 125–30, 138; clothing made from, 5, 6, 162; European, *126;* transport of, 55; types, 124, 125, 126–27, 129, 212nn. 26, 28. *See also* canoes; voyageurs; Winter
treaty negotiations, 97–98; and Cass's land greed, 100. *See also* reservations
Treaty of 1815 (Spring Wells), 89
Treaty of 1821 (Chicago), 208n. 47
Treaty of 1828 (Carey Mission), 99, 100–101, 120, *121, 122,* 208n. 47
Treaty of 1832 (Tippecanoe), 131, 132
Treaty of 1832/33 (Chicago), 154, 208n. 47
Treaty of 1833 (Chicago), 105–6, 208n. 47
Treaty of 1838 (Wabash), 122–23
Treaty of 1840, at the Forks of the Wabash, 135
Treaty of Paris (1783), 63, 74, 86
Treaty of Utrecht, 192n. 4
Trotter, Catherine, 52
Turnbull, George, 64, 196n. 46

Van Slyck (Slycke), Cornelius, 58, 59, 63
Varier, Louis de, 192n. 2
Vaudreuil. *See* Rigaud
Venango, Fort, 60
Verchere. *See* St. Pierre
Vermontville, Michigan, 145–46
Vincennes, *13, 39,* 84
violence: anti-Catholic, 10–12, 208n. 63; massacre, 86; removal, 132–33; squatter, 132, 184n. 13
voyageurs, 30, 55, 75, 151, 193n. 10, 196n. 41

Wabash River, *13,* 14, *39,* 87, 88; Native housing on the, 120, *122*
Wabash Treaties, 122–23, 135
Wabunaki people, 38
Wagansgisi. *See* L'Arbre Croche
Wakimanido, 102, 207n. 44
Wallace, David, 132
wampum, 194n. 14
warfare. *See treaties by specific name;* agriculture; Beaver Wars; forts; Fox Wars; military; Seven Years' War; War of 1812
War of 1812, 88, 93, 94, 98; aftermath, 96, 97, 117, 124
Waubojeeg, 19
Wawasee, Lake, 119
Wayne, Anthony, 85–86
Wayne, Fort, *13, 39,* 98, 136, 137, 143; villages, 96
Wea. *See* Ouiatenon
Wesaw, 102, *107,* 207n. 44
Wewissa, 130
White, Richard, 2–3, 95, 112, 168n. 6; on Rouensa, 35, 178nn. 7, 11
Wilamek (Winamek). *See* Ouilamette
Winnebago people, 32
Winter, George, 5, 119–20, 123–26, 127–31, 137–39, 147, 211n. 17
Wisconsin, 119, 151
women (Native): abused, 23–24, 177n. 4; as agriculturists, 16, 30, 32–33, 75, 77, 82, 91–92; as artisans, 125, 127; as catechizers, 29, 49; as "frontier exotics," 149, 150, 152, 155, 160; as fur traders, 45–46, 51–53, 151, 155, 156, 185n. 19; as Catholics, 21, 36; as interpreters, 20; lands of, 121; licensed, 52–53, 152; and marriage, 23–26; power held via fur trade, 5, 19–20, 148; power sources for, 24, 32; and prostitution, 40–41; as role models, 33; roles of, 32–33, 60, 148–50, 154, 159; unmarried, 26. *See also* Bailly; Bertrand; Catholic converts; Chevalier; identity; Kakima; La Framboise; marriage; rape; Rouensa; Slocum
wool, 62
Wyandot people, 89

Susan Sleeper-Smith grew up in New York City and received a B.A. from C. W. Post College, her M.A. from the University of Wisconsin, and her Ph.D. from the University of Michigan. She co-edited the volume *New Faces of the Fur Trade* (1998) and has published in *American Indian Culture and Research Journal, Ethnohistory, The Journal of American History,* and *Recherches amérindiennes.* Her work also appears in *The Sixty Years' War for the Great Lakes, 1754–1814* (2001).

1800 622 8731

Chat